International Trade Centre

Business and the multilateral trading system

UNCTAD CNUCED   WTO OMC

Business Guide to Trade Remedies in the United States

Anti-dumping, countervailing and safeguards legislation, practices and procedures

Geneva 2003

ABSTRACT FOR TRADE INFORMATION SERVICES

2003   C-20 840
                                                                    BUS

INTERNATIONAL TRADE CENTRE UNCTAD/WTO
Business Guide to Trade Remedies in the United States: Anti-dumping, countervailing and safeguards legislation, practices and procedures
Geneva: ITC, 2003. xvii, 221 p.

Guide to trade remedy procedures (anti-dumping, countervailing and safeguard) aimed at exporters from developing countries and transition economies, with particular reference to trade remedy legislation and practices of the United States - examines origins of trade remedies and their administration in the country under review; considers role of institutions responsible for trade remedy administration, and the WTO rules governing trade remedies (WTO Agreements on Implementation of Article VI of the General Agreement on Tariffs and Trade 1994, WTO Agreement on Subsidies and Countervailing Measures, and WTO Agreement on Safeguards); presents procedural framework for the United States unfair trade remedies; discusses trade remedy investigations and actions; includes Internet guide to the United States trade remedy law.

Subject descriptors: **United States, Import Regulations, Anti-dumping, Anti-Dumping Agreement, Agreement on Safeguards, Agreement on Subsidies and Countervailing Measures**.

English

ITC, Palais des Nations, 1211 Geneva 10, Switzerland

Digital image on the cover: © Eyewire, Getty Images (image modified).

ITC/P150.E/TSS/BAS/03-II   **ISBN 92-9137-253-6**
                                    United Nations Sales No. E.03.III.T.3

Foreword

Under the WTO Agreements, members have the right to apply trade remedies in the form of anti-dumping, countervailing or safeguard measures subject to specific rules. The importance of these rules was highlighted at the WTO Ministerial Conference in Doha, where Members agreed to 'negotiations aimed at clarifying and improving disciplines under the Agreements on Implementation of Article VI of the GATT 1994 and on Subsidies and Countervailing Measures...' (paragraph 28 of the Ministerial Declaration).

From 1995 to 2002, more than 2000 anti-dumping investigations were initiated worldwide. For almost three-quarters of these cases, exporters in developing and transition countries were the main targets. According to information from ITC's World Tr@de Net programme, businesses in developing countries and transition economies engaged in the production and exportation of 'sensitive' products, consider anti-dumping investigations, or the threat thereof, as a significant market access barrier to a number of major markets.

Parties involved in anti-dumping and other trade remedy proceedings, namely exporters, importers and domestic producers of the product in question, often know very little about the procedures themselves and what they entail. They are unaware of the basic substantive rules of the relevant WTO Agreements and/or implementing national legislation, and hence have very limited knowledge of their rights and are thus ill equipped to defend their business interests. There has been a growing demand from a number of partners of the International Trade Centre for a publication explaining to business people the essential laws applicable and practices followed in such proceedings.

It is in response to this demand that the International Trade Centre has published this series of Business Guides to Trade Remedies. The four publications in this series concern the relevant trade remedy rules and practices of the European Community, the United States of America, Canada and South Africa and the Southern African Customs Union. The first three of these are the biggest traditional users of trade remedy measures. Over the last few years, an increasing number of developing countries and transition economies have begun to implement trade remedy actions at an accelerated pace.

This volume focuses on the United States, which is the largest market for many developing countries and transition economies and a frequent user of trade remedy measures. The main objective of this guide is to highlight those aspects of the law and practice of the United States and the appropriate provisions of the relevant WTO Agreements that may be of practical interest to business managers, exporters and importers of developing countries and transition economies. The guide is not for specialists; special emphasis is therefore given to practical definitions, problems and recommendations.

J. Denis Bélisle
Executive Director
International Trade Centre

Acknowledgements

James Durling, a partner in the Washington D.C. office of Willkie Farr & Gallagher, wrote this publication. He is entirely responsible for the views expressed herein. He would like to thank his colleagues, and particularly his partner, **Daniel Porter**, for their substantial contributions in preparing this volume.

Peter Naray, Senior Adviser on the Multilateral Trading System, coordinated the preparation of this publication.

R. Badrinath, Director, Division of Trade Support Services, and **Sabine Meitzel**, Chief, Business Advisory Services, provided strategic guidance in the planning and preparation of this publication.

Alison Southby copyedited the book. Isabel Droste prepared the copy for printing.

Contents

CHAPTER 3

CHAPTER 4

CHAPTER 8
Section 337: Protecting intellectual property

CHAPTER 9
Section 301: Market access and trade policy issues

CHAPTER 10
Conducting verification

CHAPTER 11
Injury determinations

APPENDIX
Internet guide to United States trade remedy law under Title VII and Section 201

Note

Unless otherwise specified, all references to dollars ($) are to United States dollars, and all references to tons are to metric tons.

The following abbreviations are used:

AD	Anti-dumping
ALJ	Administrative law judge
APO	Administrative protective order
CAFC	Court of Appeals for the Federal Circuit
CEP	Constructed export price
CIT	Court of International Trade
COGS	Cost of goods sold
CONNUMs	Control numbers
CVD	Countervailing duty
DSB	Dispute Settlement Body
DSU	Dispute Settlement Understanding
EP	Export price
EU	European Union
FOB	Free on board
GAAP	Generally accepted accounting principles
GATT	General Agreement on Tariffs and Trade
GSA	General, selling and administrative
MOI	Market-oriented industry
NME	Non-market economy
OECD	Organisation for Economic Co-operation and Development
R&D	Research and development
SCM	Subsidies and Countervailing Measures
USTR	The Office of the United States Trade Representative
WTO	World Trade Organization

Chapter 1

Scope of United States trade remedy laws

The United States of America has a wide variety of trade remedy laws. Many foreign companies are genuinely shocked when they learn how many different ways they can run afoul of United States trade laws. Most foreign companies have heard about anti-dumping laws, which are the most commonly used trade remedy laws. But there are many other laws as well.

This chapter provides a brief overview of the United States trade remedy arsenal – the variety of ways that domestic companies can try to limit their foreign competition. First the trade remedies themselves are discussed, then the frequency of use of these different trade remedies, and the range of products and countries that have been attacked.

Purposes of trade remedy laws

At their most basic level, all United States trade remedies are about restricting competition from foreign companies, so as to benefit domestic companies. The particular rationale for the trade restrictions varies from trade remedy to trade remedy. All of these restrictions, however, are created by United States statutes, statutes that were written with significant input from the domestic industries that benefit from the trade remedies.

Foreign companies often complain that these trade remedy laws are anti-competitive. This point is an intellectually fair criticism, but the very purpose of the trade remedy laws is to restrict competition – although only foreign competition. Domestic competition law in the United States focuses on protecting competition, not protecting competitors. Since both sides of an antitrust struggle are usually domestic companies, the law has generally evolved in a more balanced way, with no bias favouring one set of competitors at the expense of other competitors. Trade law is different; it explicitly favours domestic competitors at the expense of foreign competitors.

Trade remedies thus have become tools that United States companies use regularly to achieve corporate objectives. In many foreign countries, managers focus on engineering, marketing and other traditional business disciplines and rarely focus on legal proceedings. In the United States, in contrast, management often focuses on legal proceedings as a competitive tool. In the United States, the chief legal officer of the company is frequently promoted to become the CEO. Most United States business schools require their MBA students to take a mandatory course in the relationship of government to business. Students are taught case studies illustrating how legal proceedings, including trade remedy cases such as an anti-dumping proceeding, can be used as competitive weapons. It is not surprising, therefore, that United States companies have historically been among the most aggressive users of trade remedy laws.

Variety of trade remedies

In subsequent chapters the various trade remedies are discussed in some detail. This section simply sketches the laws and provides a general overview.

Anti-dumping duties

Anti-dumping duties address allegedly unfair pricing by a foreign company. There is no allegation of government involvement; only that the company itself is selling at prices that are so low as to be deemed 'unfair'. Although the rules are complex, the basic idea is that companies should not be allowed to sell in the United States market at prices lower than they sell in their home market or in other export markets. If a company is found to be 'dumping', the United States Government can impose offsetting anti-dumping duties. These laws are discussed in more detail in chapters 3, 4 and 5.

Countervailing duties

Countervailing duties address allegedly unfair pricing that has resulted from improper government subsidies to a company. Unlike anti-dumping cases, the focus here shifts to the government and the subsidies being provided. The basic idea is that companies should not be allowed to charge unfairly low prices because of special government benefits that allow such low pricing. If the company is found to have received improper subsidies, the United States Government can impose offsetting countervailing duties. These laws are discussed in more detail in chapter 6.

Section 201: Safeguard measures

Safeguard remedies address surging imports, regardless of whether they are 'fairly' or 'unfairly' traded. Unlike anti-dumping and countervailing duty cases, which target specific countries accused of unfair practices, safeguard actions include all sources of imports. If it finds that increasing imports are causing serious injury to the domestic industry, the United States Government can impose a wide variety of restrictions, including tariffs, quotas, or a combination of remedies. These laws are discussed in more detail in chapter 7.

Section 337: Intellectual property

Section 337 addresses imports that infringe intellectual property held by a United States company. Such actions target the specific countries and companies allegedly infringing the intellectual property. If it finds a violation, the United States Government can prohibit the importation of the product at issue. This restriction is much more severe than anti-dumping and countervailing duties, which do not involve prohibitions on imports, only additional duties. These laws are discussed in more detail in chapter 8.

Section 301: Market access

Section 301 does not directly address imports, but rather focuses on market barriers that may limit United States exports to another country or other violations of United States international rights under treaties. If it finds such a violation, the United States Government can impose trade sanctions – such as punitive tariffs – to create leverage on the other country to open its market or change its practices. Although the law itself does not focus on imports, the remedy under this law often involves imports. These laws are discussed in more detail in chapter 9.

Other trade remedies

These five trade remedies are the most important for foreign companies, particularly those in developing countries, and are the most commonly used trade remedies. Moreover, several of these remedies involve either limited or no discretion. If the legal requirements are met, the trade restriction must be imposed. Since broader policy judgements do not come into play for anti-dumping or countervailing duty cases, these remedies are particularly popular with United States companies. The probability of actually obtaining the trade restriction is much higher than it would be under other trade remedies.

There are other trade remedies. These remedies are less frequently used, and less frequently lead to restrictions. They involve more discretion before the remedy is imposed, and often that means remedies are not imposed.

For example, Section 232 allows the imposition of trade restrictions when imports threaten United States national security. Since this standard is very difficult to meet, this law is rarely invoked, and even more rarely applied.

There are also special laws, such as Section 406, that allow trade restrictions on communist countries. These laws are a legal relic of the cold war, but even during the cold war they were rarely used. Since the anti-dumping law has special provisions to address 'non-market' economies (see 'Special rules for non-market economies' in chapter 4) most domestic companies have found the anti-dumping law to be a more effective tool to use against imports from communist and former communist countries.

There are also various trade remedies that can be applied to agricultural products, to address environmental concerns, or to reflect political concerns. These laws are also rarely used, because anti-dumping and countervailing duty cases provide more effective trade remedies.

These specialized and rarely used laws are beyond the scope of this book. From a practical perspective, there is little a foreign company can do to avoid the invocation of these laws; if it happens, the company simply copes as best it can.

The main trade remedy laws addressed here, however, are laws for which advance knowledge can help. Knowing about the law allows a company to reduce its risk of being targeted by such actions. Moreover, knowing about the law allows the company to better prepare itself to cope with the law. That is the focus of this book.

Frequency of use of different trade remedies

As table 1 shows, the United States has applied its 'unfair trade' laws – anti-dumping and countervailing duties – to a variety of countries. Even excluding Japan, the Republic of Korea, the various European Union (EU) countries and other OECD countries – all frequent targets – there is an amazing number and range of cases against developing countries.

Table 1   Anti-dumping and countervailing duties applied, by country, 1980–1999

Country	Anti-dumping duties	Countervailing duties
Argentina	15	14
Armenia	3	0
Azerbaijan	3	0
Bangladesh	1	1
Belarus	3	0
Brazil	45	33
Chile	5	2
China	70	4
Colombia	5	4
Costa Rica	5	2
Cuba	0	1
Czech Republic	4	1
Dominican Republic	1	0
Ecuador	2	1
Egypt	1	1
El Salvador	1	1
Estonia	2	0
Georgia	3	0
Hong Kong (China)	5	0
Hungary	6	0
India	15	13
Indonesia	7	4
Iran, Islamic Republic of	1	3
Iraq	1	1
Kazakhstan	5	0
Kenya	1	1
Kyrgyzstan	2	0
Latvia	2	0
Lithuania	2	0
Macao (China)	1	0
Macedonia	1	0
Malaysia	5	7
Mexico	30	30
Republic of Moldova	3	0
Pakistan	0	2
Panama	0	1
Peru	1	7
Philippines	1	2
Poland	9	1
Romania	12	1
Russian Federation/USSR	16	1
Saudi Arabia	1	3

Table 1 (cont'd)		
Country	*Anti-dumping duties*	*Countervailing duties*
Singapore	*6*	*7*
Slovakia	*1*	*0*
South Africa	*8*	*12*
Sri Lanka	*0*	*1*
Taiwan Province (China)	*57*	*8*
Tajikistan	*3*	*0*
Thailand	*11*	*10*
Trinidad and Tobago	*3*	*2*
Turkey	*7*	*7*
Turkmenistan	*3*	*0*
Ukraine	*8*	*0*
United Arab Emirates	*0*	*1*
Uzbekistan	*3*	*0*
Venezuela	*18*	*14*
Yugoslavia	*8*	*0*
Zimbabwe	*0*	*1*

The frequency of such investigations increases or decreases depending on the economic cycle in the United States. When the United States economy is strong, it is harder for the domestic industry to show 'injury', which is necessary to win the case; they are therefore less likely to file. But when the economy weakens, the number of cases increases. Figures 1, 2, 3 and 4, based on official United States Government summaries, show these trends.

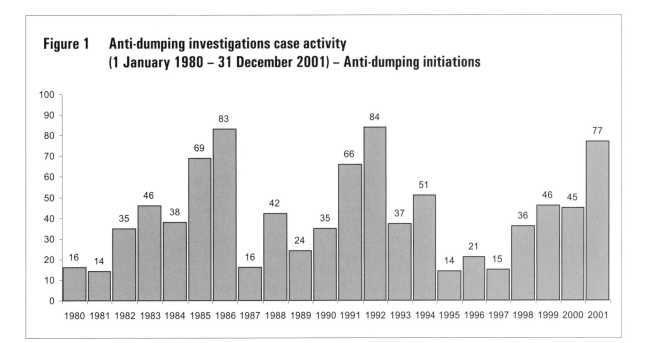

**Figure 1   Anti-dumping investigations case activity
(1 January 1980 – 31 December 2001) – Anti-dumping initiations**

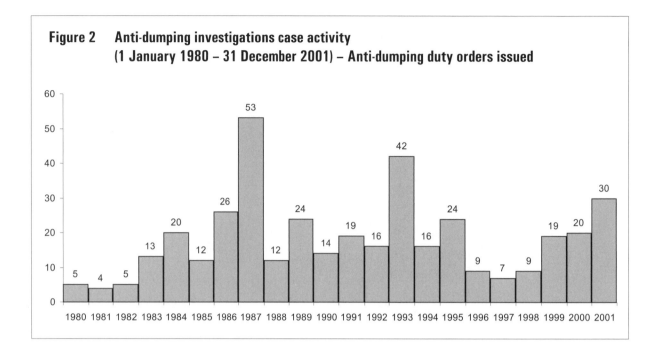

**Figure 2   Anti-dumping investigations case activity
(1 January 1980 – 31 December 2001) – Anti-dumping duty orders issued**

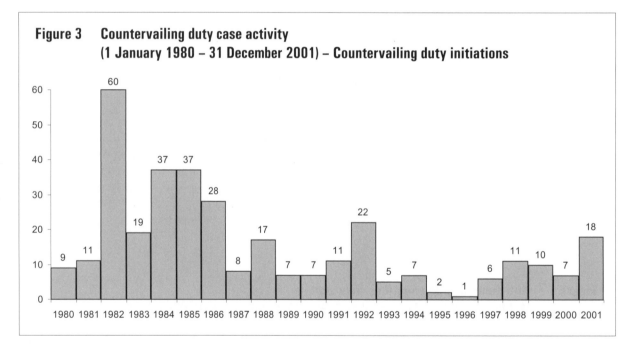

**Figure 3   Countervailing duty case activity
(1 January 1980 – 31 December 2001) – Countervailing duty initiations**

Thus, based on these Commerce Department statistics, the United States has conducted 910 anti-dumping investigations over the past 22 years, averaging 41 investigations per year. Anti-dumping investigations are by far the most frequently used trade remedy. (Note that these statistics for anti-dumping and countervailing duty investigations reflect each country as a separate investigation, even if the same product is involved.)

Over the same period, the United States conducted 340 countervailing duty investigations, averaging 15 investigations per year. As figure 3 shows, the frequency of countervailing duty investigations has dropped somewhat over time. The reason is that countervailing duty investigations have historically yielding lower duty margins than anti-dumping investigations. As a result, domestic industries generally prefer anti-dumping investigations as more likely to lead to severe trade restrictions.

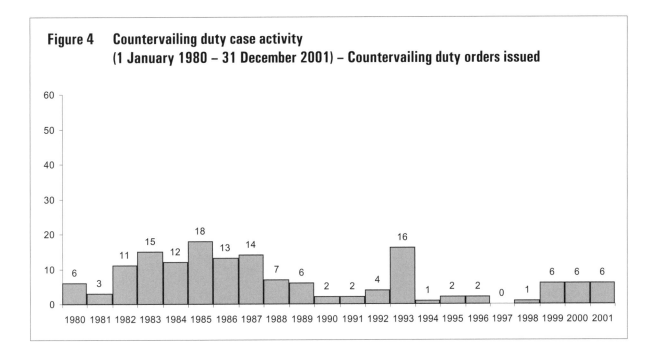

**Figure 4   Countervailing duty case activity
(1 January 1980 – 31 December 2001) – Countervailing duty orders issued**

For both anti-dumping and countervailing duty investigations, these numbers reflect the number of times foreign companies have been burdened by these investigations. The investigations sometimes end with negative determinations, and no duties are imposed. In addition, five years after the order goes into effect, there is a 'sunset review' (see 'Sunset reviews to terminate orders' in chapter 15) to decide whether the order should be continued or terminated. As at 22 March 2002 there were about 260 outstanding anti-dumping orders against 44 different countries and about 50 outstanding countervailing duty orders against 23 different countries.

These cases have also hit a very wide range of products. The most frequently targeted product is steel in any form. The United States domestic steel industry is the single most aggressive user of these laws, and alone accounts for about half of the recent cases. The remaining cases still cover a remarkably wide variety of products, as shown in table 2.

Table 2   Non-steel products affected by anti-dumping duties, by country, 30 April 2001

Country	*Product*
Bangladesh	*Cotton shop towels*
Belarus	*Solid urea*
Belgium	*Sugar*
Brazil	*Frozen concentrated orange juice* *Industrial nitrocellulose* *Silicomanganese*
Canada	*Brass sheet and strip* *Pure and alloy magnesium*
Chile	*Fresh Atlantic salmon* *Preserved mushrooms*

Table 2 (cont'd)

Country	Product
China	*Chloropicrin*
	Cotton shop towels
	Barium chloride
	Greig polyester cotton print cloth
	Natural bristle paint brushes
	Petroleum wax candles
	Porcelain-on-steel cooking ware
	Tapered roller bearings
	Industrial nitrocellulose
	Heavy forged hand tools
	Sparklers
	Sulphur chemicals (sodium thiosulfate)
	Silicon metal
	Sulphanilic acid
	Helical spring lock washers
	Sebacic acid
	Paper clips
	Pencils, cased
	Silicomanganese
	Coumarin
	Garlic, fresh
	Pure magnesium
	Furfuryl alcohol
	Glycine
	Polyvinyl alcohol
	Melamine institutional dinnerware
	Brake rotors
	Persulphates
	Freshwater crawfish tail meat
	Preserved mushrooms
	Apple juice non-frozen
	Bulk aspirin
	Creatine monohydrate
Estonia	*Solid urea*
France	*Sorbitol*
	Industrial nitrocellulose
	Sugar
	Anhydrous sodium metasilicate
	Brass sheet and strip
	Antifriction bearings
Germany	*Large newspaper printing presses*
	Sugar
	Brass sheet and strip
	Antifriction bearings
	Industrial nitrocellulose
	Sulphur chemicals
India	*Sulphanilic acid*
	Preserved mushrooms
Indonesia	*Melamine institutional dinnerware*
	Preserved mushrooms
	Extruded rubber thread

Table 2 (cont'd)

Country	Product
Iran, Islamic Republic of	In shell pistachios
Italy	Pressure sensitive plastic tape Brass sheet and strip Granular polytetrafluoroethylene resin Antifriction bearings Pasta, certain
Japan	Polychloroprene rubber Tapered roller bearings, under 4 inches Melamine in crystal form Tapered roller bearings, over 4 inches Internal combustion IND forklift trucks Brass sheet and strip Granular polytetrafluoroethylene resin Antifriction bearings Electrolytic manganese dioxide Mechanical transfer presses Drafting machines and parts thereof Industrial nitrocellulose Grey Portland cement and clinker Polyvinyl alcohol Large newspaper printing presses and components Gas turbo compressors Vector super computers
Lithuania	Solid urea
Malaysia	Extruded rubber thread
Mexico	Porcelain-on-steel cooking ware Grey Portland cement and clinker
Norway	Fresh and chilled Atlantic salmon
Republic of Korea	Stainless steel cooking ware Industrial nitrocellulose Polyethylene terephthalate (PET) film Polyester staple fibre
Romania	Urea
Russian Federation	Solid urea Ferrovanadium and nitrided vanadium
Singapore	Ball bearings, antifriction
Taiwan Province (China)	Porcelain-on-steel cooking ware Stainless steel cooking ware Helical spring lock washers Polyvinyl alcohol Melamine institutional dinnerware Static random access memory Polyester staple fibre
Tajikistan	Solid urea
Thailand	Furfuryl alcohol Canned pineapple fruit
Turkey	Aspirin Pasta, certain

Table 2 (cont'd)

Country	Product
Turkmenistan	Solid urea
Ukraine	Solid urea
United Kingdom	Antifriction bearings Industrial nitrocellulose Sulphur chemicals
Uzbekistan	Solid urea

Section 201 'safeguard' actions are much less commonly used. Since the legal standards to obtain safeguard remedies are higher than in anti-dumping cases, domestic industries generally prefer anti-dumping cases. In addition, even if the tough legal standards are met, the President still has discretion under Section 201 to deny relief to the domestic industry – and often does. Thus, from 1974 to 2000 the United States conducted about 70 safeguard investigations. In about half of these investigations the International Trade Commission found no injury, and in about half of the affirmative findings the President decided not to grant any relief. Thus, only about 20% of the cases led to any import restrictions. Not surprisingly, domestic industries do not view Section 201 as their trade remedy of first choice. More recently, however, relief has been granted in some cases, leading to renewed interest in Section 201.

Section 337 is used more frequently. According to the International Trade Commission database, by 1 August 2001 there had been 460 investigations under Section 337. Of these there were 30 outstanding exclusion orders, barring certain products from entering the United States. Since these cases frequently force companies into licensing agreements for the intellectual property at issue, there is less need to impose trade restriction sanctions.

Section 301 has also been used frequently, with more than 120 different investigations since the law was enacted. Few of these investigations have resulted in actual trade sanctions. Prior to the WTO decision in 2000 declaring sanctions under Section 301 to be WTO inconsistent, the United States did threaten or impose sanctions in some cases. There was a very high-profile case involving Japanese automobiles, in which the United States threatened 100% duties on Japanese exports of luxury automobiles. That case, however, was settled before the duties went into effect. One case involving Japanese semiconductors resulted in the imposition of 100% tariffs on Japanese exports of computers to the United States for several years, before they were finally lifted. Note that although many of these cases focused on the EU, Japan and other developed countries, over 45 of them involved various developing countries.

As this discussion shows, there are many different ways in which domestic companies can seek trade restrictions against their foreign competitors. If your company has not yet had the unpleasant experience of coping with one of these legal proceedings, the risk of future problems remains very real. The remaining chapters in this book are designed to help you better understand how these different laws work, and how you can best cope with proceedings under these laws.

Chapter 2

Procedural framework for United States unfair trade remedies

As the preceding chapter explained, the most frequently used trade remedy is the anti-dumping duty investigation. The next most frequently used trade remedy is a close cousin – the countervailing duty investigation. Both of these proceedings involve allegations of 'unfair trade' – either prices that are set too low by companies, or prices that have been lowered by government subsidies. Because they are closely related, the United States procedural frameworks for dealing with both types of cases are quite similar.

This chapter provides a procedural overview of an unfair trade investigation. The sections below describe what happens during each major phase in the investigation, and explain the major concepts involved. Although not every procedural detail is included, this chapter discusses all the major phases of the investigation and important concepts. Readers who have already been involved in such investigations may find much of this material familiar. These readers may want to skim this chapter and move immediately to the more detailed discussions of the substantive principles of anti-dumping and countervailing duty law discussed in later chapters.

What is an anti-dumping or countervailing duty investigation?

An anti-dumping or countervailing duty investigation is an administrative proceeding through which two United States Government agencies – the United States Department of Commerce (or Commerce Department) and the United States International Trade Commission (the Commission) – decide whether unfairly traded imports are injuring a United States industry.

The Commerce Department handles the part of the investigation that determines whether the imports are unfairly priced – whether they are being sold at 'less than fair value', otherwise known as 'dumping' – or being sold with the benefit of impermissible government subsidies. The dozens of complicated issues that arise in trying to make the fair value or subsidy determinations are resolved only at the end of the long and complex Commerce Department phase of the investigation.

The International Trade Commission (an independent, quasi-judicial agency, whose six Commissioners serve nine-year terms) handles the other part of the investigation, and determines whether a United States industry is suffering 'material injury by reason of' imports, or is threatened with material injury. The two key aspects of this legal test – whether there is 'material injury' and whether it is 'by reason of' imports – are discussed in more detail in later chapters. For present purposes, the important point is that two parallel investigations take place in an anti-dumping investigation. If a foreign producer is successful in either the dumping or injury investigation, no anti-dumping order will be issued.

This bifurcated approach is somewhat unique to the United States. Most countries have a single administering authority that considers both issues, decides the dumping or subsidy margin, and also decides whether there is injury caused by unfair trade imports. The United States separates these two functions, largely for historical reasons, but also in an effort to give more independence to the International Trade Commission.

Procedural framework for unfair trade investigations

Before beginning a detailed examination of the most crucial substantive aspects of an anti-dumping investigation, it is necessary to have an overview of the general procedural framework, and what happens at each stage. This chapter discusses the following stages:

❏ Initiation of the investigation

❏ Preliminary injury determination

❏ Questionnaire response

❏ Preliminary dumping determination

❏ Verification

❏ Post-verification legal arguments

❏ Final dumping determination

❏ Final injury determination

❏ Anti-dumping duty order

❏ Judicial review

❏ Administrative review

Some aspects of the procedure are fixed while other aspects are flexible. Although no two investigations are conducted in exactly the same way, there are a number of basic features common to all anti-dumping investigations.

Filing of the petition and the initiation of the investigation

An unfair trade investigation can begin in two different ways. The investigation usually begins when an 'interested party' (a domestic producer of the product in question, a labour union, or a trade association) files a petition with the Commerce Department and the Commission alleging that dumping or subsidization is taking place. The Commerce Department may also initiate an investigation by itself – without waiting for a formal petition – whenever it determines that an investigation is warranted. Such 'self-initiation' of anti-dumping investigations is quite rare, however, and happens only in very political cases, such as those involving lumber or semiconductors.

Initiation of the investigation

Initiation of the investigation is virtually automatic. The Commission begins its investigation almost immediately, and imposes virtually no requirements on the petitioner before beginning the investigation. Any problems are resolved during the pre-filing consultation with the agency that most petitioners undertake.

The Commerce Department follows a somewhat different practice. Within 20 days after a petition is filed, the Commerce Department must determine whether the petition meets the technical requirements for the initiation of an investigation. If not, the petition will be dismissed and the proceeding terminated. As a practical matter, however, the Commerce Department almost always initiates investigations. The Commerce Department encourages domestic companies to submit their proposed petitions for informal review prior to a formal filing. Because the Commerce Department advises the companies of any technical problems in the petition or areas where additional information is necessary, the petition is almost always acceptable when it is formally submitted to the Commerce Department and the Commission.

Foreign companies often wonder whether there is anything they can do to encourage or persuade the Commerce Department not to initiate an investigation, especially when the petition seems to have little basis in fact. Unfortunately, there is very little that can be done. Current United States law prohibits the Commerce Department from having any contact with potential targets of an anti-dumping investigation before the investigation is initiated. Although contact with other United States government agencies [such as the Office of the United States Trade Representative (USTR)] is legally permissible, it is virtually impossible to persuade those agencies to intercede in the early stages of an anti-dumping investigation. If a petition is filed, foreign companies therefore have little choice but to wait for the inevitable initiation of the investigation.

Once the petition is filed, a timetable set forth in the statute and required by law begins. Table 3 summarizes the important deadlines imposed by the statute in anti-dumping cases.

Table 3   Anti-dumping schedule

Phase	Deadline
Initiation	Petition + 20 days
Preliminary Commission	Petition + 45 days
Preliminary Commerce Department	Petition + 160–210 days
Final Commerce Department	Petition + 235–345 days
Final Commission	Petition + 280–420 days

A similar, but shorter, set of deadlines apply in countervailing duty investigations, as shown in table 4.

Table 4   Countervailing duty schedule

Phase	Deadline
Initiation	Petition + 20 days
Preliminary Commission	Petition + 45 days
Preliminary Commerce Department	Petition + 85–150 days
Final Commerce Department	Petition + 160–225 days
Final Commission	Petition + 205–270 days

Because of the various possibilities for extensions, it is best to think of the timetable as periods of time during which a particular decision can be made, rather than precise dates.

In addition, if the Commerce Department decides that it needs to conduct a special investigation to determine whether the domestic industry has 'standing' to bring to case, the agency can take more time. The United States law allows an extra 20 days before initiating the case to conduct this special review. The topic of standing is discussed under 'Examining petitioner's standing' in chapter 3.

A special rule applies if the Commerce Department decides that it needs to investigate so-called upstream subsidies. In such cases, the agency is allowed an additional period of time – another 160 days – to make the preliminary determination. The topic of upstream subsidies is discussed under 'Upstream subsidies' in chapter 6.

These are the major deadlines required by the statute. As discussed below, there are a number of other deadlines, some formal and some informal, imposed by the Commerce Department during the course of the investigation.

Preliminary injury determination

Within 45 days after the petition is filed, the Commission must make a preliminary determination of whether there is evidence of injury to the domestic industry. Unlike most other phases of the investigation, there is no possibility of an extension. The Commission must make its determination in 45 days, based on whatever information is available.

The standard of proof in the preliminary injury determination is quite low. The domestic industry need only show that there is a 'reasonable indication' that an industry in the United States has been materially injured or is threatened with material injury. If the preliminary injury determination is negative, the anti-dumping investigations by the Commerce Department and the Commission will be terminated. If the preliminary injury determination is affirmative, the investigations will continue.

This first stage in an anti-dumping investigation is the threshold determination required by the General Agreement on Tariffs and Trade (GATT) to stop cases that are groundless. Unfortunately, the standard of proof is so low that most preliminary injury determinations are affirmative. In the past several years, the Commission has made negative preliminary injury determinations in approximately 15% of the cases filed.

The procedure for a preliminary injury determination is simple and quick. Approximately one week after the petition is filed, the Commission publishes a schedule for the preliminary determination in the *Federal Register*. A public hearing is held, but only the Commission staff attends, not the Commissioners who ultimately make the decision. During the hearing, interested parties can submit arguments and information that they feel would help the Commission in its decision-making. The Commission staff sends out questionnaires to members of the domestic industry, to importers of the merchandise under investigation, and to foreign producers to collect information needed for the investigation. Because of the severe time constraints, however, the quality and quantity of information collected for the preliminary injury determination is often extremely limited.

Even though a foreign company's chances of success are small, there are two important reasons to participate actively in the preliminary injury determination. First, sometimes domestic industries bring anti-dumping cases with fundamental flaws that foreign respondents can help reveal to the Commission. For example, in 2002 one United States company filed an anti-dumping case even though the company was itself one of the largest importers of the merchandise against which the case was filed. The Commission made a negative determination in that case. The chances of success may be small, but the benefits of avoiding the remainder of the investigation are worth the effort.

Second, even if the case survives the preliminary injury determination, many anti-dumping cases can be defeated in the final injury determination. In the past several years, the Commission has made negative final injury determinations in approximately 30%–40% of the cases. By participating actively in the early stages of the investigation, foreign exporters can often persuade the Commission to frame the issues in a favourable way and thus increase the likelihood of success later when the Commission conducts its more detailed final injury investigation. Not participating in the preliminary investigation runs the risk that the petitioner will be able to frame the issues in the investigation in the way most favourable to the petitioner's point of view. The defence of a preliminary injury case is discussed in detail in chapter 12.

The foreign company should note that injury determinations – at both the preliminary and final stages – are based on all United States imports from the exporting country. The Commission does not make separate injury determinations for individual companies. If there is injury 'by reason of' imports from a country, all companies exporting to the United States from that country will be included in the injury finding. In most cases, the Commission will also consider together all the imports from different countries under investigation. This doctrine of 'cumulation' is discussed in detail under 'Cumulation of imports' in chapter 11.

Questionnaire response

Shortly after the investigation is initiated, the Commerce Department sends out a detailed questionnaire to foreign manufacturers and exporters of the merchandise under investigation. This questionnaire is given either to the lawyer representing the foreign company or to the country's embassy in Washington DC, or to both.

The questionnaire in an anti-dumping case asks for general background about the company and its sales practices (section A), information on domestic sales in the exporter's home market (section B), export sales to other countries (also part of section B), and export sales to the United States (section C). It sometimes also asks for information about the cost of producing the merchandise under investigation (section D) and constructed value (section E). All of this information is needed to enable the Commerce Department to make a comparison between 'United States price' and 'foreign market value' (usually either foreign home market prices or prices to export markets other than the United States), which determines whether there has been dumping as defined by United States law. The questionnaire is very detailed and requires much of the information to be submitted on appropriate computer media in a specified format.

In the dumping context, the questionnaires have become quite standardized. The products and period of time being investigated change from case to case, but much of the remainder of the questionnaire is the same. The Commerce Department has a standard questionnaire posted on its website, at *www.ita.doc.gov*, in the 'IA Document Library'.

The questionnaires in countervailing duty case are different in two respects. First, the government of the country in question receives a very detailed questionnaire about the operation of the various alleged subsidy programmes, and about various economic issues that may affect the assessment of whether the programmes are impermissible subsidies. Second, the foreign exporters also receive questionnaires, but the focus is on the utilization of the programmes and on general questions about the company, not the transaction-by-transaction examination of prices and costs that is requested in an anti-dumping questionnaire.

A response to the questionnaire usually must be made within 30 to 45 days after it is received. The response is normally due within 30 days after the questionnaire is presented. An extension of 15 days is normal and is usually granted routinely. Extensions beyond 45 days are unusual, and will be granted only if the foreign company can provide a good justification for the delay. For example, in some investigations the Commerce Department has considered national holidays and the closing of a company's financial year to be good justifications for extensions.

There is normally a great deal of activity during the period following submission of the questionnaire responses. The Commerce Department, based on its review of the questionnaire response, usually has follow-up questions and usually requires supplemental responses. These responses are often called 'deficiency responses', an unfair name since the deficiency is sometimes with the questions and the Commerce Department's understanding of the response, not with the answer itself.

Complaints from the domestic industry can also trigger supplemental responses. If the United States industry is represented by an aggressive lawyer, that lawyer (and any consultants working with the lawyer) carefully reviews all the submissions made by the foreign company and presents arguments to the Commerce Department that the information submitted is incomplete or inaccurate, and that additional information should therefore be requested from the company. The United States industry wants to have as much information submitted in writing as possible. The United States industry also wants to make the defence of the case as burdensome as possible for its foreign competitor. Requests from the petitioner sometimes lead to supplemental responses, if the Commerce Department decides that it agrees with the criticisms and arguments made by the petitioner.

Preparation of the responses and supplemental responses to the questionnaire is one of the most crucial parts of the defence effort. The foreign company must devote substantial time and effort to preparing thorough and accurate responses to the Commerce Department questionnaire.

Preliminary Commerce Department determination

Timing of the determination

Within 85 days (countervailing duty) or 160 days (anti-dumping duty) after the petition is filed, the Commerce Department must make its preliminary determination of whether sales have occurred at less-than-fair-value or whether impermissible subsidies exist. The statutory deadline for this preliminary determination by the Commerce Department can be extended up to the 150th day (countervailing duty) or 210th day (anti-dumping duty) after the petition is filed in cases that are deemed to be 'extraordinarily complicated' by the Commerce Department, or where the petitioner requests an extension. If the Commerce Department decides to extend the preliminary determination, it must notify the parties before the scheduled date of the determination.

An 'extraordinarily complicated' case is one that presents a large number of complex transactions or adjustments, raises novel issues, or involves a large number of firms under investigation. An additional practical consideration, although not specifically mentioned in the statute or regulations, is the workload of the Commerce Department at the time. If other investigations are absorbing all of the available personnel, it is more likely that the Commerce Department will decide that a case is complicated and extend the deadline.

Legal significance

The date of the preliminary dumping determination is legally significant. The date an affirmative preliminary determination is published in the *Federal Register* is the date on which the United States Customs Service (Customs) 'suspends liquidation' of all future imports of the product under investigation. 'Suspension of liquidation' means that Customs will not make a final decision about the import duties that are owed on the merchandise, because the question of whether special anti-dumping or countervailing duties should be added to the normal customs duties is now at issue.

This date also has business significance. With the suspension of liquidation, Customs begins to require a bond (a legal promise to pay the duties) to cover estimated duties. The importer (often a United States subsidiary related to the parent company) must pay for this bond, and must bear the risk of future anti-dumping duty. The legal responsibility to pay the duties falls to the so-called 'importer of record', which is often the United States subsidiary of the parent company.

Suspension of liquidation takes place only if the preliminary determination is affirmative. A negative preliminary determination allows merchandise to continue entering the United States without any risk of future duty liability as the case proceeds. A negative preliminary determination by Commerce, however, unlike a negative preliminary injury determination, does not end the case. It will continue at least to the Commerce Department's final determination, at which time the case will end if the determination is still negative.

The estimated duties set in the preliminary determination represent the maximum liability for the importer until the Commerce Department's final determination. The actual liability (to be determined later in the investigation) can be lower, but it cannot be higher. This cap on liability changes after the final dumping determination, and again after the final injury determination is issued. Note that the 'importer of record' must pay any duties, not the foreign exporter. In many cases exporters ship to related companies in the United States, who serve as importers of record, so the liability is still within the corporate family.

De minimis *rules*

The Commerce Department's threshold for making an affirmative preliminary determination is a margin of 2.0% in anti-dumping cases and 1.0% in countervailing duty cases. Margins below these levels are regarded as *de minimis* by the Commerce Department and result in a negative determination. Margins at or above these levels result in an affirmative determination. The same thresholds apply to both the Commerce Department's preliminary and final determinations. (Note that a somewhat lower threshold – 0.5% – applies in administrative reviews of both anti-dumping and countervailing duty orders.)

Note that there is a special rule for developing countries in countervailing duty cases, but not anti-dumping cases. Countries certified by the United States Trade Representative as 'developing countries' are entitled to a special 2.0% or 3.0% level for *de minimis* subsidies, depending on their level of development. This special rule applies only in original investigations, however, not in the so-called administrative reviews that take place annually after a countervailing duty has been imposed. (See 'Developing country rules' in chapter 6 for further discussion.)

The Commerce Department's preliminary determination (and ultimately the final determination) is company-specific. The Commerce Department estimates dumping margins for each company that participates in the anti-dumping investigation. In addition, the Commerce Department calculates an 'all others' rate which applies to any company not involved in the investigation that decides later to begin exporting to the United States.

Basis of the determination

The Commerce Department generally bases its preliminary determination on the information provided by the foreign company in the questionnaire response. Although the Commerce Department is permitted to conduct a 'verification' of the response before the preliminary dumping determination, as a practical matter such an early verification virtually never takes place. The Commerce Department thus takes all of the company's claims at their face value. Usually the claims are accepted as long as they nominally satisfy the Commerce Department's standards; sometimes the Commerce Department misunderstands the claims and rejects them.

The Commerce Department explains how it reached its preliminary determination in two ways. First, a notice summarizing the methodologies and results is published in the *Federal Register* approximately a week after the preliminary determination is made. This notice is usually too general to be very useful, but does set forth the basic methodology used by the Commerce Department. In the past the full rationale was published in the *Federal Register*. Now the published version is much shorter, but the full decisional memoranda are published on the Commerce Department website.

Second, the Commerce Department holds separate disclosure conferences for both the attorneys for the foreign company and the attorneys for the United States industry. At these disclosure conferences, the Commerce Department discusses the methodologies in more detail, and provides the actual calculation sheets and computer printouts.

The disclosure conference often reveals errors in the Commerce Department's calculations, but these errors are difficult to correct. The Commerce Department leaves the preliminary determination as it was published and tells the parties to make their arguments for corrections in written submissions later in the investigation. The predominant attitude at the Commerce Department is that since 'it is only a preliminary determination', there is no urgency to correct errors that can be corrected in the final determination. The fact that the preliminary determination has legal significance (i.e. it is the date on which liquidation is suspended) has not persuaded the Commerce Department to make corrections. In at least one case, for example, the Commerce Department refused to correct clerical errors in a preliminary determination that would have changed the result from an affirmative determination (with suspension of liquidation) to a negative determination (with no suspension of liquidation).

Critical circumstances

In most cases, the publication date of an affirmative preliminary determination is the first time the importer of the merchandise becomes potentially liable for anti-dumping duties. The one exception is when a petitioner successfully argues that 'critical circumstances' exist. If the Commerce Department and Trade

Commission both find critical circumstances, then suspension of liquidation can be retroactive as far back as 90 days prior to the date of the affirmative preliminary dumping determination.

The two agencies apply different standards to determine whether 'critical circumstances' exist. The Commerce Department must find first either that there has been a history of dumping, whether in the United States or elsewhere, or that the importer should have known it was receiving dumped merchandise. The Commerce Department will assume that the importer knew the merchandise was dumped if the dumping margins are greater than 20%. For countervailing duty cases, the parallel requirement is a finding that the subsidy is inconsistent with the Subsidies Agreement, a requirement easily met in most cases.

The Commerce Department must also find that there have been massive imports over a short period of time. To make this determination, it will examine the extent to which imports have gained market share in the United States market and the historical pattern of imports. If imports have increased at least 15% over the period immediately preceding the petition, the Commerce Department will usually find 'massive' imports.

The period of time analysed by the Commerce Department became contentious in the late 1990s. Largely as a favour to the United States steel industry, it adopted a new policy that allows it to examine earlier time periods to find a 'surge' whenever it decides that the exporters knew the unfair trade case was coming, and thus may have begun moderating their behaviour. With the flexibility to pick and choose different time periods for the comparison, it is now much easier to find the necessary increase.

This particular Commerce Department policy was challenged by Japan in a recent WTO case involving hot-rolled steel, but the panel upheld the WTO consistency of the United States practice.

The Commission considers whether retroactive dumping duties are necessary to prevent the reoccurrence of injury. Recent changes to the United States law specify the various factors the Commission is to review in making this determination: the condition of the domestic industry; whether there have been massive imports to evade the effect of the anti-dumping or countervailing duties (in other words, did the exporter increase shipments before the Commerce Department's preliminary determination to avoid duties); and whether the massive imports will have a lingering effect in the marketplace after the duty liability comes into effect.

The domestic industry is free to make allegations of critical circumstances throughout the investigation. Allegations are often made in the petition. The allegations can be made as late as 21 days before the Commerce Department's final determination. Petitioners have an incentive to raise the allegations before the preliminary determination, however, to obtain protection more quickly.

The effect and timing of a critical circumstances determination is intertwined with the Commerce Department's determination of dumping or subsidization. If the Commerce Department makes an affirmative preliminary determination of dumping or subsidization, a finding of critical circumstances means that suspension of liquidation can be retroactive for 90 days prior to the preliminary determination. Even if the preliminary critical circumstances determination itself is negative, and thus there is no retroactive suspension of liquidation after the preliminary dumping determination, the Commerce Department can still reach back 90 days prior to the preliminary dumping determination if the final critical circumstances determination is affirmative. If the Commerce Department makes a negative preliminary determination of dumping, however, any retroactive suspension of liquidation can only go back 90 days from the date the suspension of liquidation was first ordered – the date of the Commerce Department's final determination.

Verification by the Department of Commerce

After the preliminary determination, the Commerce Department conducts a 'verification' of the response to the questionnaire. It sends a team of two to four people to the headquarters and production facilities of the foreign company to verify the accuracy of the information that has been submitted. In a countervailing duty investigation, this verification includes the government agencies who responded to the questionnaires. The verification normally lasts one or two weeks, depending on how many companies and topics are involved. The inquiry can be wide-ranging and it is important that the foreign company prepare as thoroughly as possible for the verification.

The timing of the verification and the post-verification activities is somewhat flexible. Although in theory the verification may take place before the Commerce Department's preliminary determination, the standard practice recently has been to conduct the verification afterwards. One or two weeks before the verification is scheduled to begin, the Commerce Department normally issues a verification outline.

This outline is sometimes detailed, but it often provides only a skeletal explanation of what the Commerce Department will examine during the verification. In recent years, outlines have become more standardized.

After the verification, the Commerce Department staff will prepare detailed verification reports summarizing the results. These reports are usually ready two to three weeks after the verification has been completed, although reports are sometimes not prepared until much later.

A more detailed description of the verification process and of strategies for a successful verification is provided in chapter 10. For present purposes, the most important point to note is that the verification is an extremely important phase of the investigation. If the foreign company is unable to verify the accuracy of its response and more generally to convince the Commerce Department of the reliability of the company's accounting system, there is a significant risk that the Commerce Department will reject the company's response and instead use the 'facts available' rule. 'Facts available', formerly known as 'best information available', is a euphemism under United States law for the use of the worst information possible. It is usually the information submitted in the petition by the domestic industry.

Post-verification legal arguments

After the verification, the attorneys for the foreign company and the attorneys for the United States industry prepare legal briefs to submit to the Commerce Department. The briefs are based largely on key issues in the case, issues raised in the verification reports, and on the various developments that have taken place during the investigation. The parties set forth their views concerning the important issues in the investigation and how the Commerce Department should treat these issues. The tentative schedule for the briefs is published in the *Federal Register* notice accompanying the preliminary determination, but the schedule sometimes changes.

The legal arguments in this phase of the investigation take place in several parts. The deadlines imposed by the statute often force the Commerce Department to move very quickly through the last few weeks of an anti-dumping investigation. First, the parties submit pre-hearing briefs. These briefs are usually due after the Commerce Department has released the verification reports.

Second, the parties submit rebuttal briefs. These briefs are usually due one week after the pre-hearing briefs. The parties are allowed to comment only on the arguments raised by the other side in its pre-hearing brief. These briefs, and any other arguments submitted by the lawyers during the investigation, are usually considered by the Commerce Department during its deliberations about the final determination.

Third, the Commerce Department usually holds a public hearing approximately one week after the pre-hearing briefs are submitted. Although such a hearing is not required by the law unless one of the parties requests it, usually one of the parties makes such a request. The hearing normally lasts between two and four hours, depending on the number of companies that wish to participate. Anyone may attend. Foreign companies may attend the hearing, but they usually choose not to do so.

Several Commerce Department officials will attend the hearing, including the Commerce Department staff members who have been working on the investigation. In theory, the purpose of the hearing is to allow the Commerce Department staff members to ask questions to help them decide the important issues in the investigation. In practice, the Commerce Department officials seldom ask questions, although this varies depending on the particular officials and issues involved. This hearing will be one of the opportunities to draw their attention to important issues in the case.

Final Commerce determination

Timing of the determination

Within 75 days after the preliminary determination (for both anti-dumping and countervailing duty investigations), the Commerce Department must make its final determination. Depending on whether there was an extension of the preliminary determination, this final determination will take place sometime between 160 and 225 days (in a countervailing duty case) or 235 and 285 days (in an anti-dumping case) after the petition is filed.

It is also possible for the final determination to be extended in anti-dumping cases. If the preliminary determination was affirmative, then the foreign producers who account for a 'significant portion' of the exports under investigation have the legal right to request an extension of up to 60 days. If the preliminary determination was negative, then only the United States industry has the right to request an extension. Occasionally there are battles over whether extensions will be granted, but in most situations extensions have become somewhat routine whenever one party wants an extension. Sometimes the Commerce Department decides an extension is necessary, in which case it applies informal pressure on the appropriate party to make the formal request for the extension.

If an extension is granted, the final dumping determination is due 135 days after the preliminary determination. Depending on whether there was an extension of the preliminary dumping determination, the final determination can take place between 295 and 345 days after the petition is filed.

In countervailing duty cases, the rule for extending the final determination is different. There is no general rule for extending the final determination for complicated cases. Rather, there is a special rule that applies if there are simultaneous countervailing duty and anti-dumping investigations of the same product, a fairly common occurrence. In this situation, the domestic industry (but not the foreign exporters) has a right to request that the final anti-dumping and countervailing determinations be aligned to occur at the same time. This request, if made, has the effect of delaying the countervailing duty determination.

Legal significance

The final dumping determination states whether there have been sales at 'less than fair value' or impermissible subsidies within the meaning of the United States law. The Commerce Department calculates a weighted average margin of dumping or subsidy.

As noted above in the discussion of preliminary dumping determinations, if the margin is less than 2.0% in an anti-dumping case or 1.0% in a countervailing duty case, the Commerce Department considers the margin to be *de minimis* and makes a negative determination. In such a situation, the investigation ends. If the margin of dumping is above these thresholds, the Commerce Department makes an affirmative determination and the investigation then returns to the Commission for a final injury determination. In either case, the Commerce Department publishes a notice of the final determination in the *Federal Register*, and summarizes the various arguments made by the parties and the comments of the Commerce Department concerning those arguments.

The date of publication of the final dumping determination in the *Federal Register* is legally significant. This date marks a change in the potential liability for duties. United States law provides that between the Commerce Department's preliminary and final determinations, the duties eventually collected can be no higher than the rate set in the preliminary determination (and can be lower). This rate is sometimes called the 'cap'. After the final dumping determination, the Commerce Department changes the cap to reflect the margin of dumping or subsidy found in its final determination. The new cap remains in effect until the Commission's final injury determination; it can be lower or higher than the cap established by the Commerce Department's preliminary determination.

Note that there is a special rule for countervailing duty cases. Sometimes a 'gap' period opens up, under which the liability for potential countervailing duties ends and then resumes once the final decision has been made. This special rule is discussed under 'Final Commerce Department subsidy determination' in chapter 6.

The final determination in the original investigation, however, is not really 'final'. Like the preliminary dumping determination, the final determination is only an estimate of the present dumping or subsidy margin, and only establishes the bond or cash deposit rate. The final liability is not fixed until much later.

Basis of the determination

The final determination is generally based on the information provided in the questionnaire response, and follows methodologies similar to those used in the preliminary determination. There are important exceptions, however, to this general pattern. First, the Commerce Department is legally permitted to use only information that has been 'verified'. Therefore, if any of the information changes during the verification, the Commerce Department must use the verified information. If too much changes at the verification, the Commerce Department is permitted to disregard the response entirely and instead use the 'facts available' rule as a penalty to the foreign respondent.

Second, the methodologies in the final determination sometimes vary considerably from those used in the preliminary determination. The preliminary dumping determination may be based on a price-to-price comparison while the final determination is based on a price-to-cost comparison, with cost based on 'constructed value' as defined in the United States law. Foreign companies are thus deprived of the opportunity to see what types of methodologies the Commerce Department is considering for the investigation.

After the final determination, the Commerce Department usually holds a disclosure conference to describe the methodologies and calculations used to reach the decision. The degree of disclosure depends a great deal on the individual persons involved. In deciding on the amount of disclosure, the Commerce Department faces a tension between competing policies. On the one hand, complete disclosure is fair to the parties and can sometimes avoid the need to begin a court action just to find out what the Commerce Department actually did in the investigation. On the other hand, the Commerce Department is frequently concerned that complete disclosure could weaken the defence of its decisions in any court action that might result.

This historical reluctance to discuss fully the results of a final determination has been changing. In a recent innovation, the Commerce Department implemented a procedure through which various parties can call the Commerce Department's attention to 'clerical' errors (such as arithmetic mistakes and inadvertent decisions to exclude certain data) after the final determination, and the Commerce Department can correct those errors. This new administrative policy, codified in amendments to the United States law in 1988, has required the Commerce Department to begin providing more complete information so that the various parties can review the calculations looking for clerical errors. This process takes place soon after the final determination is made, so it is important to be prepared to make this review as quickly as possible.

Final injury determination

The final injury determination is the last chance to avoid imposition of the anti-dumping or countervailing duty order. Foreign companies and their lawyers therefore devote a great deal of time and effort to this stage, especially if the Commerce Department has calculated high dumping or subsidy margins.

Timing of the determination

The timing of a final injury determination is somewhat complicated. If the Commerce Department's preliminary dumping determination is affirmative, the Commission must make its final decision either 120 days after the Commerce Department's preliminary determination or 45 days after the Commerce Department's final determination, whichever is later. If the Commerce Department's preliminary determination is negative, the Commission must make its decision 75 days after the Commerce Department's final determination. Depending on whether there have been extensions of either the preliminary or the final Commerce Department determinations, this final Commission determination could take place between 280 and 420 days after the anti-dumping petition was filed, or earlier in a countervailing duty petition without any extensions.

Because the statutory deadlines work in complex ways, the earliest deadline determines when the Commission must do its work and make its decision. It is not uncommon for multiple cases against the same product to end up with different schedules and deadlines. The Commission sets its schedule based on the earliest deadline. Once all the work is done, the subsequent investigations use the same basic data set, and usually reach the same decision as the first case to go through the process (unless some of the countries have an argument that they should not be cumulated with the others – see 'Cumulation of imports' in chapter 11).

Legal significance

The date that the Commission's final injury determination is published in the *Federal Register* is the date on which the limited liability comes to an end. The cap on liability that becomes effective after the Commerce Department's preliminary determination, and is revised after the Commerce Department's final dumping determination, no longer applies. Beginning with imports entered on or after this date, the importer's final liability is theoretically unlimited. The importer, therefore, has no way to determine the final cost of the imported merchandise.

Legal standard

The legal standard for a final injury determination is different from that in the preliminary injury determination. Although in the preliminary injury determination the domestic industry need show only a 'reasonable indication' of injury or threat of injury, in the final injury determination this standard is raised to a requirement to show that the domestic industry is actually being materially injured or threatened with material injury. This higher standard of proof makes it more likely that a foreign company will be able to succeed in showing that there has been no injury or threat of injury to the United States industry. As noted above, approximately 30%–40% of recent final injury determinations have ended in negative determinations.

Procedures

The process of the final injury investigation is longer and somewhat more complex than that for the preliminary injury investigation. Chapter 13 will describe the final injury investigation in some detail, but a brief overview here will be helpful.

First, the Commission begins collecting information. After an affirmative preliminary determination, the Commission formally initiates its final injury investigation. The Commission thus begins its investigation even before it knows what the Commerce Department's final determination will be. The Commission staff collects all of the responses to the various questionnaires and any other information that it has obtained and drafts a preliminary staff report. This report is provided to all the parties for their comments and criticisms.

Second, the various parties submit pre-hearing briefs to the Commission, participate in a hearing, and submit post-hearing briefs. The briefs provide comments on the draft preliminary staff report, as well as present any legal arguments that the parties wish to raise in the investigation. The Commission also conducts a public hearing. Unlike the hearing in the preliminary injury determination, which is attended only by Commission staff people, this hearing is conducted by the Commissioners themselves, the individuals who actually make the determinations in the investigation. (A full Commission has six members.) The post-hearing briefs are usually limited to those issues raised in the pre-hearing briefs of the other parties, and those issues raised at the hearing itself.

Finally, the Commissioners vote on whether they believe there is injury or threat of injury to the domestic industry. The basis for the vote is the final staff report, summarizing the data collected in the investigation, and the briefs submitted by the various parties in the course of the investigation. This vote is usually scheduled about two weeks before the actual decision is due. One of the many curiosities of the United States law is that a tie vote of the Commissioners results in an affirmative finding of injury.

If during the course of this process the Commerce Department decides that there have been no sales at less than fair value or no impermissible subsidies, the Commission immediately stops its investigation. If the Commerce Department decides that there have been sales at less than fair value or impermissible subsidies, the Commission's investigation continues to a conclusion.

Anti-dumping or countervailing duty order

Approximately seven days after the final injury determination, the Commerce Department publishes an anti-dumping or countervailing duty order in the *Federal Register*. This notice is the official announcement of the size of the estimated margins, and sets forth the amount of the cash deposit for estimated duties that importers are expected to pay whenever they import the merchandise that has been under investigation. Customs will continue suspension of liquidation on prior entries, and maintain the bonds with respect to those entries. Any new entries will require a cash deposit rather than a bond. As discussed below, the actual duties owed are determined later during administrative reviews of the anti-dumping order.

At the same time as the order is published, the Commerce Department sends a message to the United States Customs Service, giving the specific instructions that Customs is to follow regarding importation of the merchandise. This message is sent to all ports, so that Customs officers can implement the new anti-dumping or countervailing duty order. Sometimes the message contains errors in the cash deposit rates or the description of the merchandise, so it is usually a good idea to obtain a copy of the actual message that has been sent so that errors can be discovered and corrected.

The anti-dumping or countervailing duty order is the stage at which the importer must begin paying cash deposits rather than just posting security. The cash flow burden on the company becomes much more severe – instead of paying as a premium on the bond a fraction of the estimated duties (usually approximately 1% of the total amount of the bond per year), the company must pay the entire amount. Even if the company eventually obtains a refund of the cash deposits in a Section 751 administrative review, the financial burden can be considerable.

Judicial review

If either the domestic industry or the foreign company is dissatisfied with the results of the Commerce Department or Commission determinations, there is an option to file an appeal of the particular determination to the United States Court of International Trade. The various issues involved in court appeals – such as the right to judicial review, the nature of the proceedings, and the standard of review – are discussed in chapter 16 in more detail.

The most important point for this overview is that the initial paperwork for the court appeal must be filed rather quickly. Within 30 days of publication of the anti-dumping or countervailing duty order in the *Federal Register*, a party must file a summons with the court. This document is very simple, and does little more than notify the various parties that a court appeal is being made. Within 60 days of publication of the order, however, the party must file with the court a formal complaint outlining the particular issues that the party wishes to raise in the court appeal. Although this document need not be extremely detailed, it must at least set forth the broad outlines of why the party is dissatisfied with the decision made by either the Commerce Department or the Commission, or both.

Administrative reviews

The original investigation determines only *estimated* anti-dumping duties. The *actual* duties are established during the administrative reviews under Section 751 of the Tariff Act of 1930, usually known as 'Section 751 reviews'. The most important aspects of administrative reviews are:

❑ Reviews begin each year in the anniversary month of the anti-dumping order.

❑ Although reviews were once automatic, recent amendments to United States law now require one of the parties to request a review. If no one requests a review, the Commerce Department uses the estimated duties from the preceding investigation as the basis for the actual duties.

❑ Reviews take approximately one year to complete; historically the Commerce Department has been slow to publish the final results of administrative reviews, with delays sometimes taking several years; the current practice is more disciplined and timely.

❑ Reviews continue indefinitely until a company satisfies the requirements for termination of the anti-dumping order. Meeting these requirements can take several years.

Under the new law, there will be a 'sunset review' every five years to determine whether the duties will be continued. Sunset reviews involve work by both the Commerce Department and the Commission, and are discussed under 'Sunset reviews to terminate orders' in chapter 15.

In general, the Commerce Department applies the same basic rules in an administrative review as in the original dumping investigation. A detailed examination of how the detailed methodologies vary in administrative reviews is beyond the scope of this book. Foreign companies should simply keep in mind that if they find themselves in an administrative review situation, they need to be sure to discuss with their advisers how the rules might vary for their particular case.

Selecting a lawyer

Needless to say, the trade remedies process is quite complex. Most foreign companies cannot navigate these complex proceedings without the advice of a lawyer or some other specialist.

Often a foreign company already has a relationship with a lawyer specializing in international trade matters. This lawyer may have helped the company in prior trade remedy investigations, or may have been advising the company on how to avoid the risk of an anti-dumping case. If the company already has a lawyer, and is happy with the quality of the lawyer's work, the company should continue the relationship. The ability to move quickly to begin preparing the defence is a major advantage.

Other companies may have to select a lawyer to handle the case. Since most companies use the same lawyer to handle both the Commission and Commerce Department phases of the investigation, the selection of the lawyer will have an effect on the remainder of the case. How a company should select a lawyer for the overall defence of the anti-dumping case is discussed below. When choosing a lawyer, the company should consider the following factors:

Experience – This factor is the single most important consideration. If the company wants an effective defence, it is crucial to select a lawyer with specific experience in this specialized area of law. The company should ask specifically how much experience the law firm and its lawyers have with such investigations.

The company should also evaluate the experience carefully. Does the experience relate to anti-dumping investigations or the specific problem the company faces? For example, while a former United States Trade Representative may be the ideal lawyer for certain types of problems, USTR does not handle anti-dumping cases and USTR officials learn little about the defence of anti-dumping cases. Similarly, a person may have been a senior official in the Commerce Department, but if their job did not directly involve anti-dumping investigations they may not be very effective in defending the company.

Staffing – The company should ask about the team of people the law firm proposes to handle the case. This consideration is important for two reasons. First, the company should make sure that experienced lawyers are assigned to the case. A law firm may have some experienced lawyers, but if they are busy on other matters, the company may find inexperienced lawyers assigned to its case. Second, the company should ask for a proper balance of senior and junior lawyers. The proper balance ensures that the company receives cost-effective, high-quality legal advice.

Cost – The market for international trade lawyers has become very competitive. Companies can choose from a wide variety of law firms, and can receive a wide range of estimates for the cost of the defence. Although foreign companies want to limit their legal costs as much as possible, it is important to remember there is a trade-off between price and quality.

Virtually all of the reputable law firms practising international trade law charge for legal services based on hourly rates. The per hour charge varies depending on the seniority of the lawyer. The rates vary from firm to firm, and may seem high. Unfortunately, the market for lawyers in the United States is such that good lawyers are very expensive. It is not unusual for senior lawyers to charge $300–$500 per hour for their time.

Three variables determine the cost of the defence. First, how complex is the case? Obviously, the more complex the case, the more time the lawyers must spend. A case involving only a price response will be less expensive than a case that also involves a cost response. A case involving only a few domestic producers and a few foreign producers will be less expensive than a case involving many parties.

Second, how much experience does the company have? Companies with highly experienced staff can do much of the work themselves, especially at the Commerce Department stage. Companies involved in their first anti-dumping case require more time from the lawyers, which increases the cost.

Third, how efficient are the lawyers? Experienced lawyers work much more quickly than lawyers new to anti-dumping law. It is a mistake, however, to have too many senior lawyers involved. Much of the work is routine. One senior lawyer can easily supervise two or three more junior lawyers handling more routine tasks.

The cost of the defence can vary dramatically. Most anti-dumping cases involving a single company cost $300,000–$500,000. It would be unusual for a case to cost less than $200,000. It is also unusual for a normal case to cost more than $500,000. Complex cases for large foreign multinationals, however, can easily cost over $1,000,000. It is impossible to defend an anti-dumping case properly for less than $200,000. If a company receives an estimate of less than $200,000, they should be suspicious of the quality being offered.

Conclusions and caveats

This overview has sketched the procedural framework for anti-dumping and countervailing investigations. Many of the topics discussed here are developed in more detail in later chapters. The United States laws, however, are very complex. This chapter – indeed, the entire book – cannot discuss exhaustively every conceivable scenario or exception under such a complex law. Although this book covers the rules that apply in the vast majority of cases, a foreign company involved in any particular case should remember to consult with its advisers about how United States law might apply to its own situation.

Chapter 3

Anti-dumping duties: comparing prices to determine dumping margins

As noted previously, the United States anti-dumping law is administered by two different federal agencies in two separate, but overlapping, proceedings. The United States Commerce Department investigates whether the targeted foreign exporters have engaged in 'dumping' as defined by the law. The United States International Trade Commission investigates whether the targeted imports have caused (or threaten to cause) the domestic industry to suffer material injury. This chapter addresses in detail defending the company's interest in the Commerce Department proceeding. Issues relating to injury investigations are discussed in more detail in chapters 11, 12 and 13.

The Commerce Department determines whether each exporter has made sales to the United States at dumped prices. This means it must obtain sufficient information from each exporter to determine whether prices of the exporter's United States sales are below the prices of identical or similar products sold in the exporter's home market. This topic will be the focus of this chapter. In addition, in most cases the Commerce Department must determine whether such prices are below the exporter's cost of production. This second topic is addressed in chapter 4.

Although simple in concept, in practice evaluating relative prices involves a very intensive undertaking. For example, the Commerce Department's *initial* questionnaire alone typically consists of more than 130 single-spaced pages of instructions and questions. The exporter's response to this questionnaire must include computerized databases that provide a *transaction-by-transaction listing* of every shipment that the exporter made to the United States and in the home market during the previous four fiscal quarters. The listing must also include for each transaction more than 20 different pieces of information and data concerning the product and price adjustments (e.g. selling expense items). Moreover, the Commerce Department requires the exporter to adopt the Commerce Department's particular methodologies for calculating the various price adjustments. Such methodologies are often inconsistent with the manner in which the exporter keeps data, and sometimes the methodologies defy common business sense.

Responding to the Commerce Department's initial questionnaire (as well as several supplemental questionnaires), therefore, becomes a burdensome undertaking. This chapter details what is expected of a foreign exporter who wishes to participate in the Commerce Department proceeding. It also provides some useful advice on how to cope with the information demands of the Commerce Department. The chapter is structured to follow the chronology of a typical Commerce Department proceeding.

Recommended initial preparation by the company

When an anti-dumping case is filed, a foreign company faces the 'fair value investigation' conducted by the Commerce Department. In many ways, this is the most difficult part of the anti-dumping investigation for foreign companies. In a very short time period, the company is expected to understand a complex legal process, prepare a large amount of very detailed information, and overcome a strong cultural bias against disclosing sensitive information to outsiders. For foreign companies not previously exposed to the anti-dumping law, the two or three months until the first response is due is a very short time within which to achieve all of these goals.

There is no single right way to defend the company's interests in a Commerce Department anti-dumping proceeding. Many different companies have undoubtedly developed methods that work for them. Nevertheless, based on our many years of advising foreign companies in numerous different countries, we make the following suggestions. These ideas and approaches have been successful for us. We are confident that these approaches will help foreign companies to prepare more effectively their price response.

Understand the timing of the investigation

The deadlines for the price response are usually the same in each investigation. The Commerce Department initiates the investigation 20 days after the petition is filed. The questionnaire is typically issued about two weeks after the initiation of the investigation. Once the questionnaire is issued, the response is due in 30 days, with a likely 15-day extension. Extensions beyond 60 days are very unusual.

It is a mistake, however, to wait until the questionnaire is issued to begin the preparations. The questionnaire is quite standardized, with very little change from case to case. There is thus no need to wait for the questionnaire to find out what the Commerce Department wants to know. Those few areas that will be changed (e.g. the product description and period of investigation) can usually be predicted, based on the petition, with a great degree of certainty by the lawyers. Waiting is also a mistake because the 30–45 days for completing the response is very short. Foreign companies, especially those without a great deal of experience in anti-dumping investigations, usually find this time period too short. The sooner the company starts with the basic preparations, the better.

It is also a mistake to wait until the International Trade Commission makes its preliminary injury determination. It is unlikely that the Commission will make a negative preliminary injury determination, so a company usually should not delay its preparations on the small chance that the Commission decision might make the preparations unnecessary.

Deadlines are very important in anti-dumping investigations. A foreign company should make every possible effort to meet all of the deadlines, including those for submission of the response. The Commerce Department has been becoming increasingly strict about the deadlines it issues in anti-dumping investigations. If a company misses a deadline, even by just a few days, the Commerce Department can use that failure to justify the use of 'facts available' as punishment. Although the Commerce Department might be more reasonable in a particular case and not use facts available, it is better to avoid the risk.

If it appears likely that a response, or some other submission, might be late, it is important to consult with the Commerce Department. It is usually possible to obtain a short extension. The Commerce Department regulations impose strict standards on who within the Commerce Department may grant extensions, so it is important to plan far enough in advance to receive the necessary approval. Generally the Commerce Department issues a written approval of the extension. If the Commerce Department does not issue such written approval, the lawyers for the company should at least send a letter to the Commerce Department summarizing for the administrative record the oral conversation in which the Commerce Department approved the extension. Such written evidence may be important later in the investigation if a dispute arises over whether the late submission was approved or not.

Create an effective anti-dumping team

In many ways, this stage of the defence effort is one of the most crucial. If the right team is assembled, the rest of the defence effort will proceed much more smoothly. If the wrong team is assembled, or if key people are missing, the rest of the defence will be difficult, and may even fail. The team should consist of at least the following members:

❑ At least one member of senior management;

❑ Salespeople of the product under investigation;

❑ Financial accountants;

❑ Cost accountants;

❑ A specialist in United States anti-dumping law.

Depending on the circumstances, the team might also involve members of the company's in-house legal department and the company's regular outside lawyers (either foreign or United States). The role of each of these team members is discussed below.

Senior manager

Defending an anti-dumping investigation is a very complex undertaking. The investigation eventually involves many different parts of the company. Many people have to spend a great deal of time working on numerous projects that seem irrelevant and not part of their jobs. Many of the key people are already quite busy, and therefore are reluctant to cooperate. Various subsidiaries of the company may also be reluctant to cooperate.

The key to resolving all of these issues is to have a respected member of senior management take charge. The involvement of a senior manager is an indication that the company views the anti-dumping problem seriously, and considers solving it a priority. Moreover, someone needs to resolve the disputes and disagreements among the various parts of the company, and ensure that the defence effort continues as smoothly as possible.

In most foreign companies, this person will need to be a director of the company. There may be a number of general managers and managers involved; resolving the disputes among these other managers is one of the major tasks facing the director.

Salespeople of the product

Many foreign companies staff their defence team with the salespeople of the product under investigation. After all, they are the ones selling the product in the United States. They have the greatest interest in preserving access to the United States market, and thus many companies feel that the salespeople should do most of the work.

The salespeople have an important role to play on the defence team. They know the most about the United States market, and are often able to develop information about competition in the United States market that can help the lawyers prepare a more effective defence of the Commission phase of the investigation. The salespeople are also very knowledgeable about the selling practices of the company, and can usually answer most of the questions about the exports to the United States.

The salespeople cannot defend the case by themselves, however. They usually do not have accounting backgrounds, and know very little about the underlying accounting records that are crucial for verifying the responses to the Commerce Department questionnaires. Even if the salespeople can develop the information to prepare the price response, they often do not know the accounting system well enough to verify the information they prepare. This problem is even more severe if the investigation involves cost of production. The salespeople usually know the cost of the product, but they have no idea how the cost information was derived or how to tie the cost back into the accounting records of the company. Because of these limitations, relying on the salespeople alone to defend the company's interests is usually a serious mistake.

Financial accountants

Financial accountants supplement the salespeople in a very important way – they are familiar with the underlying accounting system of the company, and are able to use the accounting records to verify the information in the price response. It is important to remember that the responses to the Commerce Department's questionnaires are useless unless the company can verify the information. (The Commerce Department's verification process is discussed in chapter 10.)

The amount of time the financial accountants need to spend on the case varies. Depending on their experience, the salespeople working on the defence team may be able to do most of the work themselves, only using the accountants to answer specific questions. In some cases, it may be necessary for the accountants themselves to prepare much of the information. Companies face an internal dilemma – the accountants can usually prepare the information more quickly and accurately than the salespeople; but the accountants feel that such work is not part of their job. The company can assign the work to either the salespeople or the accountants, provided someone assumes the responsibility for making sure the work is finished.

Cost accountants

If the investigation becomes a 'cost case' (and most do), it is essential to assign cost accountants to the defence team. The financial accountants are usually not familiar enough with the cost accounting system of the company to prepare the cost information by themselves. They need assistance from the cost accountants.

It is usually a good idea to assign a cost accountant to the defence team from the beginning. Since more and more anti-dumping investigations involve cost of production issues, foreign companies are spending more time trying to anticipate and resolve cost issues earlier in the investigation, even before the formal cost case is begun. Moreover, having a cost accountant involved from the beginning avoids the need to repeat a great deal of background information when the cost accountant joins the team later in the process.

Specialist in anti-dumping law

The United States anti-dumping law is extremely complex. It is almost impossible for a foreign company to defend itself adequately without the advice of an expert. Usually companies choose to retain an American lawyer who specializes in this area of law. Sometimes companies instead work with accountants, consultants, economists or other professionals with experience in this area.

Companies normally choose lawyers because only lawyers are able to defend the company throughout the entire course of the investigation. Non-lawyer professionals can assist in the Commission and Commerce Department phases of the investigation. If the case later involves court litigation, however, the non-lawyer must transfer the case to a lawyer. It is usually more efficient to have the lawyer involved from the beginning. Moreover, only a lawyer is sensitive enough to the issues involved to prepare the administrative record (the collection of all the papers and documents submitted to the Commission and Commerce Department during the course of the investigation) in such a way as to improve the chances of success during a court appeal. Only lawyers receive the professional training necessary to make those judgements.

When choosing the specialist, the company should inquire very carefully into the experience of the person being considered. How much experience does that person and their firm have in defending anti-dumping investigations? Which person would actually do most of the work? Very often law firms have one or two people with some experience, but they are busy working on matters for other clients. In that case, mostly junior people, without experience, could be assigned to the case. For complex anti-dumping cases, it is important that the firm chosen have a number of experienced people. For example, in some cases it may be necessary to have lawyers at the foreign parent company, at the United States subsidiary, and at another foreign subsidiary all at the same time. Staffing such a case requires a number of experienced people. Foreign companies should make sure that their lawyer has the resources necessary to handle the particular case.

Establishing who is involved

Examining petitioner's standing

An anti-dumping investigation is usually commenced by a United States producer (or several producers) filing a petition simultaneously with the Commerce Department and the International Trade Commission. Under the law, the Commerce Department has the responsibility for formally initiating the United States Government's anti-dumping investigation.

Once the petition has been filed, the Commerce Department has 20 days to assess the accuracy and adequacy of information contained in the petition and to determine whether the petition 'alleges the elements necessary' to justify initiating an anti-dumping investigation. The Commerce Department must make this determination, however, only on the basis of 'sources readily available' to it; it may not solicit or accept information from parties other than the domestic industry or domestic unions concerning the adequacy of the petition.

In addition to determining whether the petition sets forth the requisite elements of an anti-dumping case, the Commerce Department must determine whether the petition has been filed 'by or on behalf of' a domestic industry producing a like product. This requirement – often referred to as the 'standing' issue – was not specifically defined in United States law until 1995, when it was incorporated as a result of the anti-dumping agreements in the Uruguay Round.

Under United States law, the issue of standing has now been clarified to involve two separate questions: (1) whether the petitioners represent at least 25% of total domestic production of the like product in the United States; and (2) whether the petitioners represent a majority of those producers who express an opinion in support of the petition. Both questions must be answered in the affirmative for the Commerce Department to rule that the petition has been filed 'on behalf of' an affected industry.

Foreign exporters are not expected to participate in the Department's process of initiating the anti-dumping investigation and examining the petitioners' standing. This does not mean, however, that foreign exporters should ignore this early part of the case. The foreign exporter should be aware of those situations in which it is unclear whether the petitioners have met the standing requirements under the law. This is often evident from the public version of the petition. (Anyone can obtain a copy of the public version of the petition the day after it is filed with the agencies.)

If the petition states unequivocally that petitioners account for more than 50% of United States production of the product at issue, then there is usually no dispute that petitioners have standing. However, if the petition does not make this claim, and therefore it is unclear what portion of total United States production is represented by petitioners, then the foreign exporter may want to examine this issue. If the foreign exporter has credible information that either (1) petitioners account for less than 25% of total United States production or (2) other United States producers actually oppose the anti-dumping petition, then the foreign exporter should submit this information to the Commerce Department and request that the Commerce Department conduct a formal poll of all United States producers.

Although there usually is only a small chance that such efforts will cause the Commerce Department to dismiss the case for lack of standing, such efforts could cause the Commerce Department to delay its initiation by 20 days. Such delay is usually beneficial to respondent exporters.

Mandatory foreign respondents

In principle, the Commerce Department investigates all the known exporters of the merchandise being investigated. In many cases, however, such a comprehensive investigation is not possible and it must limit its investigation to so-called mandatory respondents, the particular foreign exporters chosen to respond.

Usually, the two or three largest exporters from each country are selected to be mandatory respondents. The precise number varies, based on the number of countries involved in the particular case, the number of exporters per country, and the overall workload level at the Commerce Department. The Commerce Department almost always selects exporters that together represent at least 60% of total exports from a country. If there is a very large number of small exporters, United States law allows it to conduct sampling to decide which specific exporters to investigate.

Exporters not selected have two options. The most common choice is to celebrate: most exporters are quite happy to be spared the burden of responding to the Commerce Department questionnaires. Particularly if you think your company's dumping margin is no different to anyone else's, you may be quite content to receive the 'all others rate' – the dumping margin announced for all those exporters not specifically investigated.

The other option is to request to become a so-called voluntary respondent. The Commerce Department regulations envisage that some companies may feel that their own situation is different – that they are not dumping, even if others may be dumping – and allows foreign exporters to request to participate. Depending on the circumstances, Commerce may be more or less sympathetic to accepting voluntary respondents. The regulations give Commerce wide discretion to accept them if it can, but to reject them if the workload is too much.

Establishing the model-match methodology

The Commerce Department's first step after selecting the mandatory respondents is to invite the foreign exporters to provide comments on the appropriate model-match methodology. 'Model-match methodology' refers to the manner by which the Commerce Department determines which products sold in the home market should be compared to the products sold to the United States market. In an attempt to ensure 'apples-to-apples' comparisons, the Commerce Department first strives to compare United States export prices to home market prices of *identical* products. If the identical product was not sold in the home market during the investigation period, the Commerce Department will then compare the United States price to the *most similar* home market product, and make an adjustment for the difference. The model-match methodology is the approach that the Commerce Department uses for determining which home market products are identical or most similar to those products sold to the United States.

Overview of Commerce Department model-match methodology

Although the overall product-matching concept is straightforward, the manner in which the Commerce Department engages in appropriate product comparisons has some quirks. First, it is the Commerce Department (and not the foreign manufacturer) that determines which products sold in the home market are 'identical' and 'most similar' to the products sold to the United States. This approach is a relatively recent change from the Commerce Department's prior approach of *asking respondents* to inform it which home market models were identical or most similar.

Throughout the 1980s and early 1990s, the Commerce Department asked respondents to indicate which home market products were identical and similar to the United States merchandise and to rank each home market similar product according to its similarity (first most similar, second most similar, etc.) using the physical criteria the respondent believed best identified the product. In addition, it required detailed narrative explanation and documentation supporting the respondent's selections and ranking. Although in certain cases the Commerce Department may have identified the physical criteria upon which products were to be compared, it rarely defined a hierarchy among these characteristics and, if a hierarchy was established, it was usually very general in nature.

In the mid-1990s the Commerce Department adopted a new approach under which it assumed responsibility for product comparisons. It is currently the Commerce Department's practice to identify itself which home market products are identical and most similar to the United States merchandise. Not only does it identify the most important physical characteristics of the targeted merchandise, but it establishes a specific hierarchy among them. In this way the Commerce Department conducts its own analysis to determine similarity.

Under its new approach, in theory, the Commerce Department identifies a hierarchy of physical characteristics based on those *physical characteristics* which the industry considers most important with respect to pricing. In practice, however, the Commerce Department's approach to product-matching is sometimes incomprehensible to the foreign manufacturer. For example, in the flat-rolled steel cases the Commerce Department determined that whether a corrosion-resistant coil was painted or not painted was an important physical characteristic. However, the Commerce Department did not allow for any differences among painting types, even though such differences could result in several hundred dollars' difference in prices. That is, in the flat-rolled steel cases the Commerce Department ruled that a home market product was 'identical' to a United States product, and therefore no difference-in-merchandise adjustments would be allowed when comparing prices, even though there could be significant differences in the painting type.

Accordingly, the foreign company needs to be prepared for the methodology that the Commerce Department adopts for determining which home market products are the best matches for products sold to the United States for purposes of the anti-dumping calculation to be quite different from the methodology that the company would adopt. Such difference may cause the Commerce Department's dumping margin calculation to be different from the foreign company's own guess as to the estimated margin.

Ability of exporter to influence model-match methodology

Soon after it issues its initiation notice, the Commerce Department will send to all interested parties a proposed model-match hierarchy. Such proposal will consist of a several-page list of important physical characteristics of the product at issue. The physical characteristics will be arranged in a hierarchy of importance (as defined by the Commerce Department). The Commerce Department will invite parties to submit comments on the model-match hierarchy.

Although the Commerce Department's invitation will occur very early in the process, and usually before much analysis can be done, the company should try to take advantage of the opportunity. Often, how the Commerce Department establishes the model-match hierarchy has a big impact on the dumping margin calculation. (The only exception is if the foreign exporter sold identical products (models) in the United States and home markets, and the relative quantities of each product (model) sold were the same in each market. In this situation, the dumping calculation will result in identical matches and therefore the model-match hierarchy becomes less important.)

To take advantage of the Commerce Department's invitation, the company needs to examine three questions: (1) does the Commerce Department's list omit an important physical characteristic; (2) does the Department's hierarchy of physical characteristics correctly reflect the relative importance of each physical characteristic; and (3) are any of the individual physical characteristics listed too broadly defined and more appropriately split into several sub-categories.

The company should submit any comments by the deadline given by the Department. Before submitting any changes, however, the company should undertake a quick examination (if possible) as to whether the changes would help or hurt the dumping margin calculation for the company.

Section A of the questionnaire – general information and establishing the response framework

The first part of the questionnaire, section A, seeks information about the general background of the company and its sales in various markets. The information in section A provides the factual basis for many of the choices to be made later in the questionnaire (the basic form of the questionnaire, not yet adapted for use in a specific case, can be found on the Commerce Department website: *www.ita.doc.gov*). Section A of the questionnaire contains 10 question categories:

❑ *Quantity and value of sales.* This question seeks numerical data on the quantity and value of sales of the targeted merchandise to different markets, e.g. United States, home market and third countries. The question also requests a breakdown of sales between sales made to affiliated customers and sales made to unaffiliated customers. The answers to this question will dictate the composition of the sales databases that will need to be prepared.

❑ *Corporate structure and affiliations.* This question requests general information on how the company is organized and whether the company is affiliated with any other company involved in the production or sale of the targeted merchandise.

❑ *Distribution process.* This question requests a flow chart of how the targeted merchandise is sold and shipped to customers in each market, and an explanation of the flow chart. This question also seeks general information on the different categories of customers (e.g. end-users versus distributors) in each market. In addition, the question seeks general information on the types of selling activities undertaken in each market.

❑ *Sales process.* This question seeks a detailed explanation (and chronology) of how the targeted merchandise is sold in each market. In particular, the question seeks an explanation of the process the company employs to negotiate the price with its customers. The answers to this question will influence selection of the appropriate 'date of sale' for each transaction (discussed below).

❑ *Sales to affiliated persons in the foreign market.* This question seeks additional information on sales made to affiliated customers, and in particular, whether the affiliated customers consume or resell the targeted merchandise.

❑ *Accounting and financial practices.* This question seeks a general explanation of the company's accounting and financial practices and requests copies of the company's most recent financial statements.

❑ *Merchandise.* This question seeks a detailed description of the different types of the targeted merchandise that are sold in each market. The question also seeks information on the production process utilized for producing the targeted information, and seeks a full explanation of the company's product coding system.

❑ *Further manufacture or assembly in the United States.* This question asks whether the company's United States shipments of the targeted merchandise are made to an affiliate in the United States who undertakes further processing before the merchandise is sold to the United States customer. If so, the Commerce Department employs a special methodology for calculating the anti-dumping margin.

❑ *Exports through intermediate countries.* This question asks whether the company is aware if any of its shipments of the targeted merchandise made to a third country were subsequently exported to the United States.

❑ *Sales of merchandise under investigation supplied by an unaffiliated producer.* This question is for companies who do not produce the targeted merchandise, but rather only export the merchandise produced by another company.

The responses to these sections do not need to be exceedingly detailed. A typical section A response is usually only 15–20 pages long (although the supporting documents attached as exhibits will make the response much longer). The most important point is to ensure consistency between this information and the claims made later in the response.

Because of the interrelationship between section A and the rest of the questionnaire, it is important to prepare the response to the entire questionnaire as a whole. It is a mistake to submit the response to section A before the company has fully analysed the consequences in section B (foreign prices) and section C (United States prices) of making certain claims in section A.

In particular, preparing the answers to the section A questionnaire will make the company decide how to approach two critical issues for the anti-dumping investigation: (1) the universe, or specific transactions, of United States sales to be examined, and (2) the universe of sales in the foreign market to be examined. These are discussed below.

Determining the universe for the United States sales database – export price versus constructed export price

During its investigation, the Commerce Department will require that the foreign company report *all* of its United States sales during the investigation period. The 'period of investigation' consists of the previous four calendar quarters. The sales to be included are those to *unaffiliated* United States customers.

In addition, a foreign respondent is required to report all sales of the imported targeted merchandise which has undergone further processing or manufacturing in the United States, even if the final product that is sold to the first unaffiliated customer no longer meets the definition of the targeted merchandise. For example, assume an anti-dumping investigation on colour picture tubes: if a foreign manufacturer has shipped colour picture tubes to an affiliated company in the United States which incorporated the colour picture tubes into colour televisions prior to sale to an unaffiliated customer, the Commerce Department would require the sales of the colour televisions to be included in the foreign company's United States sales database. For the dumping margin calculation, the Commerce Department would deduct the further processing expenses in order to derive the 'sale price' of the targeted merchandise, that is, the colour picture tube.

Under United States anti-dumping law, sales made directly from the foreign company to the United States company are called 'export price' (EP) sales. Sales which are processed in any fashion through the foreign company's United States affiliate (even if the merchandise is shipped directly) are called 'constructed export price' ('CEP') sales. As will be discussed later in this chapter, United States law adopts a different dumping margin calculation methodology depending on whether the foreign company's United States sales meet the definition of EP sales or CEP sales.

Determining the universe for the foreign market sales database

Determining which foreign market (home market or third country) sales will be used in the calculation

Under United States anti-dumping law, although the preference is to compare United States sales prices with home market sales prices (i.e. prices of the merchandise in the targeted country), home market sales will be used only if they are deemed 'viable'. One of the most significant changes in anti-dumping law resulting from the Uruguay Round implementing legislation is the statutory change for determining whether home market sales are 'viable'. Under the new

United States law, home market sales will normally be considered to be viable as long as they constitute 5% or more of United States sales of the subject merchandise. (Under the old law, the 5% test measured home market sales against all third country sales.)

The 5% test is typically performed on the basis of volume or quantity, rather than value. Consequently, if the foreign company's home market sales by volume of the targeted merchandise constitute more than 5% of the foreign company's United States sales of the targeted merchandise, then the home market sales will *normally* be used in the dumping margin calculation.

Note the word 'normally'. It is important not to forget that United States law contains a possible exception to the new viability standard. Under the new statutory provisions, even if home market sales are greater than 5% of the volume shipped to the United States, the Commerce Department is allowed to refuse to use home market sales in the anti-dumping calculation if it determines that a 'particular market situation' exists in the home market that would not permit a proper comparison.

Neither the statute nor the Department's regulations define 'particular market situation'. The legislative history suggests that this exemption is to be invoked only to address particularly unusual situations, for example, when there is only a single home market sale, when there is government control over pricing or when pricing depends on different seasons. Recent cases suggest, however, that the Commerce Department is still struggling with defining the existence of a particular market situation, and in doing so appears willing to entertain applying the exception to more common scenarios. For example, in the recent Commerce Department preliminary determination *Salmon from Chile*, the Commerce Department ruled that a 'particular market situation' existed in the home market (and therefore home market sales would not be used as the basis of comparison) primarily because the grades of salmon which were sold in Chile were quite different from the grades sold in the United States. A foreign company should be aware of the possible application of this exception.

If the foreign company's home market sales are not viable, the Commerce Department will seek to examine the foreign company's sales of the targeted merchandise to a third country. The question then becomes which third country sales should be used. Typically, the Commerce Department requires the third country that accounts for the foreign company's largest volume, provided that such volume constitutes at least 5% of the volume sold to the United States. In some situations, however, the Commerce Department may allow (or require) selection of another third country if it can be demonstrated that the type of targeted merchandise sold to another third country more closely resembles the type of targeted merchandise sold to the United States (provided that the volume to this other third country satisfies the 5% test).

Which home market sales must be reported – the issue of affiliated customers

As with United States sales, the Commerce Department typically requires a respondent to report *all* sales of the targeted merchandise in the home market (or third country) to *unaffiliated* customers, *and* to *affiliated* customers that *consume* the merchandise. It is important to note, however, that sales to an affiliated customer who *resells* the subject merchandise are *not* to be included in the home market sales universe; that affiliated reseller's sales to its unaffiliated customers are included instead. That is, sales by the foreign company's affiliates in the home market are potentially subject to inclusion in the home market sales anti-dumping universe.

The only exception to the requirement to report all home market sales is for affiliated resellers who sell only limited quantities of the subject merchandise. Under the Department's regulations, if all of the sales by affiliated resellers of the subject merchandise amount to less than 5% of total home market subject merchandise sales, then the respondent need not report those affiliated resellers' sales of the subject merchandise. In this situation, the respondent can simply report the sales to the affiliated resellers instead.

Given these requirements, whether a customer is deemed 'affiliated' or 'unaffiliated' takes on tremendous importance. The United States statute and the Department's regulations have significantly expanded the definition of 'affiliated persons'. In particular, the new provisions expanded the concept of affiliation by control. Under the new provisions, a customer or supplier will be considered 'affiliated' or 'related' to the respondent if the respondent is 'legally or operationally in a position to exercise restraint or direction over' the customer or supplier (or vice versa). It is important to emphasize that the expanded definition of affiliated persons can include entities even when there is *no equity relationship*. Under the Commerce Department's regulations, companies may be considered to be affiliated if a company is 'in a position to exercise restraint or direction, for example, through corporate or family groupings, franchises or joint-venture agreements, debt financing, or close supplier relationships in which the supplier or buyer becomes reliant upon the other'.

Because both reporting burdens and the anti-dumping calculation change significantly depending on whether the customer is considered 'affiliated', the new changes in the law on this issue are important. In general, if the customer is not related at all to the manufacturer, and the customer is a *retailer* that purchases the targeted merchandise from multiple suppliers, it is unlikely that there would be any concern. However, if the customer is a distributor that purchases the product from only a single manufacturer, (i.e. the customer is a single brand distributor) there may be a concern that the customer is deemed to be affiliated, notwithstanding the absence of an equity relationship.

Note that if there is any doubt as to whether a home market customer (who resells the targeted merchandise) is affiliated, the Commerce Department will require the foreign company to submit, as part of its response, all of the affiliates' sales transactions of the targeted merchandise, just in case the ultimate decision is that the customer meets the definition of 'affiliated' under the law. This means that the foreign company could very well be forced to obtain significant sales and cost data from an affiliated customer over which it has little control. This is one of the biggest burdens of the Commerce Department's anti-dumping investigation. Accordingly, this issue needs to be examined closely during the preparation of the section A response.

When confronting sales to affiliated customers, the Commerce Department also has a test for determining whether sales are at 'arm's length'. Traditionally, it has used the so-called 99.5% test, which analyses whether the prices on transactions to an affiliated customer were at least 99.5% of or *more* than the prices on transactions to unaffiliated customers.

Not surprisingly, the strict and one-sided test (it did not matter if prices were very high – high home market prices mean high dumping margins) has often led to the rejection of the prices as being unreliable.

This test was recently challenged in WTO. The Appellate Body ruled in *United States – Anti-dumping measures on certain hot-rolled steel from Japan* that this Commerce test violated Article 2.1 of the Anti-Dumping Agreement. The Commerce Department has adjusted its old 99.5% test in light of this WTO decision. The new rule measures whether the average price falls outside the range of 98% to 102% of the average price to unrelated customers. It remains to be seen how the Commerce Department will actually apply this test in practice.

Determining which shipments to include in each database – the date of sale issue

Once it is determined how the United States and foreign market databases will be structured – which entity's sales must be included in the United States and foreign market sales databases – the company must then decide how to determine the appropriate universe of sales to submit.

On this issue the Commerce Department's questionnaire requires that the company report all United States and home market shipments that have a 'date of sale' within the 12-month period of investigation. Commerce Department regulations state that the Commerce Department 'normally' will define 'date of sale' as 'the date of invoice as recorded in the company's books and records'. Most often, using the invoice date will be easiest for the company. The company would simply need to assemble data on all shipments made pursuant to invoices issued during the investigation period.

Commerce Department regulations also provide a significant exception to this general rule, however. If the price and quantity for the sale are both established at some time other than the date of invoice, the Commerce Department can decide that the 'date of sale' is some other date, such as the order confirmation date.

As a practical matter, if the foreign company can demonstrate that price and quantities can and do change after the date of order (or whatever other date the price and quantity are generally set), the Commerce Department will generally fall back to the regulatory presumption of using the invoice date. But if the domestic industry complains about the point, the Commerce Department can become quite persistent in investigating it. The foreign company should therefore be prepared for possible battles on this issue.

Sections B, C, and E of the questionnaire – the sales databases

Sections B, C, and E of the Commerce Department's questionnaire seek detailed information and data on sales, and in particular selling prices, of the targeted merchandise. Section B of the questionnaire focuses on sales made in the home market (or third country); section C focuses on the company's United States sales; and, if applicable, section E focuses on 'further manufactured' sales made by a United States affiliate. Responses to all three sections are typically due together (about 45 days after the questionnaire is issued) and therefore response preparations for all three sections should begin at the same time (and as early as possible).

Although each section of the questionnaire asks a few questions that require narrative responses, the heart of these sections of the questionnaire is the request for the company to prepare detailed, computerized sales databases. Typically, a separate sales database is submitted in response to each section of the questionnaire. These databases are what the Commerce Department uses to calculate the dumping margins for the company.

The Commerce Department requires these computerized databases to contain incredible amounts of detailed data. Foreign companies reviewing Commerce Department questionnaires for the first time are usually shocked at the level of detail. Essentially, the Commerce Department requires a transaction-by-transaction listing of every single shipment that the company made of the targeted merchandise to all customers in the particular market (United States market for section C, home market for section B.) In addition, for each transaction the company must provide a great deal of data on the particular product characteristics and on all selling expenses incurred in selling and shipping the merchandise to the customer. (These selling expenses are used in calculating the price adjustments needed to derive ex-factory prices made at the same level of trade.)

The Commerce Department wants three types of data for each transaction: (1) data on the actual sales price; (2) data on the physical characteristics of the merchandise being sold and the quantity of the transaction; and (3) data on the different types of selling expenses and circumstances of sales to calculate appropriate price adjustments.

The sales price

The Commerce Department requires the foreign company to prepare a computerized listing of *all* transactions (i.e. shipments/invoices) of the targeted merchandise during the period under investigation – the last four calendar quarters. The sales price for each of these transactions should be the per-unit invoice price. In preparing this computerized listing, the foreign company should be aware of the following points.

First, it is preferable to list separately the original invoice price and all subsequent modifications. This will make the verification process much easier. Accounting systems usually track these adjustments but companies too quickly jump to the final invoice price.

Second, the company should be sure the final net sales price provided can tie to the company's *financial* accounting records. Often a company will use some internal salesperson's management sales system to prepare the required computerized database because, typically, this is the only system that has a product-specific sales database. Such an internal system often does not concern itself with minor price adjustments, such as credits for mistakes in invoicing. Sole reliance on such a system could lead to problems if the total sales value does not tie to the actual amount recorded in the company's financial accounting records as net sales of the targeted merchandise. That is, the Commerce Department requires that the net sales prices reported be the *final* price charged to the customer.

Product characteristics and quantity

The sales databases must also contain, for each reported transaction, specific information on the physical characteristics of the product being sold. Usually, the Commerce Department's questionnaire will detail exactly which physical characteristics need to be reported and how. Although conceptually such an exercise is straightforward, foreign companies often encounter a couple of difficulties.

First, the Commerce Department often requests reporting of certain product characteristics that are not retained in the company's shipment databases, but rather can only be found in the company's production records. (For example, in many steel cases the Commerce Department questionnaire requires that the yield strength for each shipment be reported.) The company will therefore be required to 'marry' its production databases with shipment/sales databases. This often is a hugely time-consuming exercise.

Second, the Commerce Department's questionnaire often requests product characteristic information that the company does not retain for individual shipments. In such a situation, the company should attempt to provide a best guess based on other available information about the shipment.

The other very important aspect is always to remember that these product characteristics must be based on some verifiable source of information. Since these characteristics often determine whether a product is subject or not subject to the investigation (for example, whether the product fits the definition of 'carbon' rather than 'alloy' steel), the Commerce Department often investigates the product characteristics closely at verification. Foreign companies need to keep this point in mind as they assemble data. Often companies have the necessary detailed data, but only retain the data for 6 or 12 months; when the verification comes, the data have been purged from computer systems or thrown away from paper records. It is important to save the data the company will need at the verification.

Price adjustments

The United States law recognizes that differences in prices between sales to the United States and sales to other markets may result from numerous legitimate business considerations. In general, the Commerce Department tries to compare United States prices to home market or third country prices on an 'ex factory' basis – in other words, the price of the merchandise when it leaves the factory. The Commerce Department also tries to compare United States prices to home market or third country prices at the same 'level of trade' and in the same quantities. Various adjustments are permitted to United States price and foreign market value to account for differences that can affect the relative prices in different markets. The objective is to adjust invoice prices back to a common point of comparison, that is, an ex-factory price. Essentially, the goal of these adjustments is to ensure comparison:

❑ Of identical or similar merchandise;

❑ To customers at the same level of trade;

❑ At the same point in time (i.e. at the factory gate); and

❑ Under similar selling conditions.

This section first discusses some common methodological issues for all adjustments and then looks briefly at the major adjustments that arise in most anti-dumping investigations.

General methodological issues concerning price adjustments

Price versus cost

The Commerce Department has struggled for many years with the proper treatment of adjustments to price for selling expenses and other costs. The issue is whether the adjustments should be based on the actual costs incurred, or based only on the extent to which the costs are reflected in the sales price. On the one hand, since the objective of the law is to create a comparison of ex-factory *prices*, one might argue that only costs that are included in the price should be eligible for adjustment. On the other hand, one must recognize that it is often impossible to measure how a particular cost, especially a selling expense, affects the price.

Although this issue is worthy of academic study, the foreign businessperson affected by the anti-dumping law also must understand enough about the issue to know that dumping can occur under United States law even when prices and costs in the home and export markets are the same. Rather than treat this subject theoretically, important instances in which the so-called cost versus price issue arises are identified below:

❑ Home market delivery costs prior to sale do not qualify for any adjustment because Commerce believes that only 'after-sale' delivery costs are reflected in the price. United States delivery costs prior to sale, however, are deducted fully from the United States price.

❑ The Commerce Department's adjustment for packing costs includes materials, labour, and factory overhead, without regard to any theoretical effect on the price.

❑ The adjustment for physical differences in merchandise ('difference-in-merchandise' or 'difmer' adjustment) is expressly limited by law to costs reflected in the price. The Commerce Department limits the adjustment to differences in materials, labour, and *variable* factory overhead under the theory that variable overhead, but not fixed overhead, is reflected in the price.

❑ The anti-dumping law adjusts for the entire amount of duty drawback, i.e. home market import duties rebated or forgiven upon exportation. The theory is that import duties are entirely reflected in the sales price.

❑ The Commerce Department also includes in the difference-in-merchandise adjustment any differences in import duties paid on physically different components.

❑ The law expressly limits the adjustment for differences in quantities sold to differences affecting the price. The Commerce Department administers this requirement through a complex set of rules that are almost impossible for respondents to satisfy.

❑ The adjustment for further manufacturing performed in the United States assumes that the United States price equals the cost of production plus all selling expenses and allocated profit or loss. Thus, the further manufacturing calculation is a cost-based methodology.

There are two lessons in all this for the foreign exporter. First, in preparing a response, the exporter must examine the particular requirements of each adjustment to ensure that the response contains the information necessary to satisfy the requirements of *that* adjustment. A general approach will not do. Some of the price–cost criteria used by the Commerce Department simply do not square with common business sense.

Second, in setting prices so as to avoid dumping, the exporter cannot assume that equal profits in both the United States and the home market means that dumping is not occurring. This assumption is true only under a purely cost-based approach. As the preceding discussion shows, the assumption might be true of the business world but it is not true of United States anti-dumping law, which in many instances denies adjustment for costs on the theoretical ground that they are not reflected in the price.

Burden of proof

The United States anti-dumping law imposes on the foreign exporter almost all of the burden of proof associated with adjustments to price. The exporter has both positive and negative burdens of proof.

With respect to foreign market value, the exporter has a positive burden of proving entitlement to every adjustment. The exporter not only must provide information necessary to satisfy all of the criteria for the adjustment, but also must show that the information can be verified from the exporter's records. This double burden is often very difficult to meet in the case of adjustments that are granted only if the cost is reflected in the price.

With respect to United States price, the exporter has both positive and negative burdens. The exporter has the positive burden of proving the amount of a particular expense known by the Commerce Department to exist. If the exporter cannot prove that the expense is X dollars, then Commerce has the discretion to *increase* the expense to X multiplied by two or three or whatever amounts Commerce deems 'reasonable'. Commerce, naturally, is not inclined to decrease the amount of an unverified United States selling expense.

Commerce also sometimes places on the exporter the burden of 'proving the negative'. If the exporter claims that it did not incur a particular expense alleged by the petitioner, Commerce might ask the exporter to demonstrate the non-existence of the expense. There is no standard by which to prove the non-existence of something that truly does not exist. Whether the exporter succeeds in such an exercise usually depends on (1) whether the exporter's records are organized well enough to permit a systematic search for the alleged expense; (2) whether the exporter expends a sufficient amount of time and effort to please the Commerce Department's verifiers; and (3) whether the verifiers believe that the exporter is telling the truth.

This exercise does not occur just with United States selling expenses. Whenever the petitioner alleges the existence of some damaging fact relating to any aspect of the exporter's operations, the exporter must be prepared to 'prove the negative'.

Averaging

As a general matter, the Commerce Department prefers adjustments to be calculated on a transaction-specific basis. If a sale-by-sale calculation is not possible, the Commerce Department will usually accept a weighted average calculation of the adjustment. A single average for the entire period of investigation is usually acceptable, unless there is significant variation in the average from month to month. The average also may not be acceptable if there is a significant time lag between when the expense is incurred and when the company pays.

Sometimes the Commerce Department unreasonably attempts to force a respondent to calculate expenses customer-by-customer or sale-by-sale, even when the normal records of the Company do not permit such a calculation. Not only can this be impossibly burdensome, but reporting expenses on a sale-by-sale basis in the home market would not enhance the accuracy of the calculations. In the case of home market sales, given that foreign market value is calculated as a weighted average of net home market prices, such reporting would amount to breaking down average figures into sale-specific amounts only to average them again in the final anti-dumping calculation.

Discounts and rebates

The Commerce Department requires the calculation of adjustments to reflect all discounts that are not reflected in the net invoice price. The starting point for all sales is the net invoice price. Accordingly, if the discount is granted at the time of payment (as a reduction in the amount due), an adjustment needs to be made. If the net invoice price already reflects a discount, however, no further adjustment is warranted. The Commerce Department defines 'rebates' as payments or credits made to customers *after* the invoice has been issued. All rebates to the customer must be accounted for.

The Commerce Department prefers that discounts and rebates be tied to specific invoices. The calculation methodology for calculating invoice or model specific discounts and rebates depends on how they are granted and recorded on the company books. If such incentives are granted as a fixed percentage of the sales price, the company should calculate the adjustment by multiplying this percentage factor by the unit price of the product.

Delivery costs

Delivery costs are usually not controversial, either in the way they are calculated or in the effect they have on the outcome. The statute and Commerce Department policy are quite clear. The Commerce Department subtracts United States delivery costs from United States price and foreign market delivery costs from foreign market value, provided the cost has been included in the gross price. If the item is charged separately and is not included in the price, the Commerce Department does not deduct the item. Examples of delivery costs (sometimes called 'movement charges') include inland freight, inland insurance, warehouse charges, ocean freight, ocean insurance and brokerage fees. Delivery costs include all of the expenses of moving the product from the place of shipment (usually the factory) to the customer; the costs of moving the product within the factory, however, are not subtracted from United States price and foreign market value.

As a practical matter, delivery costs seldom affect the outcome of an investigation. Often the delivery costs in the two markets being compared are virtually the same – for example, when the Commerce Department compares exports to the United States with exports to another market. Even if the delivery costs are somewhat different, they are well known by the company when it makes its pricing decisions. The prices charged in the various markets therefore generally reflect differences in the delivery costs.

To the extent possible, a foreign company wants to maximize the delivery costs in the home market or third country market, and minimize the delivery costs in the United States market. Lowering the net price in the home market or third country market and raising the net price in the United States market will lower the dumping margins. Unfortunately, foreign companies have limited discretion in how they calculate delivery costs. Such costs are usually quite unambiguous.

Historically, movement expenses have raised four areas of controversy – shipment-by-shipment versus average calculation, the proper numerator for an average, the proper denominator, and expenses from factory to sales warehouse.

Shipment-by-shipment versus average calculation

If the freight company charges the foreign exporter for inland freight each time a shipment is made, the Commerce Department might expect the inland freight charge to be reported using the freight invoice for that particular shipment. As discussed earlier in this chapter, to calculate shipment-by-shipment expenses on home market sales serves no purpose, as the averaging of the prices washes out any sale-by-sale differences.

Proper numerator for average calculation

Companies often ship a variety of products at the same time. These will include the products that are subject to the investigation but perhaps many more that are not. In this case the Commerce Department usually understands the problem and accepts a calculation based on the average expenses for all the products, as long as it does not appear to distort the expense factor for the subject products.

The company should be especially careful in this case to ensure that the calculation is not open to a charge of distortion. Whether or not there is a distortion with a multi-product average often boils down to what denominator is used for the allocation among products.

Proper denominator for average calculation

When charges are not reported on a shipment-by-shipment basis, the Commerce Department accepts a reasonable allocation of total expenses to individual units. The allocation methodology should be based on the same method used to calculate the charge. This is normally by weight or volume. For example, suppose the exporter sells ten units of Product A and five units of Product B. The volume of Product A is 5 m^3 for each unit, and that of Product B is 7 m^3 for each unit. The total volume is 85 m^3 and the total freight charge is $2,000. The freight charge can be allocated as follows:

$$\frac{\$2,000}{85 \text{ m}^3} = \$23.5/\text{m}^3$$

Product A: $(5 \text{ m}^3)(\$23.5/\text{m}^3) = \$117.5$

Product B: $(7 \text{ m}^3)(\$23.5/\text{m}^3) = \$164.5$

If the information in the company's accounting records does not permit the precise calculation of per-unit charges, the foreign company should develop an allocation based on cost of goods sold or sales value. The Commerce Department will accept these denominators when the company can show that nothing else is available. Commerce will almost never accept an allocation based on quantity, unless the charge is incurred on that basis.

The exporter can use the same basic methodology for other movement expenses. The only difference is that the basis for the allocation will change. The general rule is that the expense should be allocated using the same basis on which the expense is incurred. Following this basic principle, the bases below are commonly used for these various expenses:

Expense	Allocation basis
Freight	Volume or weight
Insurance	FOB value
Warehousing	Volume
Brokerage/handling	FOB value
Bank charges	FOB value
Port charges	FOB value

In any particular case, however, the foreign company should try to use the basis on which it actually paid the expense.

Expenses from factory to sales warehouse

When home market products are sold out of a distribution centre or warehouse after transfer from the factory, the Commerce Department regularly denies any direct adjustment for the movement expenses between the factory and warehouse. Commerce adjusts only for movement expenses from the warehouse to the unrelated customer in the home market. What is the reasoning? The Commerce Department believes that the expenses between factory and warehouse are incurred 'prior to sale' and therefore are not directly related to the home market sale. The inconsistent part of this reasoning is that movement expenses from the factory to the port on *United States sales* are deducted entirely from the United States price, even when these expenses occur prior to the sale in the United States.

The Commerce Department's reasoning does not hold up to any serious scrutiny. A simple example will show why. Assume Producer A and Producer B both sell on delivery terms of 'FOB producer's warehouse'. Prior to sale, however, Producer A has stocked its warehouse with 10 units, while Producer B's warehouse is empty. Customer X orders 10 units from both Producer A and Producer B, FOB producer's warehouse. To put the 10 units in a condition necessary to satisfy the delivery terms to Customer X, both Producer A and Producer B must ship the units to the warehouse, incurring freight expenses between the factory and the warehouse. Producers A and B incur the same expenses and the customer in each case receives the same benefit – delivery terms of 'FOB producer's warehouse'.

Nevertheless, the Commerce Department's methodology arrives at two different calculations. Producer B's home market sales price will be net of the factory-to-warehouse freight expense because shipment to the place of delivery occurred after sale. Producer A's home market sales price, by contrast, will have no such adjustment because the goods were shipped to the place of delivery before sale. The Commerce Department's calculation, in other words, erroneously distinguishes two situations in which delivery terms are identical, costs to the producers are identical, and benefits to the customer are identical, purely on the detail of whether movement of the goods to the warehouse occurred before or after the customer's order.

The purpose of adjusting for differences in inland freight is to make a fair value comparison based on *ex-factory* prices. By including all inland freight incurred on United States sales, while excluding a portion of inland freight incurred for the home market, the Commerce Department ends up making an 'apples-to-oranges' comparison between ex-factory United States prices and ex-warehouse home market prices. Exporters involved in anti-dumping cases should challenge this practice until the Commerce Department gives it up.

Packing costs

Packing costs are treated somewhat differently from delivery costs. Rather than subtracting the packing costs from both United States price and foreign market value to achieve a fair comparison, the Commerce Department subtracts any packing charges from foreign market value and then adds back the amount of United States packing. Suppose the packing cost for the United States market is $10 and the packing cost for the Mexican market is $8.

The total net price for sales to the United States and Canada (after making all other appropriate adjustments), including packing, is $100 in each market. The adjustment for net Mexican price would be: gross price, less Mexican packing, plus United States packing, or $100 – $8 + $10 = $102. In this example, the lower packing cost in Mexico has created a dumping margin (the United States price of $100 is lower than the adjusted Mexican price of $102).

This result is consistent with the law. The anti-dumping statute explicitly requires the comparison of United States price and foreign market value to be on an 'ex factory' basis, *packed as if the merchandise were to be shipped to the United States*. Thus, the term 'ex-factory price' under United States anti-dumping law really means 'ex-factory price of goods packed for the United States'.

As a practical matter, the adjustment for packing costs often does not make much difference. Packing for export to different markets is usually the same. (Rare exceptions do occasionally arise.) Foreign companies also often pack merchandise for sale in the home market and export markets using the same materials. When there is a substantial difference in packing, the adjustment can be more important, but the company does not have a great deal of flexibility in calculating packing costs. Like delivery costs, the costs of packing are usually unambiguous. To the extent possible, the foreign company would like to lower United States packing costs and raise the packing costs used to calculate foreign market value.

The Commerce Department requires packing costs to be calculated on a per-unit basis. When the company subcontracts packing, establishing the per-unit charges that are paid is quite easy as they are usually listed on the invoices. Even when the packing is not subcontracted, foreign companies usually have detailed packing cost figures for each product that they produce. The Commerce Department asks for detailed information about the material, labour and factory overhead costs of packing merchandise for shipment to the United States and to the foreign market. (The Commerce Department does not have a consistent practice with regard to factory overhead. Sometimes Commerce includes only variable overhead; sometimes it includes both variable and fixed overhead. Whether or not Commerce makes the distinction often depends on what the exporter reports in the response. The distinction normally has no significant effect on the anti-dumping calculation.) Packing materials are usually very easy – most foreign companies keep cost sheets showing the precise cost of packing materials. Packing labour and overhead can be calculated by determining two factors:

❑ The average labour and overhead rates, usually per minute, based on either packing labour and overhead expenses or overall labour and overhead expenses; and

❑ The per-unit time needed to complete packing, usually drawn from engineering time studies.

Multiplying the labour and overhead rates by the per-unit time yields the per-unit cost of packing labour. If the company cannot derive precise per-unit figures from its records, the Commerce Department will accept some allocation of packing costs, generally based on the unit volume or unit weight of the individual products.

Differences in physical characteristics

Whenever possible, the Commerce Department compares identical merchandise in the United States market and foreign markets. When the Commerce Department must compare similar merchandise – because either identical merchandise does not exist or it was not sold in sufficient quantities – the Commerce Department makes an adjustment for any differences in the physical characteristics of the merchandise. Such an adjustment is usually called a 'difference in merchandise' or 'difmer' adjustment. The adjustment, either positive or negative, is made to foreign market value so that the foreign merchandise becomes comparable to the United States merchandise.

Difference-in-merchandise adjustments are based on differences in the cost of producing the two items that are being compared. Although United States law allows the Commerce Department to consider differences in the value of the merchandise, the Commerce Department generally does not do so. The Commerce Department's practice has been to consider only the material costs, direct labour costs, and variable overhead costs. These are the elements that, in the Commerce Department's view, contribute directly to the physical differences. Other elements of cost, such as indirect labour, fixed overhead, R&D expenses and administrative expenses, do not contribute directly to the physical differences between the merchandise.

Although difference-in-merchandise adjustments are routinely granted by Commerce, the issues can become more complex. For example, the foreign company must be able to show actual physical differences in the merchandise; it is not sufficient to show a quality difference between otherwise physically identical items. The differences cannot be too great, however, otherwise the Commerce Department may decide that the merchandise no longer qualifies as similar. As a general matter, the Commerce Department considers cost differences of more than 20% to divide the merchandise into two dissimilar categories that cannot be compared.

The adjustment is the amount of the difference between the variable costs of the two products. Under Commerce Department practice, the adjustment is always applied against the home market price. If the United States product has higher variable costs, then the difference is added to the home market price. If the United States product has smaller direct costs, then the difference is subtracted from the home market price.

Level of trade adjustment

The United States legislation implementing changes to the WTO Anti-Dumping Agreement has significantly increased attention by the Commerce Department in analysing 'level of trade' differences in anti-dumping calculations. Prior to the new law, the Commerce Department provided for a level of trade adjustment pursuant to the broad statutory requirement that it adjust foreign market ('normal') value to take into account 'differences in circumstances of sale'. Exporters claiming this adjustment were required to demonstrate costs in selling the same merchandise to different levels of trade. In practice, this proved extremely difficult and the adjustment rarely was made.

Under the new law, the Commerce Department is now required to adjust for level of trade differences between the two markets. The Commerce Department's regulations specify when it will determine that different levels of trade exist. Basically, the Commerce Department will find that sales are made at different levels of trade if they are made at different marketing stages – different places in the distribution chain – and there are substantial differences in selling activities among the proposed levels.

Essentially, in order to convince the Commerce Department that different levels of trade exist in the home market, the respondent has to demonstrate both that sales are made to different classes of customers (e.g. distributors and retailers) and that the respondent in fact performs different selling functions depending on the class of customer. For example, the respondent performs more sales-related services for a retailer than a distributor.

When United States sales are made through an affiliated company in the United States (now called constructed export price, or CEP, sales), the level of trade analysis is performed *after* all selling expenses incurred in the United States are deducted. Essentially, for CEP sales, the activities of the respondent consist of those selling activities related to the plant selling the merchandise to the affiliated United States importer. Typically, these selling activities are few, and so for the anti-dumping level of trade analysis CEP sales are generally considered to be *further back* in the distribution chain than sales from the plant to unrelated customers. Consequently, if home market sales are made to retailers, the Commerce Department will generally consider the home market and United States sales to be at different levels of trade, necessitating an adjustment.

The calculation of the appropriate adjustment depends on whether: (1) there are any home market sales of the subject merchandise to distributors; (2) the sales to those home market distributors are shown to be at a different level of trade from the home market sales to the retailers; and (3) the home market sales to distributors are considered to be at the same level of trade as the CEP sales to the affiliated company in the United States market. If *all* of these factors exist, then the level of trade adjustment will equal the percentage difference between the weighted average price of all home market sales to retailers and the weighted average price of all home market sales to distributors. The percentage difference would then be applied to the weighted average price of the home market model sold to retailers that is the match for the CEP sale.

If there is only one level of trade in the home market – if all home market sales are made to retailers – then the Commerce Department will use home market indirect selling expenses in lieu of a calculated level of trade adjustment. That is, in this situation, home market indirect selling expenses will be deducted from the weighted average home market price, but only up to the amount of the deduction for United States indirect selling expenses.

Profit deduction for United States (CEP) sales

Another significant change to the United States anti-dumping law from the legislation implementing the Uruguay Round is the requirement that Commerce deduct from the *United States price* an amount for profit (attributable to United States operations) in *all* situations in which United States sales are made through an affiliated company. There is no corresponding profit deduction for home market sales made through an affiliated company in the home market. This is just another example of the asymmetrical comparisons under the United States anti-dumping law. Given the manner in which the Commerce Department undertakes the calculation, this new deduction from the United States price could play an important part in the calculation of the anti-dumping margin.

In September 1997 the Commerce Department published fairly detailed guidelines on how the profit deduction is to be calculated for United States CEP transactions. Essentially, the Commerce Department undertakes a two-step process. First, the Department calculates the 'total actual profit' for *all* sales of the subject merchandise in *both* the United States and the foreign market. This example illustrates the Commerce Department methodology:

Net home market sales revenue	$7,250,000
Net United States market sales revenue (converted to home market currency)	<u>$6,750,000</u>
Total revenue for both markets	*$14,000,000*
Cost of manufacturing for home market products	-$4,000,000
Cost of manufacturing for United States market products	-$5,000,000
Home market selling expenses (both direct and indirect)	-$350,000
United States market selling expenses incurred in country of manufacture	-$300,000
United States selling expenses incurred in United States (both direct and indirect)	-$1,750,000
Home market movement/distribution	-$50,000
United States movement expenses incurred prior to entry into United States (e.g. freight, brokerage etc.)	-$75,000
United States movement expenses incurred in United States	<u>-$90,000</u>
Total costs and expenses for both markets	<u>*-$11,615,000*</u>
Total profit for both markets used in profit deduction calculation	*$2,385,000*

Second, the Department then allocates the total profit derived in step one to individual United States transactions based on the ratio of total expenses incurred in the United States to total costs and expenses incurred in both markets.

Note that 'total home market sales revenue' is equivalent to invoice prices to all customers minus discounts and rebates. In this regard, *all* home market sales of subject merchandise should be included, except sales to affiliated customers that do not pass the arm's-length test. In particular, unlike the calculation of the profit for constructed value purposes, the law explicitly allows inclusion of sales below cost price in the calculation of CEP profit deduction. Also note that the total cost of production should equal a fully allocated cost – including fixed overhead, general, selling and administrative (GSA), and financing expenses.

As indicated, the actual amount of the profit deduction is based on a factor equal to total expenses incurred in the United States divided by total costs and expenses of all products in both markets. This factor applied against total profit yields the total amount of profit to be allocated across all United States sales. The allocation should be based on the relative value of each United States model.

To illustrate, in the example above those expenses associated with the United States market total $7,215,000 (the sum of $5,000,000 plus $300,000 plus $1,750,000 plus $75,000 plus $90,000). This United States total is 62.1% of the total ($7,215,000 divided by $11,615,000). Therefore, the Commerce Department would attribute 62.1% of the total profit to the United States transactions. The allocation to each particular model would be based on the total value of sales of that particular model relative to total sales value in the United States market.

Circumstance-of-sale adjustments

Some of the most important adjustments in every anti-dumping case relate to the particular circumstances of the sale. The law recognizes that different prices in the United States when compared to prices in other countries can result from the different conditions under which a company sells in various markets.

Circumstance-of-sale adjustments are made for the differences in selling expenses between the United States and foreign markets. The treatment of these selling expenses under the United States anti-dumping law depends on two factors. First, the treatment depends on whether the expense is classified as a 'direct' or an 'indirect' expense. This distinction is critical because it is more difficult to claim adjustments for indirect expenses. Second, different rules apply depending on whether the basis of the United States price is export price (EP) or constructed export price (CEP).

The Commerce Department recognizes various categories of expenses that could be considered for circumstance-of-sale adjustments, including:

❑ Credit expenses

❑ Inventory carrying costs

❑ Commissions

❑ Warranty and servicing expenses

❑ Advertising

❑ Technical services

❑ Warehousing

Each of these adjustments is discussed briefly below. Our goal is to provide enough background for a foreign company to understand the nature and calculation of the adjustment. Each case, however, will raise its own unique issues.

Credit expenses

The Commerce Department adjusts its comparison of United States price and foreign market value to account for differences in credit costs between the two markets being compared.

Credit cost adjustments are one of the most common sale adjustments, and arise in virtually every anti-dumping case. Credit costs incurred after a sale are considered a direct selling expense. Pre-sale credit costs (inventory carrying costs) are considered an indirect selling expense.

The Commerce Department calculates the difference in credit costs by using what is known as 'imputed interest'. The Commerce Department does not measure the actual interest costs incurred in each market. Rather, the Commerce Department calculates the *hypothetical* interest cost that the company would have incurred, and then 'imputes' that cost to the individual sales transaction. This imputation is done on a sale-by-sale basis.

Although the questionnaire does not explain Commerce Department practice very well, the Commerce Department's policy for calculating post-sale credit costs is well settled. Post-sale credit costs are considered a direct selling expense, and can thus always be claimed as a circumstance-of-sale adjustment. The Commerce Department uses the following formula in its calculations of credit costs:

$$(\text{interest rate}) \times (\text{transaction amount}) \times (\text{number of days}/360)$$

This formula is based on three elements. The 'interest rate' is the average short-term interest rate paid by the company. Note that the figure '360' varies depending on the period base of the interest rate. For annual interest rates, the figure 360 is used. For monthly interest rates, the figure 30 is used. The 'transaction amount' is the value of the individual sale in question. The Commerce Department always calculates credit costs on a transaction by transaction basis. The 'number of days' can either be an average number of days between sale and payment, or a precise number of days, if such a calculation is possible.

Many believe that the Commerce Department's approach is unfair. Suppose a company does not actually borrow from banks to finance its accounts receivable – the promise from the customer to pay at some time in the future. Such a company does not incur any actual credit costs, regardless of how long the sale is outstanding, so why should the Commerce Department impute a hypothetical cost? Indeed, the Commerce Department's prior policy in the early 1980s was to limit the amount of the credit adjustment to the actual borrowing of the company.

However, the Commerce Department has rejected its old policy, as well as this argument about unfairness. The Commerce Department's current position is that its policy determines the effect of different credit terms in different markets, and it does not care how (or even whether) a company chooses to finance its credit terms. If a company offers longer credit terms in a particular market, the period during which the customer does not have to pay provides some 'value' to the customer and has the effect of lowering the price to the customer. This rationale, and the Commerce Department policy of using hypothetical rather than actual credit costs, has been upheld by the Court of International Trade.

Imputed inventory carrying cost

The Commerce Department also imputes a credit cost associated with pre-sale credit expenses – the imputed cost of carrying inventory. The inventory carrying cost attempts to measure the cost of holding *finished goods* inventory. Inventory carrying expenses are typically calculated using the following formula:

$$A \times (B/360) \times R = C$$

where

C = inventory carrying expense

A = sales price

B = average number of days between end of production and shipment (on a model-specific basis)(inventory period)

R = weighted average short-term interest rate

Imputed inventory carrying cost is considered an indirect expense. Accordingly, although such expense will always be deducted from United States (CEP) sales price, the imputed inventory carrying expense will be deducted from home market sales only if there are different levels of trade between the two markets.

Commissions

Different commissions paid in different markets can significantly affect the comparability of prices. The Commerce Department therefore makes adjustments to United States price and foreign market value to reflect these differences. Since commissions by their nature vary on a sale-by-sale basis, they are always considered to be a direct expense. The way in which the adjustment is made depends on whether the United States price is based on export price (EP) or constructed export price (CEP).

When the United States price is based on export price, the Commerce Department makes the following adjustments:

❑ If the commission is paid only in the United States market, the Commerce Department adds the amount of this commission to the foreign market value. The United States price is higher to reflect the cost of the commission, and adding this same amount to the foreign market value ensures that the prices being used for United States price and foreign market value are comparable.

❑ If the commission is paid only in the domestic or third country market, the Commerce Department subtracts the amount of the commission from the foreign market value to ensure comparability of the prices.

❑ If the commission is paid in both the United States and foreign markets, the Commerce Department deducts the foreign market commission from the foreign market value and adds the amount of the United States commission to the foreign market value. In the past, the Commerce Department sometimes subtracted the commission amounts from both prices, but the Commerce Department has since recognized that it does not have statutory authority to adjust the United States price in this situation.

When the United States price is based on constructed export price sales price, different rules apply because of a specific statutory provision requiring the Commerce Department to subtract commissions from the exporter's sales price:

❑ If the commission is paid only in the United States market, the Commerce Department subtracts the amount of the commission from the United States price.

❑ If the commission is paid only in the domestic or third country market, the Commerce Department subtracts the amount of the commission from the foreign market value.

❑ If the commission is paid in both the United States and foreign markets, the Commerce Department deducts the commissions from both markets. This treatment is possible for CEP but not purchase price, because of special statutory provisions.

Generally, the Commerce Department makes adjustments only for commissions paid to unrelated parties. The underlying concern is that commission payment between related parties could be used to hide dumping margins. In some cases foreign companies have been able to convince the Commerce Department that the sale on which the commission was earned was an 'arm's-length' transaction, and the Commerce Department therefore granted the adjustment even though the parties were related. It is safer to assume, however, that the Commerce Department will reject such arguments. The courts have upheld this Commerce Department policy.

The existence of commissions also affects the treatment of indirect expenses. As noted above, if a commission is paid in one market, but not the other, the Commerce Department allows a 'commission offset' in the other market to ensure that the prices remain comparable. In such a situation, the Commerce Department suspends the basic rule that circumstance-of-sale adjustments are made only for direct selling expenses. Any selling expenses – direct or indirect – can be used to offset the commission. In an export price (EP) situation, this suspension of the basic rule means that indirect selling expenses can be used for a circumstance-of-sale adjustment, up to the amount of the commission in the other market. In an constructed export price (CEP) situation, the commission has the effect of raising the limit on the exporter's sales price offset to all United States indirect selling expenses plus the amount of the commission.

Commissions, if paid in one market but not the other, thus have a dual affect. The commission, as a direct selling expense, leads to a circumstance-of-sale adjustment – usually the subtraction of the commission from the gross price. The commission also triggers a circumstance-of-sale adjustment for the indirect selling expenses in the other market – up to the amount of the commission.

Whether the offset helps or hurts the foreign company depends on the market in which the commissions are paid. If the company pays commissions in the United States market, the offset to the foreign market price lowers the dumping margin. If the commission is paid in the foreign market, the offset to the United States price raises the dumping margin. Note, however, that if the United States price is based on exporter's sales price, the Commerce Department already reduces the United States price by the full amount of any indirect selling expenses.

Warranty expenses

The Department also makes a circumstance-of-sale adjustment for warranty expenses incurred for each market's sales. For consumer products, such as colour television sets, this adjustment can be rather significant. Warranty costs incurred during the period of investigation are used to estimate the eventual warranty costs for the sales under consideration.

The Department's warranty expense adjustment concerns only the 'direct' portion of the expenses. Direct expenses are those that vary with the quantity sold, and typically include the cost of parts and payments made to unaffiliated service companies (if paid by the respondent). Any indirect warranty expenses, such as the salaries and benefits of employees in an in-house after-sale service centre, are included in the calculation of indirect selling expenses. This distinction could be important because, although all indirect selling expenses are deducted from the United States price (in CEP situations), indirect selling expenses are deducted from home market sales prices only if the Department finds that the home market sales are made at a different level of trade.

To the extent possible, the adjustment for direct warranty expenses should be calculated on a model-specific basis, less any reimbursement received from the customer or unaffiliated parts supplier. If it is not practical to report the expenses on a model-specific basis, then direct warranty expenses should be calculated on the most product-specific basis possible.

Advertising expenses

The advertising expense adjustment consists of expenses for advertising and sales promotion *only to the extent* that these expenses are incurred on behalf of the customer's customer (e.g. advertising aimed at the ultimate end-user of the product). Expenses incurred to advertise to the respondent's customer, e.g. the retailers, should be included in the calculation of indirect selling expenses (detailed below).

Technical services

Technical services include service advice, repair work, or other customer consultations relating to the product under investigation. Such work is typically outside the scope of the warranty coverage. The principle issue concerning technical services has been whether the expenses are related to the particular sales under investigation. Sometimes a company can specifically link particular technical services expenses to particular sales (usually when the expenses relate to a specific project). In such cases, the Commerce Department allows the technical services expenses as a circumstance-of-sale adjustment. More commonly, the technical services are related to future sales, or to the company's products in general. In such cases, the Commerce Department disallows the technical service expense.

Even if the expenses are related to particular sales, the company must also show that they are direct expenses. The Commerce Department considers non-variable costs, such as the technicians' salaries, to be part of a company's fixed costs. Such expenses are indirect and the Commerce Department does not allow an adjustment. The Commerce Department considers variable expenses, such as material costs and travel expenses of the technicians, to be directly related to sales. Other kinds of expenses may not be so clear-cut, and the parties can argue about the proper characterization.

Even if the technical service expense is disallowed as a circumstance-of-sale adjustment because it is indirect, it may be possible to claim the expense nonetheless. The expense could be included with an ESP offset, or with a commission offset, if either of them are involved in the investigation. Depending on the circumstances of the particular case, claiming the technical service expense as an offset may have the same effect for the company.

Warehousing

The treatment of warehousing expenses depends on whether the warehousing is pre-sale or post-sale, and on the way in which the foreign company uses warehousing. Pre-sale warehousing is always considered to be an indirect expense; by definition, pre-sale warehousing cannot be linked to specific sales.

Post-sale warehousing depends much more on the circumstances. If the post-sale warehousing is considered part of the production process, and units of the finished merchandise are stored routinely regardless of whether they have been sold, the Commerce Department does not grant a circumstance-of-sale adjustment. In contrast, if the post-sale warehousing is a condition of the sale and the merchandise is stored while waiting for shipment to a particular customer, then the Commerce Department may consider the warehousing to be a direct expense of the selling process rather than the production process, and grant a circumstance-of-sale adjustment.

Post-sale warehousing expenses that are not directly linked to specific sales can be treated as indirect selling expenses, provided the foreign company can link the warehousing expenses to a particular market. If not, the Commerce Department ignores the expenses.

Chapter 4

Anti-dumping duties: analysing costs and determining constructed value

More and more foreign companies are finding their costs of production under investigation by United States authorities. In the early 1980s, few anti-dumping cases involved cost of production. This has changed. United States industries began to realize that a cost investigation gives them a significant strategic advantage in anti-dumping investigations, and pushed for changes in United States law and practice to make such investigations easier to trigger and more burdensome to defend. Even if the foreign company eventually proves that its sales are 'above cost', the company will have devoted enormous resources to defending against the cost allegations and will have shifted some attention away from the issues involved in defending the price investigation.

In many cases, however, the foreign company will not be able to prove that its sales are 'above cost'. In periods of rapidly changing exchange rates, it is not unusual for companies to sell merchandise at prices that, in dollar terms, do not fully cover the cost of producing the merchandise. Even if exchange rates are stable, companies sometimes consciously sell their products below cost for some period of time. From a business and economic perspective, it can make sense for a company to sell below its average costs, as long as the company is recovering its marginal costs. But the anti-dumping law is not based on a similar economic rationality.

Defending a 'cost case' – an anti-dumping investigation that involves issues of cost of production and the related concept of 'constructed value' – is becoming an increasingly common challenge facing foreign companies. These issues are therefore discussed at some length in this chapter, which offers suggestions for how a foreign company should organize its defence of a 'cost case'. The chapter also discusses how these general rules vary when applied to 'non-market economies'.

When cost information is necessary

Cost as a basis for foreign market value

Foreign market value is based on cost (or more precisely 'constructed value', which is discussed in more detail below) in two situations. First, prices cannot serve as the basis for foreign market value unless those prices are above the cost of producing and selling the merchandise. If the Commerce Department finds that home market prices or third country prices are below cost, then the Commerce Department must reject those prices and instead use constructed value as the basis for foreign market value.

Second, in some situations the foreign company does not sell identical or similar merchandise to any other market. When there are identical or similar sales in other markets, the United States law requires the Commerce Department to look first to the prices of those sales in determining foreign market value. When there are no appropriate home market or third country prices to use – either because there are no sales or because the merchandise sold is too dissimilar – the Commerce Department turns to constructed value as the only remaining alternative for determining foreign market value.

Allegations by the petitioner

Allegations that the foreign market prices are below cost can arise in two ways. First, the petition itself may be based on cost of production data. It is increasingly common for petitioners to allege dumping based on a comparison of export prices to the United States market and the petitioner's estimate of cost. Often petitioners do not have access to information about home market prices or third country prices when they prepare their petition. It is sometimes easier for the petitioner to examine its own costs of production, adapt those costs to estimate the costs that should exist in the home market of the target country, and use the adjusted costs to calculate constructed value and estimated dumping margins. If the petitioner can obtain home market prices, it can make the 'below cost' allegation in the petition. Otherwise, the petitioner makes a specific allegation when the home market or third country prices are submitted in the initial questionnaire response by respondents.

Cost allegations can also arise later in the investigation. Even if the petition is not based on the United States domestic industry's costs, it is possible that the petitioner will develop such costs later in the investigation. It is common for petitioners to wait for the foreign company's responses and then use the information in those responses, especially information submitted to support a claimed difference-in-merchandise adjustment, to document an allegation of sales below cost. As a practical matter, the requirements for difference-in-merchandise adjustments (see 'Differences in physical characteristics' in chapter 3) now essentially require respondents to develop quite detailed cost information.

Timing of cost allegations

Legal standards concerning the timing of cost allegations have changed over the years. Initially, neither the statute nor the Commerce Department regulations imposed any specific requirements. In recent revisions to its regulations, the Commerce Department has finally set forth more precise deadlines concerning cost allegations. The basic rule for original investigations and administrative reviews is that a cost allegation must be filed 20 days after the foreign respondent has submitted its questionnaire responses.

The new regulation also provides that if there is some delay in the release of important information to the petitioner's lawyers, these deadlines may be extended. This provision seeks to prevent foreign companies from intentionally withholding certain critical information until late in the investigation so that the petitioner does not have time to analyse the information and file an allegation of sales below cost based on it.

In most cases, this new regulation means that foreign companies know when they face the risk of a cost investigation. In the early stages of the investigation, before the preliminary determination, there is a significant risk that the petitioner may make an allegation of sales below cost. After the new deadline, and especially after the preliminary determination, the foreign company can be reasonably certain that the investigation will not involve cost.

General considerations in calculating costs

Before discussing the specific elements of cost of production, this section reviews the basic principles that underlie the Commerce Department determinations. This section also illustrates the basic accounting concepts and terminology used in cost investigations.

Fully distributed, actual costs

The Commerce Department determines the cost of merchandise under investigation based on the 'fully distributed, actual costs' of production. This principle means that all of the costs of the product must be included. Obvious costs such as materials and labour, as well as less obvious costs such as interest expenses and various overhead expenses, must all be included. If several related companies are involved – for example, a subsidiary manufactures subassemblies, which are sold to the parent company for final assembly, and then shipped to a related subsidiary in the United States for distribution – all of the costs of production and distribution must be included. How the costs are allocated to different products will be the subject of extensive arguments during the cost investigation. All of the costs must go somewhere, however.

The costs must also be 'actual' costs, not estimated costs or hypothetical costs. In general, this means that the Commerce Department looks at the costs actually paid by the foreign company and recorded in its accounting records. Although there are some exceptions to this principle, especially in the area of interest and R&D expenses, the Commerce Department generally uses actual costs in anti-dumping investigations. The Commerce Department does not always classify or allocate costs in the same way as the company's accounting system, but the magnitude of the costs usually corresponds to the company's accounting records.

Product-specific costs

The Commerce Department requires cost data to be submitted on a product-specific basis. It is not acceptable to submit general cost information for a whole product line – these general costs must be allocated to individual models. This requirement is sometimes very frustrating for foreign companies, especially for companies that record costs on a product line basis, rather than model by model. The Commerce Department, however, has consistently required companies to develop model-by-model costs for use in anti-dumping investigations. Depending on the type of cost accounting system used by the company, developing model-by-model costs can be easy or difficult.

Standard cost systems

Many foreign companies use 'standard cost' accounting systems. The Commerce Department will accept cost of production information based on such a system, provided the company adjusts its standard costs to reflect the actual costs of production.

Under such a system, the company has a 'standard cost' for each product, usually based on some combination of (1) cost estimates made when the product was first introduced, and (2) actual costs collected during the initial production phase. The company also calculates 'variances' – the difference between the standard cost of the product and the actual cost of the product. Variances are normally calculated based on 'cost centres'. Cost centres are simply accounting conventions for determining how best to organize the cost data. They vary from company to company. Sometimes an entire factory will be a cost centre. Sometimes a particular product, or even an individual production line at a factory, will be a cost centre. Regardless of how they are calculated, the variances are applied to the standard cost of the individual product to yield the actual cost of the product.

Other cost accounting systems

If a foreign company does not use a standard cost system, the company needs to develop some way of allocating general costs to individual products. For example, in a number of investigations of steel pipe the Commerce Department has insisted that the companies calculate costs on a size by size basis (1-inch pipe, 2-inch pipe, and so on), even though the foreign companies maintained cost accounting records only on an aggregate basis, such as how much steel and zinc was used to produce all of the pipe. These companies were forced to develop allocations from scratch.

There are no specific rules for allocating costs, as long as the allocation meets two general criteria: all of the costs must be allocated, and the allocation must not distort the relative costs of products. Within these constraints, the company and its lawyers are free to develop the most favourable allocation methodology that can be defended as reasonable. The lawyers for the domestic industry will undoubtedly challenge the allocation methodology proposed by the foreign company, and try to persuade the Commerce Department to adopt a less favourable allocation methodology. These issues will be the source of much contention during the course of the investigation.

Time period and form for cost information

Annual costs

Although its practice has varied over the years, the Commerce Department now has a basic rule of requiring foreign companies to submit cost information for the completed calendar or fiscal year that most closely corresponds to the period being investigated. The idea is to simplify the task of linking costs of production back to the company's financial statements. This period for reporting costs can change depending on the circumstances of a particular case, however. If petitioners believe that costs have been changing over time, they will argue for a different period. The Commerce Department often agrees, and requires companies to go through the burden of preparing cost of production information for some other period of time that overlaps two different fiscal year periods.

Weighted average costs

Once the Commerce Department has identified the particular 12-month period for costs, it must decide how to calculate the costs during that period. In a normal case, the Commerce Department calculates a single weighted average cost for the 12-month period under investigation (remember that the period of investigation for the cost response need not be the same as the period of investigation for the price response). This weighted average cost is then used to determine whether the sale prices have been above or below cost.

If the costs have been changing rapidly, however, the Commerce Department sometimes calculates quarterly or even monthly costs. In anti-dumping investigations involving high tech products, where the 'learning curve' is very steep and costs therefore drop rapidly as the company becomes more familiar with the production process, it is common for the Commerce Department to calculate costs for narrower periods of time. Similarly, in hyper-inflationary economies the Commerce Department often insists on monthly costs. Although foreign companies may in fact look at broader time periods, the Commerce Department assumes that the companies monitor their per-unit costs on a monthly or quarterly basis and believes that companies should recover their total costs at each point in the product life cycle. Although this practice may seem unreasonable, it is the current Commerce Department policy. The Commerce Department normally specifies in its questionnaire whether it wants costs on a quarterly or monthly basis.

When the foreign company produces the merchandise under investigation in two or more factories, the Commerce Department asks for cost information from all of the factories and calculates a single weighted average cost of production. Even if a single factory produces for export to the United States and the other factories produce only for domestic consumption, the Commerce Department insists on a weighted average cost of production. The Commerce Department is more concerned about the possibility of the company's distorting its costs by shifting costs among the various factories than it is with the burden on the responding company.

Prior year models

For products that are sold on a model-year basis, prior year models can create a tremendous burden in cost investigations. If a company sells only 5 or 10 units of a 1999 model in 2001, and sells thousands of 2000 and 2001 models, it seems unreasonable to require the company to prepare detailed cost information for the 1999 model. Sometimes the Commerce Department agrees with this argument, and does not require the cost information. Other times the Commerce Department insists, and uses 'best information' against companies that do not provide the information. Foreign companies must handle such situations on a case-by-case basis.

Commerce Department requests for information

The Commerce Department usually asks for cost information for the most recently completed fiscal year, and for any other months or quarters necessary to include the entire 12-month period under investigation. The fiscal year data is necessary for verification, since it should trace easily to the accounting records and financial statement of the company. The additional months or quarters may be more difficult to verify, but are necessary to provide the Commerce Department with information for the complete period. Although it generally calculates a single weighted average for the entire period of investigation, the Commerce Department sometimes asks for the various cost elements (such as materials, labour, overhead) to be provided on a quarterly basis.

Because of this uncertainty about how it will eventually decide to calculate the costs, the Commerce Department often makes very broad and expansive requests for information. It is easier for the Commerce Department to ask for much more information than it needs, and decide later what information it will actually use. Unfortunately, this attitude often results in great burdens for the foreign company forced to prepare the information. It is sometimes possible for the lawyer to negotiate with the Commerce Department staff and encourage them to think about what information is really necessary, and to narrow the request. Other times the unreasonable request will remain, and the company has little choice but to comply.

Use and misuse of GAAP

As a general matter, the United States statute requires the Commerce Department to follow the local 'generally accepted accounting principles'

(GAAP) used by the company under investigation. This principle was acknowledged by the United States Congress when it added the cost of production provisions to the United States anti-dumping law, and the Commerce Department has generally followed this basic principle in its decisions.

Unfortunately, the Commerce Department sometimes deviates from the local GAAP. The Commerce Department's justification for these deviations is that GAAP was designed to reflect the overall profitability of a company, and was not designed to calculate per-unit costs of particular products. Whenever the Commerce Department feels that following local GAAP distorts the per-unit costs or does not adequately reflect certain costs, it ignores the local GAAP and creates its own accounting rules.

Two areas that often involve disputes are interest costs and R&D costs. The Commerce Department often disagrees with how the foreign country GAAP classifies such expenses, or how the foreign country GAAP allocates such expenses over time. The Commerce Department has a general preference for whatever approach leads to higher costs in the period of time being investigated – which sometimes involves expensing all costs in the current year, and sometimes involves spreading costs out over a longer period of time.

As it prepares its cost information, the foreign company should be sensitive to areas where the Commerce Department might depart from foreign GAAP. The sooner the company identifies a possible issue, the sooner the company can begin to develop arguments to persuade the Commerce Department not to reclassify the cost.

Commerce department uses of the cost information

The cost information can be used in two ways. First, the Commerce Department uses the cost information to determine whether foreign market prices are above the cost of producing the merchandise. If a sufficient number of sales are above cost, the Commerce Department can use the prices of those sales as the basis for foreign market value. Second, if few or none of the sales are above cost then the Commerce Department uses the cost information to calculate constructed value. Use of constructed value also has the effect of increasing dumping margins. Each of these two possible uses is discussed below.

Cost of production versus home market price

When comparing cost of production to prices, the goal is to determine whether the home market or third country prices can serve as the basis of foreign market value. In making this determination, the Commerce Department follows several established policies.

The cost of production test – 'substantial quantities'

The anti-dumping law requires the Commerce Department to determine whether a sufficient number of sales are above cost to justify using those sales as the basis for foreign market value. The statute, however, does not specify how the Commerce Department should make that determination. As a matter of administrative practice, the Commerce Department has created what has become known as the '20% rule'.

The '20% rule' specifies how the Commerce Department applies the cost of production test. First, if more than 80% of the individual sales are above cost (usually measured by volume), the Commerce Department uses all of the sales to determine foreign market value. In such a situation, the number of below-cost sales is deemed so small that the Commerce Department is not concerned about the minor distortion that results from including them in its analysis. Application of the cost test has no effect on the dumping margins in this case.

Second, when the number of below-cost sales is above 20%, the Commerce Department excludes those individual sales that are below cost. By excluding the lower priced (below cost) sales from the weighted average price, the Commerce Department raises the average foreign market price that will be compared to the United States price, and thus raises the dumping margins.

Basis for applying the cost of production test

The Commerce Department applies the cost of production test and its '20% rule' to individual categories of products. As discussed earlier (see 'Establishing the model-match methodology' in chapter 3), the Commerce Department creates specific categories called 'control numbers' or 'CONNUMs' for each investigation, which represent what the Commerce Department believes are meaningful categories for comparison in a dumping case. The cost test is applied to each of these CONNUMs. The practice means that a foreign company may be selling most of its products above cost, but may find that certain products are below cost and are rejected as the basis for normal value.

This practice is not mandated by the statute, and in some prior cases the Commerce Department did look at broader categories when applying the cost test. The current practice is quite mechanical, and often leads to rather strange results. But this practice now seems to be quite well established, and is unlikely to alter unless some new WTO rules force a change.

Constructed value versus United States price

The role of constructed value

When the Commerce Department finds that home market prices or third country prices cannot be used to establish foreign market value – either because these prices do not exist or because the prices are below the cost of production – the anti-dumping law requires the Commerce Department to use constructed value as the basis of foreign market value. Constructed value thus serves as a surrogate for the home market price that does not exist. Once this cost-based surrogate for the price is created, it is compared to the prices offered in the United States to determine if there is any 'dumping'.

Differences between constructed value and cost of production

Constructed value is basically very similar to cost of production. The basic elements are:

❑ Cost of materials

❑ Cost of labour

❑ Overhead

❑ General and administrative expenses

❑ Selling expenses

❑ Profit

❑ Packing

The various items of cost of manufacturing (cost of materials, labour, and overhead) should be the cost of manufacturing of the merchandise sold in the United States. The GSA expenses and selling expenses, however, should be for the identical or similar merchandise sold in the home market (or third country market), not the expenses from the United States market. If there are no identical or similar sales in the home market, the Commerce Department may use the expenses associated with United States sales as a 'best information' surrogate for the non-existent foreign market expenses. Profit should also be based on the home market, but packing costs should be those for packing merchandise destined for the United States.

There are several important differences between cost of production and constructed value. First, constructed value must include an amount for profit. Cost of production involves no calculation of profit. Constructed value requires the use of either actual profits for the identical merchandise sold in the home market, or some other appropriate surrogate. United States law once imposed a statutory minimum profit of 8%, but that requirement was eliminated as part of the Uruguay Round Anti-Dumping Agreement. The new practice is to use the prices and costs submitted by the foreign respondent to calculate an actual average profit on the sales actually being made by the company. When making this calculation, however, the Commerce Department uses only sales above cost, and not all sales. For example, the foreign company may have an overall average profit margin of 5% on its home market sales, but a 20% profit margin on those sales that are above cost. The Commerce Department would use the 20% profit margin.

The practice has recently come under challenge in the WTO. In a 2001 case involving a similar EU practice, the Appellate Body ruled in *European Communities – Anti-dumping duties on imports of cotton-type bed linen from India* that in some instances the authorities must include all sales in determining the profit rate, not just the above-cost sales. It is still too early, however, to say whether and how United States practice may change in reaction to this ruling. In general, the United States authorities do not change their practice until forced to do so in specific challenges to United States anti-dumping determinations. In the meantime, the standard United States rule still applies.

Second, constructed value requires the inclusion of an amount for packing. This item should be the cost of packing the United States merchandise for shipment to the United States, not the cost of packing merchandise for sale in the home market or third country markets. Since the packing figures used in the price response and the figures used in the cost response are always identical, packing rarely affects the dumping margins.

Third, if any duties or taxes on the materials are rebated when the merchandise is exported, those duties or taxes must be excluded from the cost of materials used to calculate constructed value. As a practical matter, many foreign companies usually do not need to make this adjustment because they have already found a way to avoid paying the import duties when the materials are imported.

Fourth, selling expenses are based on the foreign market, not on the United States market. As with other GSA expenses, the Commerce Department may use selling expenses from the United States market if there are no comparable sales in the foreign market. The selling expenses used for constructed value are usually taken from the price response, so it is important to ensure that any necessary currency conversions are made.

Adjustments to constructed value

Although there was initially some uncertainty, the Commerce Department has established a settled policy of making circumstance-of-sale adjustments to constructed value. The most common such adjustment is for differences in credit costs. Domestic petitioners argued that the statutory provisions on circumstance-of-sale adjustments should apply only to home market or third country prices, not constructed value. The Commerce Department rejected this argument. Since constructed value is based on the selling expenses of foreign market sales, which may be significantly different from the selling expenses for United States sales, some adjustment is necessary to ensure comparability. The courts have upheld this Commerce Department position, so the issue should remain settled.

Determining individual cost elements

This section explains in detail the various elements of cost of production mentioned earlier. For each of the major categories of cost, this section summarizes the Commerce Department's treatment of that cost element, and identifies the major issues concerning that element. While these elements are generally the same for both cost of production and constructed value, any differences are noted in the sections that follow.

Please note, however, that the following discussion is a brief overview of a very complex area of United States law. Not only are the Commerce Department cost methodologies complex, they are also constantly evolving as the Commerce Department confronts new situations. In addition, the Commerce Department often adopts special rules to deal with certain types of cases – such as countries with hyper-inflationary economies, or cases involving highly seasonal agricultural products. The following discussion should therefore be considered a basic introduction.

Material costs

Elements and allocation of material costs

'Material costs' are the actual costs of the raw materials, components, and various supplies needed to produce the merchandise under investigation. Material costs should include all of the costs associated with the materials used. Obviously the purchase price of the material is the starting point. Items such as transportation costs must also be included. Any duties or taxes paid on imported materials must be included, but if the duties or taxes are later rebated, the rebate can be used to offset the material costs. Quality control costs, and any other costs associated with the materials used, must be included. When there is some waste in the production process, the material costs must be adjusted upward to reflect this waste. If the waste (sometimes called scrap or by-product) is sold, the amount received from the sale can be used as a credit to offset the material costs.

Allocation of material costs to individual products depends completely on the type of accounting system in place at the company. For foreign companies with a standard cost accounting system, the standard costs themselves represent an acceptable allocation. As long as the company can defend the development of the standards as reasonable, the Commerce Department normally accepts the standard costs. Companies without a standard cost system need to develop some other way to allocate material costs to individual products. It is best if the allocation is completely, or at least partially, based on the existing accounting system.

Material costs are slightly different for cost of production and constructed value, but the basic methodology for calculating the costs is the same. For cost of production, the material costs should be those for the merchandise sold in the foreign market (either home market or third country market). For constructed value, the material costs should be those for the merchandise sold in the United States.

Special issues

One of the difficult issues relating to material costs is the treatment of related or affiliated suppliers. The first task is to determine when a company is to be deemed 'related' for these purposes. The Commerce Department has historically applied a 20% test – if one company owns 20% or more of the other company's stock, the company is deemed to be related. The Commerce Department has always reserved the right, however, to find 'affiliation' based on other circumstances, such as family relationships. More recently, Commerce has been casting an even wider net, examining relationships based on as little as 5% stock ownership.

Commerce now focuses its efforts on 'major inputs', those cost items that account for a significant percentage of the total product costs. There are no fixed rules but it generally focuses on items that are more than 1% of the total cost of manufacturing.

Once the Commerce Department decides that companies are related, the foreign company bears the burden of justifying the reasonableness of the prices charged between the two companies. Three methods have historically been used to validate the price charged between the related companies. First, the Commerce Department checks whether the related supplier sells to unrelated companies at the same price that it sells to related companies. Although this method is relatively simple to apply, it is often unavailable. Foreign subsidiaries often sell to their parent company on an exclusive basis, so there are no unrelated party transactions to use to validate the related party transactions.

Second, the Commerce Department checks whether the parent company buys the same materials from other, unrelated, suppliers. While this method is also relatively simple to apply, it is also usually not available, since many foreign companies use related suppliers exclusively and do not purchase from unrelated suppliers.

Third, if there are no unrelated party prices to use, the Commerce Department looks to the cost of the materials being supplied. If the price charged by the related company is sufficient to cover the cost of the materials or product, the Commerce Department accepts the price as a reasonable basis for calculating cost of production. Developing cost information for individual components or materials can be enormously time consuming, however. For many consumer products, there are hundreds or thousands of individual parts that go into the finished product. Validating each of the component prices is virtually impossible.

Labour costs

Elements and allocation of labour costs

'Labour costs' include all of the worker-related costs associated with producing the merchandise under investigation. Besides the base pay of the workers, labour costs include overtime pay, any special incentive pay, shift differentials, bonuses, employee benefits (such as vacation pay, sick pay, holiday pay, insurance), and any government-mandated benefits. The pay to all types of workers should be included – full-time employees, part-time workers, and contract workers.

The labour costs associated with supervisory personnel should also be included.

Allocation of labour costs, like material costs, depends on the accounting system. Most accounting systems calculate a unit time for each product, and then allocate total labour costs based on the unit time per product. At some companies, the unit times already exist as part of the normal accounting system; at other companies, the company staff must calculate unit times as part of the anti-dumping investigation. The Commerce Department accepts such allocations, as long as the basis for the unit time calculations is reasonable.

Note that the important point is not the accuracy of the unit time calculations themselves, but the accuracy of the relative unit time calculations. If the unit time calculation for an individual product, or for an individual step in the production process, is accurate relative to the other products or other steps in the production process, the fact that the unit time calculations for all products or all steps are too high or too low does not matter. The unit time calculations are not labour costs; they are only an accounting tool through which to allocate total labour costs to individual products.

Like material costs, labour costs are different for cost of production and constructed value, but only because the products being considered are different – cost of production involves foreign market merchandise, while constructed value involves United States market merchandise. The basic methodology for determining the labour costs is the same.

Special issues

In many foreign companies, a major part of total compensation is paid in the form of annual bonuses. Since the Commerce Department is well aware of this business practice, it often closely scrutinizes the labour costs reported by foreign companies to make sure that these labour costs are included. Bonuses paid outside the period of investigation are prorated and a portion is included in the labour costs. The accounting systems at most foreign companies clearly account for these bonus payments, and so there is usually no problem in satisfying the Commerce Department. Foreign companies should be sensitive to this issue, however.

In many countries, the cost of part-time labour is significantly lower than the cost of full-time labour. Part-time workers are not entitled to many of the social benefits and company benefits that can significantly increase the total cost of labour. If a company uses part-time labour disproportionately for one product, the Commerce Department might ignore the company's internal allocation of labour costs to that product, and instead use the company-wide average.

Overhead costs

Elements and treatment of overhead

Overhead costs include a wide variety of items relating to the production process. Commerce Department cost questionnaires distinguish between items of 'variable overhead' and 'fixed overhead'. Variable overhead includes miscellaneous indirect materials, utility expenses, and other expenses that change depending on the number of units of the merchandise produced. Fixed overhead includes factory rent, depreciation, property taxes, and other expenses that do not change depending on the number of units produced.

Overhead is treated the same way as material costs and labour costs for purposes of cost of production and constructed value – the merchandise for which the cost is calculated is different, but the basic methodology is the same.

The major issue concerning overhead expenses is frequently the proper allocation of these expenses. Overhead expenses are usually incurred on a broad basis (for example, an entire factory) that may include more than the particular products that are under investigation. It is therefore necessary to devise some method of allocating the overhead costs to the particular products under investigation. Usually companies have some internal system of allocating overhead expenses to different product lines. Companies have used, and the Commerce Department has accepted, allocations based on the number of hours worked, the production quantity of the merchandise, number of machine hours, the floor area of the factory, and others. As long as the Commerce Department decides that this internal allocation is reasonable – it bears some rational relationship to the nature of the expense incurred – the Commerce Department accepts the company's normal allocation.

Special issues

For many companies, depreciation may be the single largest category of overhead expense. In such cases, the Commerce Department closely examines the depreciation expenses, to make sure both that they have been allocated correctly and that all appropriate depreciation expenses have been included.

Sometimes the Commerce Department does not agree with the accounting treatment for depreciation followed by the foreign company. For example, the Commerce Department insists that capital equipment be depreciated over the useful life of the asset. If the Commerce Department believes that the depreciation rate set forth in the foreign tax law does not accurately reflect the useful life of the asset, the Commerce Department might reject that allocation of depreciation.

Another example involves idle equipment. Foreign companies are sometimes able to 'stop' the depreciation on equipment that is idle and not in use. The Commerce Department has rejected this accounting practice, and added the depreciation on idle equipment back to the overhead expenses. The Commerce Department has argued that the idle capital assets are still a 'cost' to the company, and that the cost of production should therefore reflect that cost.

Research and development

Another important category of expense involves research and development (R&D) expenses. The treatment of R&D expenses in the company's accounting records is critical. If the records are detailed enough, the Commerce Department may request the company to undertake a product-specific allocation of R&D expenses.

Sometimes the company may want to undertake such an allocation, particularly to exclude R&D expenses for products that are not under investigation. If the company's normal accounting system does not classify R&D expenses by product, the Commerce Department is reluctant to allow the company to create such a classification to exclude expenses. The Commerce Department is far more likely to consider all of the R&D expenses to be general R&D and include them in general and administrative expenses.

R&D expenses sometimes raise problems concerning amortization. If the R&D expenses are relatively low, the Commerce Department generally accepts the expenses as recorded on the company's books and does not investigate further. For high technology products with large R&D costs, however, the Commerce Department is more careful. The Commerce Department generally allocates R&D expenses prior to 'commercialization' (when the company begins to sell the product) over the expected life of the product. Since many high tech products have short lifespans – new products are constantly rendering old products outdated – the R&D expenses allocated to each year can be quite high. R&D expenses incurred after commercialization are treated as overhead expenses, and the company may expense those R&D costs in the year they are incurred.

Because of the significant effect on the overall cost of production in some cases, R&D expenses are often a major topic of dispute in anti-dumping cases. Foreign companies should therefore study these issues carefully and develop a conscious strategy for the treatment of R&D expenses.

General, selling and administrative expenses

Elements of GSA

General, selling and administrative (GSA) expenses include a variety of miscellaneous expenses that do not relate directly to the production process. Examples include office space rent, salaries for senior executives, taxes, interest expenses, selling expenses, and general R&D expenses. This category of cost is sometimes referred to as 'SGA', or simply 'G&A' (general and administrative) expenses.

GSA expenses normally are not recorded in the company's accounting records based on particular products, so they must be allocated to the products under investigation. The normal practice is to collect all GSA expenses for a period of time, usually a fiscal year but sometimes the period of investigation, and then allocate them over total cost of goods sold (COGS) from the financial statement. The resulting ratio can then be applied to individual products.

There are three points to note about this methodology. First, the Commerce Department calculates GSA expenses on a company-wide basis. There must be some allocation from each member of the corporate family involved in any way with the products under investigation.

Second, the GSA expenses are allocated over cost of goods sold, not cost of goods produced (COGP). This methodology can either help or hurt, depending on whether COGS is higher or lower than COGP. If COGS is higher than COGP, using COGS as the denominator results in a smaller ratio, and the GSA cost is therefore lower. The rationale for using COGS is that since many of the GSA expenses relate to the selling process, the expenses should be allocated over the total cost of the goods that are sold during the relevant period.

Third, selling expenses are usually treated differently from other GSA expenses. In theory, the selling expenses could be treated the same – collected for some period of time, allocated over COGS, and then allocated to particular products. In practice, however, the Commerce Department already has information on selling expenses (such as credit costs, and warranty costs) on a unit-by-unit basis. This information is normally submitted as part of the price response to support difference in circumstance-of-sale adjustments. The Commerce Department therefore usually takes these per-unit adjustments and adds them to the cost calculations for the particular product.

Special issues

Treatment of interest expenses

Interest expenses are frequently a major source of contention in anti-dumping investigations. Different methods of calculating interest expenses have enormous consequences for the calculation of the final cost of production, and the dumping margins. Since the Commerce Department frequently departs from the company's financial statements when calculating interest expenses, foreign companies are often surprised at the results.

The starting point in the Commerce Department's analysis is the concept that money is 'fungible'. In other words, the Commerce Department does not care where the money is located in the corporate family, or how the money is currently being used. If there is borrowed money somewhere in the corporate family, the Commerce Department assumes that the money could be used to finance production of the merchandise under investigation. Therefore the cost of that borrowed money should be imputed to the cost of production. Although many have argued with this conceptual starting point, the Commerce Department's policy seems well settled.

The Commerce Department uses the company's consolidated income statement to calculate financial costs. Total interest cost from the income statement is allocated over total COGS, and the resulting ratio is applied to the cost of manufacturing for each particular product. When the related companies are not normally consolidated with the company under investigation, the Commerce Department asks the company under investigation to prepare a consolidated income statement for the group of related companies.

It is sometimes possible to lower the total interest cost used by the Commerce Department. The Commerce Department normally allows an offset for short-term interest income. If the foreign company can show that a certain portion of the interest income derives from short-term sources (less than one year), rather than long-term investments, the Commerce Department treats the interest as income from the operations of the company. This interest income can offset the interest expenses. The company must decide whether the potential offset to interest expenses is worth the effort necessary to document the short-term nature of the interest income.

The Commerce Department also sometimes allows an offset for long-term interest expenses that can be linked to other projects unrelated to the products under investigation. For example, interest from long-term loans used to purchase factory equipment to produce other products can sometimes be excluded. When there is any doubt, however, the Commerce Department assumes that all financing is for the products under investigation. More recently, the more common practice is to broadly include all interest expenses.

Non-operating expenses

Non-operating expenses and non-operating income are often major items on the income statements of foreign companies. It is crucial to prepare information on these two items carefully. When presented with incomplete or unclear information, the Commerce Department assumes that all the non-operating expenses are associated with the products under investigation, and that none of the non-operating income is associated with the products under investigation. The net effect is to increase significantly the total cost.

The Commerce Department examines these items carefully to make sure that no expenses that should be included as a cost of production have been hidden in the non-operating expenses. For example, the Commerce Department considers exchange gains and losses from the sales of products under investigation to be part of the cost of production. Yet this item is usually included as a non-operating expense by the foreign company.

To minimize the risk of the Commerce Department exaggerating the non-operating expenses, a foreign company should prepare a breakdown of all the non-operating expenses, and develop arguments why various items should be excluded from the cost of production. The company should also study the non-operating income, and prepare arguments for including as much non-operating income as possible. The arguments for both areas should be coordinated. Sometimes the company will find that by agreeing to include a particular non-operating expense, the company can also persuade the Commerce Department to include an even larger non-operating income item that relates to the same expense. The net effect is thus to lower the cost.

Packing

Packing costs are usually not controversial. The Commerce Department includes the costs of packing materials and labour devoted to the packing. Sometimes the Commerce Department includes an amount for overhead, but the amount is typically so small that the Commerce Department often disregards overhead. For cost of production, the Commerce Department uses the cost of packing for the foreign market. For constructed value, the Commerce Department uses the cost of packing for the United States market. In either case, the foreign company usually takes the packing cost data presented in the price response and simply uses that same data for the cost response. The Commerce Department almost always accepts this use of data from the price response, although it insists that the information actually be submitted a second time as part of the cost response.

Defending a cost investigation

This section offers specific advice to a foreign company involved in a cost investigation. It first explains how to defend against a cost allegation – both how to reduce the risk of a cost allegation and how to respond if one is made. It then sets out a strategy for preparing a cost response. By reviewing the various parts of the cost questionnaire, this section clarifies what information must be submitted and what issues the company should consider. This section also discusses the various steps of preparing a cost response.

Defending against cost allegations

There are two basic ways in which a foreign company can defend against cost allegations. First, the company should ensure that its questionnaire responses do not include any unnecessary information that might help the United States domestic industry to file an allegation of sales below cost. Second, if the domestic industry manages to prepare an allegation anyway, there are several ways that the foreign company can try to rebut the allegations.

Minimize the risk of a cost allegation

Foreign companies can reduce the risk of a cost investigation by preparing their responses carefully. A foreign company should always keep in mind that the petitioner's lawyers will be searching carefully for any information that can be used to document an allegation of sales below cost. Whenever possible, the company should avoid providing any information that will help in that effort.

It is very difficult to prevent a determined petitioner from developing the cost information necessary to make an allegation of sales below cost. In some cases, petitioners have even hired special consultants, at great expense, to develop independently the costs of producing certain merchandise in a particular country. Nevertheless, foreign companies should prepare their responses to the Commerce Department in a way that does not help the petitioner in its efforts.

Difference-in-merchandise adjustments are particularly difficult, and should be avoided if possible. As a practical matter, however, it has become very difficult to prevent the cost allegation from being made. The current Commerce

Department expectations for detailed information to support a difference-in-merchandise adjustment almost always provide petitioners with enough information to make the below cost allegation.

Challenges to the cost allegation

Once a cost allegation has been filed, the foreign company and its lawyers usually have some time to respond. Sometimes the Commerce Department acts on the allegation almost immediately, without waiting for any comments from the various parties. In most cases, however, the Commerce Department allows comments. There are several possible bases for attacking the cost allegation.

First, if the petitioner files the allegation late, this fact should be pointed out to the Commerce Department. The petitioner may attempt to file a late allegation and to rationalize the lateness. Where possible, the foreign company should rebut any excuses offered by the petitioner.

Second, when preparing a cost allegation, the petitioner must provide the Commerce Department with 'reasonable grounds' for believing that sales in the home market or in third countries are at prices below the cost of producing the merchandise. It is not enough to show that a few isolated sales (i.e. 20%) are below cost. Although there is a legal dispute over whether the petitioner must show that 'substantial' sales are below cost as a threshold matter, current practice requires a showing that many sales are below cost as part of its determination of whether there are 'reasonable grounds'.

Moreover, the evidence offered to support the allegation must be reasonably specific. The Commerce Department has rejected allegations based on general newspaper articles about rising costs, or based on general information from a financial statement that is not specific to particular products. The allegation must be based on actual home market prices of the exporters under investigation. The Commerce Department has, however, accepted allegations based on the cost information of a single company and applied that evidence to other companies also involved in the investigation. It has also accepted allegations based entirely on the cost information of the domestic industry, modified to reflect the foreign industry's costs.

Foreign companies should make the strongest arguments possible against the Commerce Department initiating a cost investigation. They should argue about both the basis for the cost information and the number of sales that appear to be below cost. If the allegation is based on the petitioner's costs, it may be possible to persuade the Commerce Department to verify (or at least briefly investigate) the petitioner's costs, especially if there is some doubt about their reliability.

It is important to remember, however, that the Commerce Department's standard for initiation is not very high. Although the standard for initiating a cost investigation is higher than the standard for initiating an anti-dumping case in general, the evidence of sales below cost does not need to be compelling or convincing, only 'reasonable'. In most cases, the Commerce Department decides to initiate cost investigations. It may ultimately find that the evidence does not support the claim that substantial sales are below cost, but it will undertake the investigation.

Preparation of the cost response

Preparation of an effective cost response is a very difficult exercise. The company accountants usually do not know anything about the requirements of the anti-dumping law. The lawyers usually do not know anything about the company's accounting systems. The two groups need to teach each other a great deal of complex information in a short period of time, making the task even more difficult.

This section first provides an overview of the cost questionnaire, to help clarify the scope of information that is necessary. It then sets forth a step-by-step strategy for effectively preparing a cost response.

Overview of the cost questionnaire and suggested strategies

The major problem confronting foreign companies when they first review the cost questionnaire is the level of detail required. To a company that has not been involved in a cost investigation before, the level of detail seems impossible. This section therefore reviews the major sections of the cost questionnaire, and offers some general suggestions concerning the level of detail that is necessary. It also contains advice on issues and tactics a foreign company should consider for each topic. The questionnaire does not offer suggestions on how to lower costs. Although companies involved in a particular investigation should follow the specific advice of their lawyers, these general comments will help a foreign company understand the general nature and magnitude of the task that they face.

General information

At the beginning of each cost questionnaire, the Commerce Department asks basic questions about the company and its manufacturing process. The Commerce Department wants to know about the corporate structure of the company, especially the structure of any subsidiary companies. The objective is to discover whether there are any company relationships that might raise problems later in the investigation. The questionnaire also asks about the manufacturing process. The objective of this section is to help ensure that all of the costs for each manufacturing stage are reported to the Commerce Department, and that all transactions with related parties are identified. The descriptions do not need to be exhaustive. A few pages on each topic should be sufficient.

The Commerce Department also asks about both the financial accounting practices and the cost accounting system of the company. For financial accounting, the Commerce Department is interested principally in any deviations from foreign GAAP; if a company follows foreign GAAP consistently, very brief explanations of financial accounting practices normally satisfy the Commerce Department. The explanation of the cost accounting system, however, needs to be more detailed. Since this topic is one of the crucial parts of the investigation, the Commerce Department wants to understand the basic system as completely as possible. The company should use as much space as necessary to explain fully the operation of the cost accounting system.

Specific cost information

The questionnaire asks for a great deal of information about the various elements of cost. When preparing this information, the company should remember two important general principles.

First, the company should always keep in mind the delicate balance between what information to provide in the response, and what information to provide at the verification. Since the 1990s, there has been a trend for the Commerce Department to demand more and more detail in the response itself. To the extent possible, however, the foreign company should try to present partial information in the response, and save the detailed explanations for the verification, or at least for delayed submission in supplemental responses.

The response must be complete – otherwise the Commerce Department may resort to 'facts available' – but sensitive topics often can and should be saved until the verification. The best balance for a particular investigation should be chosen based on the facts of that investigation.

Second, the company should remember that very few cost methodologies are firm rules that must be followed in all circumstances. There is virtually no 'law' in this area, only Commerce Department practices and policies. The major consideration is whether the lawyers can persuade the Commerce Department to accept a certain methodology. Because of this flexibility, cost investigations present many opportunities for creative arguments. The company staff and lawyers should together develop the most favourable methodologies, and arguments to persuade the Commerce Department to accept the methodologies.

Materials and labour

Although the Commerce Department needs complete information on material costs, it often does not really mean what the questionnaire says. Part of the problem is that the Commerce Department drafts the questionnaire without knowing the type of cost accounting system the company uses. The questions sometimes do not make sense, given the nature of the product and of the particular account system. The foreign company should therefore not hesitate to explain why a certain question is irrelevant or cannot be answered.

For example, the questionnaire asks for a detailed material-by-material, part-by-part breakdown of material costs. For a complex product with thousands of parts, such a request is unreasonably burdensome. In most cases, the Commerce Department allows a sample breakdown of materials and parts for one product – to illustrate the nature of the material costs – and then accepts aggregate information for the remaining products under investigation. Much depends on the nature of the product and the constraints imposed by the company's accounting system. If the product is simple and the accounting system already records a detailed breakdown, the Commerce Department may ask for details. If the product is complex and the accounting system records only aggregate information, the Commerce Department may accept less detailed information.

The same principles apply to labour costs. The Commerce Department needs to understand the breakdown of labour costs, but the response need not itemize every labour cost element for every product. If the response makes clear that all elements of labour cost have been included, and illustrates with an example, the Commerce Department should be satisfied. Of course, during the verification the Commerce Department may investigate whether in fact all of the labour costs have been included. The response, however, does not need to be as detailed as the verification materials.

Material and labour costs are usually well-defined elements in the accounting system, and therefore there are fewer opportunities to lower these costs. If the company has well-defined accounting categories for material and labour costs, and then submits in its response material and labour costs that are significantly lower, the Commerce Department becomes extremely suspicious. The company needs extremely good reasons for reporting lower costs.

Overhead costs

The questionnaire describes various categories of overhead, and draws distinctions between fixed and variable overhead. The company need not reclassify all of its overhead expenses into these various categories. The response should explain how the company's normal accounting system includes all of these elements, and then present that data in a form that traces easily back to the actual accounting records. Reclassifying expenses not only is unnecessary, but can be dangerous. If a company reclassifies its expenses and then has trouble tracing them back to the actual accounting records during the verification, the company may fail verification.

Overhead expenses usually present more opportunities to lower costs. First, the company should examine its allocation of overhead among various products. It is sometimes possible to develop alternative allocations that shift some of the overhead expenses to other products that are not under investigation. Of course, there must be some rational basis for the allocation. Sometimes the Commerce Department changes the company's normal allocation methodologies, with the result that overhead costs of the products under investigation increase. When the company itself departs from its normal methodologies, the Commerce Department becomes quite suspicious. If the company has a persuasive rationale, however, the Commerce Department may accept the change.

Second, the company should consider carefully its treatment of R&D expenses. Especially for high technology products, this cost element can be a major proportion of total costs. Recall that the Commerce Department treats product-specific R&D as an overhead expense, but treats general R&D as a general and administrative expense. The more that can be shifted to general and administrative, the better. Foreign companies often include R&D expenses for unprofitable products with the R&D expenses for more profitable products – accounting decisions can be very political and managers sometimes try to protect their favourite projects. If the company can document that R&D expenses relate to other products, the Commerce Department may allow the company to exclude them. If the expenses are normally included in the accounts for a particular product, however, the burden of proving that the expenses really relate to another product is very high.

It is sometimes possible to shift R&D expenses outside of the period under investigation. The Commerce Department often capitalizes R&D expenses and forces the company to include an allocation of R&D expenses from early periods. To the extent possible, the company should try to avoid this problem. If the Commerce Department insists on capitalizing the expenses, the company should develop a rationale for using the longest possible amortization period, to minimize the costs that are allocated to the period under investigation.

General, selling and administrative expenses

The questionnaire is not very helpful in explaining what it means by 'general and administrative' expenses. This area is one of the most contentious parts of the cost response, and the Commerce Department wants to leave itself the maximum flexibility. The questionnaire therefore asks for everything, and the Commerce Department sorts out the various details later.

In addition to total general, selling and administrative expenses, the Commerce Department expects a breakout of two particular subcategories: selling expenses, and financing expenses. Selling expenses are relatively easy, since they are usually just taken from the price response. If the foreign market value is based on prices in the home market, the selling expenses should be for sales in the home market. If the foreign market value is based on third country prices, the selling expenses in that third country should be used.

Financing expenses are often more difficult. Under current Commerce Department policy, companies must prepare data on the interest expenses and interest income for the entire group of related companies. For complex corporate families, this is not an easy task.

Foreign companies can explore several options for lowering their overall GSA costs. First, the company should explore whether changing the allocation of GSA expenses lowers the per-unit expense. GSA expenses are normally allocated over cost of goods sold (COGS). The company must choose, however, whether to report total GSA expenses over total COGS, or to subdivide the expenses into various product groups and allocate the expense for each group over the COGS for that product group. The company's accounting system may present some limitations, but within those limitations the company should consider the most favourable approach. The Commerce Department might change the allocation later to something less favourable, but sometimes it will accept the company's allocation.

Second, the company should study its non-operating income and expenses carefully. As explained earlier, the Commerce Department includes non-operating income that can be linked to the products under investigation, and excludes non-operating expenses that can be linked to products not under investigation. Developing such documentary evidence is very time consuming, and the burden of proof on the company is quite high. Nevertheless, if the possibility for significant cost savings exists, the company should explore this possibility.

Third, the company should watch for surprise Commerce Department alterations of cost items, especially GSA expenses. The Commerce Department sometimes ignores foreign GAAP and significantly alters certain expenses. A foreign company should be sensitive to such issues as it prepares its response. An important part of lowering overall costs is to avoid having the Commerce Department raise them.

Initial meetings with the defence team

After the company has received the cost questionnaire, and reviewed the requests being made by the Commerce Department, it is time to schedule an initial meeting for the defence team. At least some of the people who were involved in preparing the price response should also be part of the team that prepares the cost response. The key addition to the team will be the company's cost accountants.

General guidelines from the lawyers

To facilitate the initial meetings, the lawyers should prepare a general memorandum on two topics. First, the memorandum should review for the company the basic principles of a cost investigation, applying those principles to the particular circumstances of the particular investigation. In the course of preparing the price response, the lawyers should have learned a great deal about the company, its accounting system, and its products. This knowledge should be used to help focus the way the general principles will apply to the particular company.

Second, the memorandum should comment on the cost questionnaire. Based on the conduct of the investigation to date, the Commerce Department staff members who have been assigned to work on the cost investigation, and the lawyers' experience, the lawyers should advise the company, in general terms, what information should be prepared. As part of this process, the lawyers can contact the Commerce Department for clarification about what the Commerce Department staff really want to know. Sometimes the Commerce Department staff members will cooperate, and focus their requests more precisely to limit the burden on the company.

Preparation of background information by the company accountants

Based on this initial memo and the cost questionnaire, the company's cost accountants should begin preparing background information for the initial meetings. It is a mistake to wait until the lawyers arrive to begin preparing information. If the lawyers spend the first few days, or even weeks, just helping the company to collect the basic information, the defence team will not have time to focus on analysing the information and developing creative arguments to make on behalf of the company.

Some examples of the type of background information needed are:

❑ *Explanations of the accounting system.* Foreign companies often have a detailed explanation of their cost accounting system that was prepared for some other purpose, such as an internal audit. If these materials are translated and sent to the lawyers prior to the meetings, the lawyers can more quickly understand the system and begin to ask more detailed questions. Waiting until the lawyers arrive to begin such translations significantly delays the process.

❑ *Internal cost analysis.* Companies often have a great deal of internal analysis of their costs of production. Although much of this information is not in a format that the Commerce Department will accept, it can be very useful to the lawyers trying to make decisions about how best to present the cost information. The cost accountants should review their files to remind themselves of any studies that have already been done. Otherwise the accountants may spend hours collecting certain information, only to learn later that the information already existed in someone else's files.

❑ *Samples of the documents.* In addition to the basic overview of the system, the lawyers will have to immerse themselves in the details of the system. There is no substitute for carefully reviewing the actual documents. If the company maintains a summary sheet of the component costs for each product, an example should be prepared. The underlying supporting documents for a few sample entries on the summary sheet should also be prepared. At this stage, the purpose is to illustrate the system.

Preparation of the draft cost response and cost calculations

Once the background information has been prepared, it is time to have a meeting between the lawyers and the accountants. Sometimes there is only time for one long meeting, at which the basic information is reviewed and the cost response prepared. Other times it is possible to have an initial meeting to clarify everyone's understanding of the legal requirements, the cost accounting system, and the information that must be prepared, and then later have another meeting to prepare the cost response.

At this meeting, it is important that the appropriate accounting personnel be present to answer questions. It is usually necessary to have manager or general manager level accounting staff attend these meetings. They are usually the only ones who have a broad enough overview and understanding of the cost accounting system to answer the variety of questions that may arise during the discussions. More junior staff responsible for specific topics can be called into the meetings as necessary. It is sometimes difficult to have senior managers trapped in long meetings with the lawyers, since these same managers have many other responsibilities. Unfortunately, there is usually little alternative.

The response is usually drafted simultaneously by the lawyers and the accountants. The lawyers prepare the first draft of the text – the narrative that answers the various questions and explains how the response has been prepared. At the same time, the accountants prepare the first draft of the exhibits – the tables and charts summarizing the cost information to be submitted to the Commerce Department. The lawyers work with the accountants to develop a format that will satisfy the Commerce Department, but that also minimizes the burden on the accountants to reformat information which already exists in the company's accounting records. The drafting is an interactive process, with the lawyers and accountants consulting each other as they proceed.

Revisions to the cost calculations

As the response is being drafted, the cost calculations are normally revised several times. This process is very frustrating for the accountants, who bear the burden of revising them. Unfortunately, there is no way to avoid revisions without hurting the company's defence. There is no single 'correct' way to calculate costs. The principles discussed earlier are simply the framework within which the Commerce Department proceeds. Depending on the particular circumstances at a company, there may be alternative ways to calculate costs.

The only way to find the most favourable method is to experiment with different alternatives. The company should undertake a preliminary analysis of the initial cost response; in other words, perform a rough calculation to determine whether a particular approach is helpful or not. If the rough calculation suggests one methodology produces higher costs than some other methodology, abandon the methodology that produces the higher costs. Many accountants find it difficult to perform such rough calculations. Their training is to stress accuracy and completeness. Unfortunately, the time pressures of an anti-dumping investigation do not always allow the luxury of detailed and careful calculations. The accountants must therefore do their best to work with the lawyers in performing rough preliminary calculations to assess alternative methodologies.

Finalizing the cost response

Finalizing the response involves several steps. First, the lawyers and accountants should carefully review the response for substantive accuracy. Have all of the questions been answered? Are all of the explanations complete, and understandable? Have all of the important issues been considered?

The second step is for the lawyers to coordinate with the lawyers for other companies under investigation. This coordination takes place throughout the process, but it is especially important when finalizing the response. To the extent possible, the different foreign companies involved in an anti-dumping case should take consistent positions. If one company claims that certain information is not available, but another company provides it, the Commerce Department becomes quite suspicious. Sometimes companies are forced to take opposing positions, in which case coordination is not possible. Companies should at least avoid unnecessary and unintentional conflicting positions.

Third, the company staff should carefully recheck the accuracy of the response. Arithmetic and transcription errors are embarrassing. Too many errors may lead the Commerce Department to reject the response and use 'facts available' instead. The sooner such mistakes are found and corrected, the better. The best time to correct them is before the response is submitted to the Commerce Department.

Finally, once the company has finished with its work, the lawyers must return to Washington DC and prepare confidential and non-confidential versions of the response. Preparing these different versions takes several days, depending on the complexity of the response and the number of documents that require non-confidential summaries.

Considerations after filing the cost response

Although preparing the cost response is the most important stage in defending a cost investigation, there are other considerations that a foreign company should keep in mind after filing the cost response. First, the company should anticipate and plan for a longer and more complex verification.

Verifications are always difficult, but the need to verify both a price response and a cost response is especially challenging. Chapter 10 discusses the work involved at a verification. The company should begin its preparations much earlier to allow for the extra work.

Second, the company and its lawyers must be alert to the need for coordination between the price response and the cost response. The foreign company usually has no trouble coordinating the preparation of the responses – since the same company and same lawyers are doing the work – but the Commerce Department often has trouble coordinating its understanding of the responses. The Commerce Department staff working on the price response and the staff working on the cost response often do not communicate. The person handling the cost response often does not even read the price response. At a minimum, the company should answer any questions the Commerce Department staff might have about the different parts of the overall response.

Moreover, the company should anticipate any problem areas where a misunderstanding about the price response could lead to mistaken cost calculations, and explain them to the Commerce Department staff. The most common problem is for the staff person handling the price response to subtract certain expense items that the staff person handling the cost response includes in the cost calculations. Such a mistake greatly increases the risk that the Commerce Department will find the sales prices to be below cost. Alerting the Commerce Department staff to areas where this problem might occur can reduce the risk.

Special rules for non-market economies

One of the more complicated areas of the anti-dumping law is the calculation of dumping margins in cases involving non-market economy countries (NMEs). NME refers to any foreign country that the Commerce Department determines does not operate on market principles of cost or pricing structures, and where, therefore, sales of merchandise do not reflect the fair value of the merchandise. To deal with this problem, the Commerce Department uses a special set of rules to build up market-based costs as a surrogate for normal value.

Determining whether a country is an NME

When determining if a country is an NME, the Commerce Department considers six factors:

❑ The extent to which the currency is convertible into currencies of other countries;

❑ The extent to which wage rates are determined by free bargaining between labour and management;

❑ The extent to which joint ventures or other investments by firms from other countries are permitted;

❑ The extent of government control over of the means of production;

❑ The extent of government control over the allocation of resources, prices, and output decisions; and

❑ Other features the Department may deem appropriate.

Status as an NME continues until the Department specifically revokes it. Thus, all new anti-dumping investigations and administrative reviews involving products from NME countries are automatically classified as NME cases, unless the issue of revocation is specifically raised by an interested party. Although issues related to NME status or its revocation are typically raised within the context of an anti-dumping investigation or administrative review proceeding, the Department may assign NME status or revoke it at any time.

Currently, NME status covers the geographic area of the former USSR, each part of which still retains the NME status the Department determined for the former USSR, and China. The presence of government controls on various aspects of these economies makes the Department's standard market economy methodologies inadequate for the purpose of dumping margin calculations.

Special rules for normal value

The Commerce Department has developed a set of specialized methodologies that address the unique issues in NME cases. There is generally little difference between the Department's calculation of United States price in market economy and NME cases. A few minor modifications, which are discussed below, are made in NME cases, but the basic analysis and methodologies discussed in this chapter remain the same.

Thus, the bulk of the special NME methodologies focus on the calculation of normal value. In market economy cases, the Department receives detailed foreign market pricing and production cost data from responding foreign market companies. Because these companies are subject to market forces, the Department considers the pricing and cost information they provide to be generally reliable and indicative of fair market value. In contrast, the Commerce Department believes that the government controls in NMEs distort the available foreign market pricing and production cost data. As a result, in NME cases the Department does not use a price-to-price or constructed value calculation to derive normal value, but rather 'builds' normal value using an entirely different 'factors of production' methodology. This is one of the more complex aspects of the anti-dumping law and involves several separate analytical steps.

Surrogate country selection

The anti-dumping law requires the Commerce Department to calculate normal value for NMEs by using market economy prices to value the NME factors of production used to produce the subject merchandise. 'Factors of production' refers to the raw materials, labour, energy, utilities, capital costs, packing materials and labour, and any other inputs used when producing a product. The Commerce Department sends questionnaires to the companies that produce the subject merchandise in the NME country requesting detailed information on the all inputs used and the quantity of each input used in the production of the merchandise.

For example, every material input, all labour, and all utilities used in the production of the subject merchandise must be described and reported in terms of number of physical units (e.g. tons, kilograms, litres), hours, or quantity (BTU, kilowatt hours) used to produce one unit of the subject merchandise.

Once the Department has identified all the factors of production, it next sets out to value those factors using cost and pricing information from a market economy country. The market economy country selected is referred to as the 'surrogate' country. The surrogate must be, to the extent possible, at a stage of economic development comparable to the NME country and a significant producer of comparable merchandise. In practice, the Department determines economic comparability primarily on the basis of per capita GDP. It does have the flexibility, however, to consider other economic indicators where applicable.

The anti-dumping law and the Department's regulations do not detail any other aspect of the surrogate selection so the selection may be somewhat subjective. The factors reviewed, the weight placed on each of the selection criteria (economic comparability and significant production of comparable merchandise), and the final selection vary on a case-by-case basis. This subjectivity, combined with the fact that the choice of a surrogate has a significant impact on the final margin calculation, explains why surrogate country selection is one of the most hotly debated aspects of NME cases. It is important to note that the Commerce Department regularly decides upon a list of surrogates for each case. It identifies not just one potential surrogate choice, but another three or four that could also reasonably serve as a surrogate. As described below, this is necessary to ensure the valuation of all reported factors of production.

Valuing the factors of production

Upon receipt of the NME questionnaire responses, the Department has detailed information concerning the type and quantity of all inputs used in the production of the subject merchandise. The next step is to determine the cost of the input in the production of one unit of subject merchandise. As mentioned above, the questionnaire requires the input quantities to be reported in terms of the quantity used to produce one unit of the subject merchandise. The Department determines the cost or value of each unit of input quantity based on surrogate country data, and simply multiplies the input quantity reported by this value to derive an overall cost of the input.

When valuing factors of production, the Department relies almost exclusively on publicly available data sources. These sources include government publications, industry publications, newspapers, magazines, international agency publications (e.g. the International Labour Organization's Yearbook of Labour Statistics, and statistics and data published by the International Energy Agency, the International Monetary Fund, the World Bank, the Asian Development Bank, the United Nations and the WTO), and various United States and foreign agency studies, reports, and publications. The Department has developed a very detailed index of all sources used in previous NME investigations and administrative reviews. Available at the Commerce Department website (*www.ita.doc.gov*), this index details all factors previously valued in all past cases, the surrogate countries used, the source of the value, and the time period of the value. When valuing factors in a new case, the Department refers to this index as a guide for determining the source of the values to be applied in the current case.

As a general rule, the Commerce Department values all factors using publicly available information regarding prices in a *single* surrogate country. There are some practical exceptions to this rule. The Department may not be able to obtain value information for a factor from the single surrogate chosen. In such cases it examines whether value information for that factor is available in any of the other surrogate countries on the list. In certain cases, the Department has gone back and subsequently added additional surrogates to the list based on the availability of public information in that country. If value information is still not available, the Department often uses the value for an input similar, but not identical, to the factor under consideration. For example, the value for one type of fuel oil may be used to determine the surrogate costs for another type of fuel oil. In addition, if an NME producer of the subject merchandise purchases the input from a market economy producer of the input and the input is paid for in the market economy currency, the Department will value the input using the actual price paid by the NME producer.

The Department's other primary concern when valuing factors of production is contemporaneity. The values used must reflect values applicable to the period under investigation or review. If the Department has available a value for a factor, but that value is outdated, it will adjust the value using wholesale price indices from publicly available sources. (Typically, the Department adjusts for inflation using the price indices published in the International Monetary Fund's International Financial Statistics). To the extent possible, the Department also attempts to value factors using tax and duty exclusive factor prices. In addition, the Department prefers factor values that are broadly available in the surrogate economy. For example, if the Department has information on what a particular producer paid for an input and information on what producers economy-wide paid for the input, it would value the input using the broader, economy-wide data.

The Department also adjusts values, where appropriate, so they reflect delivered prices. Commerce adds a surrogate freight cost to the values. Such freight costs are derived by (1) computing the distance from the supplier of the input to the subject merchandise factory, (2) identifying a surrogate freight rate, and (3) appropriately applying the rate and distance to derive a per-unit freight value for the input under consideration.

If the Department is unable to value a factor using publicly available information for the identical or comparable input in the selected surrogate country or any of the other surrogates on its list, it will use data from other sources such as the United States Foreign Commercial Service office in the United States embassy in the surrogate country. If it is still unable to value the factor, the Department will apply facts available. The most common source for facts available is information provided by the domestic industry in its petition.

Typically, all material, energy, packing and utilities are valued in the manner described above. The Commerce Department applies a different valuation methodology for labour. In the past, the Department identified labour wage rates from publicly available sources in the chosen surrogate country and applied those rates accordingly. However, the Department reexamined this practice after analysis revealed a great variation in wage rates in market economy countries that were economically comparable. Thus, the results of an NME normal value calculation could be dramatically different depending on which economically comparable market economy was chosen as a surrogate. Because of the variability of wage rates in countries with similar GDPs, the Department developed a methodology that values labour in all NME cases using a regression-based wage rate – essentially an average of the wage rates in market economies viewed as being economically comparable to a particular NME. This regression analysis reflects the observed relationship between wages and national income in market economies, is updated yearly, and is publicly available.

Upon valuing all inputs and calculating the cost of each input in the production of one unit of subject merchandise, the Department sums all costs to derive a total cost of manufacturing one unit of the subject merchandise. To this total cost it adds an amount for factory overhead, depreciation, GSA, and profit – step three of the 'factors of production' methodology.

Overhead, GSA and profit

Once the Department has 'built' a cost of manufacturing for one unit of subject merchandise, it adds to that cost an amount for factory overhead, depreciation, general, selling and administrative expenses (GSA), and profit. Again, the Department's general rule when determining these values is to use publicly available information. In the past, the Department obtained such information from government publications or industry publications in the surrogate country. However, it was generally very difficult to obtain public surrogate information for these cost elements. More recently, where available, the Department has begun using the published financial statements of producers of the subject merchandise or comparable merchandise in the surrogate country.

The Department's regulations also specifically refer to the use of non-proprietary information gathered from producers of the subject merchandise or comparable merchandise in the surrogate country. This rule allows the Department to use its own records as a source. For example, if the Department has previously conducted an investigation or review of the same subject merchandise for the surrogate country, as long as the data provided in that proceeding were non-proprietary, it will use those data (e.g. published financial statements) as a source for this information. In fact, the Department's value index lists several previous investigations of products from Brazil, India and Thailand as value sources

Normally, when valuing these cost elements, the Department expresses the value as a percentage of the cost of goods sold. For example, for factory overhead, it simply divides the total factory overhead from the surrogate financial statement by the cost of goods sold to derive a surrogate percentage factor. The Department multiplies the factor by the cost of manufacturing described above to derive the per-unit factory overhead to be added to the cost of manufacturing for the subject merchandise. The same methodology is applied to derive the per-unit GSA and profit added to the calculation as well. The end result is a per-unit value very similar to the Department's market economy constructed value. In essence, the Department 'builds' a price to which it will compare United States prices to calculate a dumping margin. The built price in NME calculations is a gross price in that it includes all costs, all selling expenses, and profit. The Department makes deductions from this price using the same methodology it uses in market economy cases. However, NME cases often pose some difficulties that require minor modifications to its standard margin calculation methodology.

Calculation of United States price

As explained under 'Price adjustments' in chapter 3, the Commerce Department makes a series of deductions from and adjustments to the final price to the first unrelated United States customer to derive an ex-factory constructed export price (CEP) or export price (EP). Likewise, it makes a series of deductions from and adjustments to the comparison market gross price to derive an ex-factory normal value. In market economy cases, the adjustments made to United States price are based on expense data reported by the foreign exporters or producers in response to the Department's questionnaires. In NME cases, the Department does not consider the expenses incurred by the NME exporter or producer for United States export sales to reflect fair market value. Thus, it revalues these expenses using a methodology similar to the normal value 'factors of production'.

For example, NME exporters incur the same types of movement expenses as market economy exporters when exporting to the United States (e.g. inland freight expenses from the plant to the warehouse and/or port, domestic brokerage and handling charges, inland insurance, ocean freight, and marine insurance). If the service is provided by a market economy supplier and paid for in the currency of the market economy, the Department will use the expense as incurred by the NME exporter in its calculations of United States price. This is typically the case for ocean freight and marine insurance costs, which are both commonly provided by market economy suppliers. However, market economy expenses are often not used for other movement expenses such as domestic inland freight. For these expenses the Department obtains detailed information from the NME exporters regarding the locations of the plant, ports or any warehouses, and distances from the factory to the port or warehouse. The Department identifies the appropriate surrogate freight rates using publicly available information and calculates the final per-unit expense amount that will be deducted from the United States price in its margin calculations.

The difficulty of obtaining detailed GSA data for NME normal value calculations also requires the Department to make some additional modifications when calculating United States price and dumping margins. In market economy dumping calculations for United States CEP sales, the Department deducts direct selling expenses incurred for United States sales to derive an ex-factory United States price. To ensure an apples-to-apples comparison, the Department deducts direct selling expenses incurred for surrogate market sales from foreign market price. When adding GSA to calculate normal value in NME cases, however, the source of the surrogate information often does not distinguish between direct and indirect selling expenses. The Department is, therefore, unable to separately quantify direct selling expenses that should be deducted from normal value. Thus, it does not deduct direct expenses when calculating the NME normal value. Similarly, if the United States sales in the NME case are CEP sales, the Department does not deduct direct selling expenses incurred for United States sales from the United States price. Likewise, in a market economy dumping calculation where the United States price is EP, the Department adds United States direct selling expenses to normal value and deducts direct selling expenses incurred for sales in the comparison market from normal value. If the Department is unable to identify direct selling expenses separately using the surrogate data, it cannot deduct them from the NME normal value. If the United States sales in the NME case are EP sales, to ensure a valid comparison, the Department will not add United States direct selling expenses to the normal value side of the equation.

Other methodologies – separate rates

In market economy cases, individual dumping margins are calculated and assigned to each exporter of the subject merchandise. In NME cases, separate dumping margins are not automatically calculated and assigned to each exporter in the NME country. Rather, the Department uses the presumption that all exporters or producers comprise a single exporter under common government control – the NME entity. The Department assigns a single rate to the NME entity unless an exporter can demonstrate that it is sufficiently independent to be entitled to a separate rate. The Department determines whether an NME exporter should receive its own individual dumping margin by means of its 'separate rates' analysis.

The analysis requires the exporter to demonstrate that its export activities, on both a *de jure* and *de facto* basis, are not subject to government control. Typically, the Department considers the following *de jure* criteria in determining whether a separate rate is warranted: (1) an absence of restrictive stipulations associated with the exporter's business and export licenses; (2) any legislative enactments decentralizing control of companies; and (3) any other formal measures by the government decentralizing control of companies. A determination of the absence of *de facto* control is based on: (1) whether export prices are set by or subject to government approval; (2) whether the exporter has the authority to negotiate and sign contracts, and can make its own management selection decisions; (3) whether the exporter retains the proceeds of its exports sales; and (4) whether the exporter makes its own decisions regarding the use of the profits or the financing of losses. If the Department determines both a *de jure* and *de facto* absence of government control, it will calculate and assign a separate rate to the exporter. If the Department finds either *de jure* or *de facto* government control, the exporter will not receive a separate rate and will be subject to the countrywide dumping margin.

If an NME exporter is owned by a parent located outside the NME, the Department forgoes the separate rates analysis based on the assumption that the exporter is not subject to the jurisdiction of the NME government. In such instances the Department automatically calculates and assigns a separate rate to the exporter.

Other methodologies – 'market oriented industry'

The anti-dumping law allows the Department, in certain instances, to apply its market economy methodologies to calculate normal value in NME cases. To determine when this exception can be applied, the Department has derived a special test referred to as the 'market-oriented industry' or MOI test. The test is applied on an industry-wide basis. The criteria for determining whether an industry is an MOI are: (1) virtually no government involvement in setting prices or the amounts to be produced; (2) the industry producing the subject merchandise should be characterized by private or collective ownership; and (3) market determined prices must be paid for all significant inputs, whether material or non-material, and for all but an insignificant portion of all inputs accounting for the total value of the subject merchandise. In addition, the Department requires the NME exporter to provide information on virtually the entire industry. All evidence submitted to the Department must cover producers that collectively constitute the industry in question. This industry-wide data requirement and the strict requirements for an affirmative MOI determination are often too difficult for an NME exporter to meet. As a result, it is not unusual for NME exporters to request the analysis and it is not unusual for the Department to conduct an MOI analysis, but it is rare for the Department to actually make an affirmative MOI determination.

Chapter 5

Anti-dumping duties: calculating dumping margins

The *methodologies* employed by the Commerce Department to calculate anti-dumping margins in an original investigation have changed dramatically over time, and particularly since the 1979 Anti-dumping Code. Many of these changes are the result of changes in the underlying statute that came into effect on 1 January 1995, with passage of the Uruguay Round Agreements Act. Other changes stem from the Department's publication for the first time in May 1997 of *substantive* anti-dumping regulations.

When preparing a price response or a cost response, a foreign company should evaluate the effect of alternative methodologies on the dumping margins. In many areas, the foreign company can choose to present information in different ways. Where there is discretion, the company should seek to minimize its dumping margins. To test the various alternatives, however, the company must understand how the Commerce Department arrives at dumping margins. This chapter explains in detail how the Commerce Department calculates dumping margins.

This chapter provides charts demonstrating, conceptually, the Department's calculation of anti-dumping margins for original investigations and administrative reviews. Before these calculation worksheets are addressed, some threshold decisions that the Commerce Department makes before it actually does the calculation are reviewed.

Interaction of model-match and cost

As discussed in previous chapters, when calculating anti-dumping margins the Commerce Department seeks to compare prices of identical (or similar) products, but wants to use only those prices in the foreign market that are above cost. The question then becomes which of these two objectives is more important.

The answer to this question has changed within the past few years. Until the mid-1990s, the Commerce Department had a practice of employing its model-matching methodology (see 'Establishing the model-match methodology' in chapter 3) *before* applying the 'cost test' (see 'When cost information is necessary' in chapter 4) to determine whether home market sales were made at prices below the cost of production. That is, the Commerce Department would first determine which home market model was the best choice to match to the United States model (i.e. identical or most similar), and then analyse whether the home market prices of that model were above cost.

Under the Department's prior practice, if the home market prices of the selected home market match were below cost, then the Commerce Department would not engage in a price-to-price comparison, but rather would compare United States price to constructed value. The Commerce Department would *not* search for the next most similar model.

In the mid-1990s, however, the courts ruled that this practice violated the law, and so ordered the Commerce Department to change its practice.

Essentially, the courts ruled that the Commerce Department must exhaust all opportunities to use a *price-to-price* comparison in the dumping calculation before resorting to constructed value. To comply with the courts' mandate, the Commerce Department now examines whether home market sales are below cost *prior* to applying the model-match methodology. Under this approach, all below-cost sales are excluded from the 'universe' before the model-match methodology is employed. This will result in more dumping margin calculations being based on price-to-price comparisons, rather than on price-to-constructed value.

Adjustments to take into account comparison of different products

'Section A of the questionnaire', chapter 3, discussed how the Commerce Department determines which products sold in the home (or third) market should be compared to products sold to the United States. If the Commerce Department is forced to compare *similar*, rather than identical, products in the two markets, it adjusts the price of the home market product to make it comparable to the United States product. The Commerce Department makes this adjustment by adding or subtracting the difference between the variable cost of manufacture of the home market product and the variable cost of manufacture of the United States product, provided that such difference is less than 20% of the total cost of manufacture of the United States product. The Department will generally not allow a United States model to be compared to a non-identical (i.e. similar) home market model if the variable cost differences between the two products is more than 20% of the total cost of the United States model. To calculate this adjustment, called the 'difmer' (for 'difference in merchandise') adjustment, the Commerce Department uses product-specific cost information.

Use of exchange rates to derive same currency calculations

Changes to the United States law in 1995 also modified the manner in which the Commerce Department converts foreign currencies to United States dollars to calculate anti-dumping margins. The Commerce Department now uses daily exchange rates rather than quarterly rates. Using the daily rates, the Department calculates a weighted average exchange rate for the investigation period for use in converting foreign currencies to United States dollars.

The Commerce Department's rather anomalous way of using exchange rates in the anti-dumping calculation still exists under the new law, however. Essentially, the Commerce Department selects exchange rates based solely on the dates that the subject merchandise was sold in the United States market. It calculates a specific weighted average exchange rate for each United States model (CONNUM). Only the daily exchange rates for those particular dates on which there were United States sales (i.e. invoices) of the model are used in the calculation of the weighted average rate.

To illustrate with an example, assume that the investigation period is a calendar year. Further assume that, for a particular model, all of the foreign manufacturer's United States sales of colour televisions occurred in the last three months of the year – October, November and December. For that model, the Commerce Department will calculate a weighted average exchange rate using the daily exchange rates only for those days in October–December on which there were United States sales of the model. That weighted average exchange rate will be used to convert all sales prices and adjustments in foreign currencies, no matter when those sales and adjustments occurred. That is, for that model, the weighted average exchange rate (based on October–December United States sales) will be used to convert *all* home market prices (of the comparison model) to United States dollars even if all the home market sales occurred in February. This approach can have dramatic effects when the exchange rate fluctuates significantly.

Average-to-average comparison and 'zeroing'

For foreign exporters, one of the most favourable changes to United States law resulting from the Uruguay Round is the requirement that the anti-dumping calculations in original investigations be based on comparison of *weighted average* home market prices to *weighted average* United States prices. Under prior United States law, the Commerce Department calculated the anti-dumping margin by comparing individual United States prices to weighted average home market prices (which resulted in much higher margins). Under current United States law, the Commerce Department is supposed to base its calculation in an original investigation on a comparison of weighted average prices.

Although the United States statute allows for departure from an average-to-average comparison (and resort to individual-to-average comparisons) upon a finding that a respondent has engaged in 'targeted dumping', to date the Commerce Department has been reluctant to apply this exception.

Normally, the Department will calculate weighted average prices *by model* (i.e. control number or CONNUM) and *by level of trade* (to the extent that there are different levels of trades) and for the entire investigation period. Although the Department also has the discretion to create further 'averaging groupings', it has done so relatively infrequently.

Note, however, that the benefit of average-to-average comparison is offset by the Commerce Department's practice of 'zeroing'. 'Zeroing' refers to the Department's practice of changing negative dumping margins (i.e. no dumping) for individual products to zero when calculating the overall anti-dumping margin for the company. This practice is best illustrated with an example.

Assume that a foreign company subject to a United States anti-dumping case sells five product models to the United States, A, B and C, and further assume that the Commerce Department's anti-dumping calculation for individual models yields the following results.

Quantity sold to United States	United States unit value	Total value of United States sales	Home market unit value	Actual amount of unit dumping	Commerce-recognized unit dumping	Total value of dumping for product sales
10 (product A)	225	2,250	280	55	55	550
15 (product B)	245	3,675	230	-15	0	-225
20 (product C)	235	4,700	230	-5	0	-100
18 (product D)	240	4,320	225	-15	0	-270
16 (product E)	225	3,600	285	60	60	960
Total		18,545				915/1,510

Calculation of overall dumping margin by
Commerce Department = 8.14%
(total value of dumping, after changing negatives to zero,
(1,510)/total value of United States sales (18,545)

Calculation of overall dumping margin without zeroing = 4.93%
(total value of dumping (915)/total value of United States sales (18,545)

Thus, depending on how the negative margins are treated, the dumping margin varies a lot. If the negative margins are allowed to offset the positive margins, the total value of dumping is only 915 and the margin is only 4.93%. But if the negative margins are set to zero, the effect of the two transaction that are dumped is exaggerated – the value is 1,510 and the margin rises to 8.14%.

A WTO panel has ruled that the EU's practice of zeroing violates the WTO Anti-Dumping Agreement. In *EC – Anti-dumping duties on imports of cotton-type bed linen from India*, the Appellate Body ruled that zeroing was inconsistent with the language of Article 2.4.2 of the Anti-Dumping Agreement, at least in the context of original investigations. The current United States position is that that decision does not apply to it. It is only a matter of time, however, before some country takes a WTO appeal on this same issue in a United States anti-dumping case, and obtains a similar ruling against the United States.

In the meantime, foreign companies should be aware of this issue in their cases, and build a record from which their country can challenge this United States practice. Since zeroing can have a significant impact on dumping margins, and often will be the difference between dumping margins and legally *de minimis* margins, it is very much in the interest of foreign companies to pursue this issue.

The dumping calculation

When making a price-to-price comparison, the Commerce Department compares *adjusted net* export prices to *adjusted net* home market prices. Accordingly, the Commerce Department's first step in the calculation is to make various adjustments to the actual sales prices in both markets. As noted in a previous chapter, the goal of these adjustments is to ensure comparison:

❏ Of identical or similar merchandise;

❏ To customers at the same level of trade;

❏ At the same point in time (i.e. at the factory gate); and

❏ Under similar selling conditions.

The summary charts in table 5 detail all the adjustments that the Commerce Department typically makes to the invoice price to derive an adjusted ex-factory price.

Table 5   Calculating anti-dumping margins

Price-to-price comparisons for constructed export price	
United States price (CEP) **Invoice price to unaffiliated United States customer**	**Home market price** **Invoice price to unaffiliated customer**
– Discounts and rebates	**– Discounts and rebates**
Movement costs – United States movement expenses – Brokerage and handling – International freight and insurance – Home market movement expenses – Home market warehousing expenses	**Movement costs** – Movement expenses from plant to customer – Warehousing
Selling expenses – Commissions – Royalties – Advertising – Warranty – Technical service – Other direct selling expenses – Indirect United States selling expenses (GSA) – Imputed credit – Imputed inventory carrying costs – Repacking costs	**Selling expenses** – Commissions – Royalties – Advertising – Warranty – Technical service – Other direct selling expenses – Indirect selling expenses (e.g. rent for sales offices, salespeople's salaries, sales administration expenses) – Imputed credit – Imputed inventory carrying goods
Other costs/benefits + Duty drawback + Interest revenue from customers – Further processing costs in United States – Profit **= Ex-factory net United States price**	**Other costs/benefits** + Interest revenue from customers **Dumping adjustments** ± Variable cost differences due to physical characteristics ± Level of trade – Packing costs for home market + Packing costs for exportation to United States **= Ex-factory net home market price**
Amount of dumping = net home market price – net United States price *Dumping margin = amount of dumping/net United States price*	
Price-to-price comparisons for export price	
United States price (EP) **Invoice price to unaffiliated customer**	**Home market price** **Invoice price to unaffiliated customer**
Discounts and rebates	**– Discounts and rebates**
Movement costs – United States customs duties and fees – International freight and insurance – Brokerage and handling – Home market movement expenses – Home market warehousing expenses	**Movement costs** – Movement expenses from plant to customer – Warehousing
Other costs/benefits + Duty drawback **= Ex-factory net United States price**	**Direct selling expenses** – Commissions – Royalties – Advertising – Warranty – Technical service – Other direct selling expenses – Imputed credit
	United States direct selling expenses + Commissions + Royalties + Warranty + Advertising + Technical service + Imputed credit

---

Table 5 (cont'd)

	Other costs/benefits + *Interest revenue from home market customers* + *Interest revenue from United States customers* *Dumping adjustments* + *Variable cost differences due to differences in physical characteristics* + *Level of trade* − *Packing costs for home market* + *Packing costs for exportation to united states* = ***Ex-factory net home market price***

Amount of dumping = net home market price – net United States price
Dumping margin = amount of dumping/net United States price

United States price to constructed value comparisons

United States price (EP) *Invoice price to unaffiliated customer*	*Constructed value (CV)* *TCOM (total cost of manufacturing)*
− ***Discounts and rebates*** ***Movement costs*** − *United States customs duties and fees* − *International freight and insurance* − *Brokerage and handling* − *Home market movement expenses* − *Home market warehousing expenses* ***Other costs and benefits*** + *Duty drawback* = ***Ex-factory net United States price***	+ *G&A (ratio*TCOM)* + *Interest expense (ratio*TCOM)* + *Profit (calculated based on home market sales data)* + *Indirect selling expenses (calculated based on home market sales data)* = *CV* *(By not including direct expenses, movement expenses, and packing in CV, the Commerce Department simulates these adjustments in a price-to-price comparison)* ***United States direct selling expenses*** + *Commissions* + *Royalties* + *Warranty* + *Advertising* + *Technical service* + *Imputed credit* ***Other costs/benefits*** + *Interest revenue from United States customers* ***Dumping adjustments*** + *Packing costs for exportation to United States* = ***Adjusted constructed value***

Amount of dumping = adjusted constructed value – net United States price

Before calculating the weighted average, the Commerce Department must determine the net prices for home market or third country sales. The foreign company will have already submitted detailed computer files containing all of the necessary data in the format specified in the questionnaire. The Commerce Department starts with the gross unit price for each individual transaction. It then makes all of the appropriate adjustments shown in those charts to the gross unit price on a transaction-by-transaction basis.

Disagreements about the adjustments can involve two separate issues. First, the Commerce Department sometimes misprograms the computer and adds an adjustment when it should subtract, or vice versa. It is important to check carefully all of the Commerce Department calculations of dumping margins.

Second, there may be a disagreement about the method of calculating the amount of the adjustment. Usually the Commerce Department uses the adjustment as reported on the computer media, so the foreign company knows how the adjustment was calculated. In some cases, however, the Commerce Department revises the methodology used to calculate the adjustment. The company should make sure it understands the new methodology and checks the accuracy of the Commerce Department calculations.

Calculation of average margins

Companies should note a number of important points about the Commerce Department's method of calculating dumping margins. First, as discussed earlier, transactions with negative dumping margins (where the United States price is higher than the foreign market price) do not offset the transactions with positive dumping margins. This policy might change if the United States decides to follow WTO decisions, but currently the United States continues to apply zeroing.

Second, large volume transactions disproportionately affect the final margin. When a company discovers such a transaction, it should carefully review the facts about the transaction. Perhaps it is possible to exclude the transaction from the investigation (for example, if it is arguably outside the period of investigation). Alternatively, perhaps there is some basis for raising the United States price (by disallowing an adjustment that would lower the United States price).

Third, the Commerce Department calculates a single margin for all models under investigation, not model-by-model margins. Dumping margins on a few models can therefore result in dumping margins for all models that the foreign company exports to the United States. In general, margins on high-value products tend to weigh more heavily than the margins on low-value products.

Application of the cost test

As explained above, the Commerce Department can only use those prices that are above cost in determining foreign market value. If the Commerce Department is conducting a cost investigation, it will test each of the proposed home market or third country prices and exclude those transactions that are below cost.

The Commerce Department calculates the net home market or third country prices to be used for comparison to the cost. The Commerce Department subtracts from the gross price all of those adjustments that are not included in the cost (for example, movement charges). Any element included in the cost (such as interest expenses) is left in the price. Note that, because of this need to ensure that the price and cost figures are comparable, the net prices for the cost test are not necessarily the same as the net prices for comparison to the United States prices.

Once it has calculated the appropriate net prices, the Commerce Department follows these steps:

❑ First, the Commerce Department tests each of the prices of individual sales transactions, to see which ones are above and below the cost of the particular product.

❏ Second, it calculates the percentage of the transactions above cost, and the percentage below cost. These percentages are calculated on a model-by-model, or product-by-product basis.

❏ Third, it applies the 20% rule, on a narrow, model-specific basis.

❏ Fourth, if more than 20% of the transactions are below cost it excludes all those transactions that are below cost from the calculation of the weighted average.

❏ Fifth, the Commerce Department calculates a weighted average price for each model, size, or type of the product; these weighted averages of the transactions that are above cost will form the basis of foreign market value.

When calculating trial dumping margins, a foreign company can go through the same steps and perform the same analysis.

The role of dumping margins in preparing the response

As it prepares its response, the foreign company collects the various items of information and begins to prepare the computer database. When it is finished, the database gives the company a powerful tool to help prepare the response. Whenever the company is unsure whether a certain methodology will increase or decrease the overall margin, it should use the database to run sample dumping margins. The company can thus check precisely the effect of alternative methodologies on the margins.

This type of checking is not necessary for every decision to be made when preparing the response. Many actions have a clear effect on the overall margin. For example, increasing the amount of downward adjustment to home market price always lowers the dumping margin.

The company may want to use the computer database to check the amount of the decrease, but the direction of the change is unambiguous. Such issues do not require any special checking.

Other issues are not so clear, however, and may require the use of the computer database. For example, suppose the company must choose between presenting average warranty costs or model-specific warranty costs. Using model-specific warranty costs raises the adjustment for some models but lowers it for other models. Some margins will go up; others will go down. The only way to measure the net effect of the various changes is to calculate overall dumping margins. If used properly, the database created as part of the response can be a powerful tool to help the foreign company present the most effective response possible.

Chapter 6

Countervailing duties: measuring subsidies

The purpose of the countervailing duty provisions of United States trade law is to permit the United States Government to collect a countervailing duty to offset any unfair competitive advantage that an exporter might gain over a United States producer because of foreign government subsidies.

Before imposing such a duty on imports, however, the United States Government must make a series of specific findings about the existence and type of subsidies provided. First, it must be determined that a subsidy is being provided by a foreign government (at either national or sub-national level) on the manufacture, production or export of any article of merchandise imported into the United States. In addition, it must also be shown that the imports from the country providing the subsidy are causing, or threaten to cause, material injury to the United States industry ('injury test').

As in the case of anti-dumping duties discussed previously, subsidy determination and the imposition of countervailing duties (CVD) follows a bifurcated approach. The Commerce Department determines whether a subsidy exists, and the amount of any duty. The International Trade Commission separately assesses whether a United States industry is materially injured by the subsidy.

This chapter addresses the issues of determining whether a subsidy exists, and the amount of that subsidy. It also expands on chapter 2 to highlight some important procedural differences between countervailing duty investigations and anti-dumping investigations. Companies that have been through an anti-dumping investigation will find their experience a good, but imperfect, guide to what they will experience in a countervailing duty investigation. Injury issues, which apply to both anti-dumping and countervailing duty cases, are discussed separately in chapters 11, 12 and 13.

What is a subsidy?

The United States countervailing duty law has a very long history – it is even older than the anti-dumping law. During much of this history, there was no clear statutory framework for determining whether a programme provided a subsidy or not. The various agencies administering this law over time adopted policies to define what was and was not a subsidy. This issue was fiercely debated during the Uruguay Round, and the Agreement on Subsidies and Countervailing Measures (the SCM Agreement) provided for the first time an internationally agreed-on definition of a subsidy. United States law now basically tracks this definition.

Not every type of government subsidy or benefit programme is considered a countervailable subsidy for the purposes of United States law. Under United States law there are three basic elements that must exist before the Commerce Department will deem a subsidy or benefit to be countervailable. First, there must be a *financial contribution* provided by a government or public body (directly or indirectly). Second, the financial contribution must provide a *benefit* to the recipient. Third, the financial benefit must be provided to a *specific* enterprise or industry. Each of these three elements is discussed below.

Financial contribution

The term 'financial contribution' is explicitly defined under the statute, and includes, but is not limited to, four common types of practices used by governments to assist industries located within their borders. The four common types of practices that meet the definition of a 'financial contribution' are:

❑ Direct or potentially direct transfers of funds (grants, loans, equity infusions, loan guarantees);

❑ A decision by the foreign government to forego or not collect tax revenue otherwise due (tax credits or exemptions);

❑ The provision of goods or services other than general infrastructure; and

❑ The purchase or procurement of goods from a producer.

Although United States law has been written to capture the most common types of subsidy programmes, nevertheless it is flexible enough to permit other types of programmes to meet the definition of 'financial contribution'. Moreover, the law is also written to make clear that the financial contribution provided can be provided either *directly* by the government or *indirectly*, as in those situations where the government entrusts or directs a private body to provide a subsidy. These decisions are made on a 'case-by-case' basis by the Commerce Department.

An example may help to highlight some of the issues. Assume a country provides to a manufacturer a direct cash benefit of 10% of the FOB value of any product exported. Such a programme clearly provides direct financial benefit (i.e. cash) to exporters. This analysis can become somewhat more complicated, however, when the benefits are more indirect or murky. For example, assume now that the country does not provide cash, but instead provides an income tax exemption for export earnings. Although a direct cash benefit is not provided, nevertheless such a programme can still provide a financial benefit to the exporters if there is taxable income. Many other scenarios are possible.

Benefit to the recipient

The mere existence of a government programme providing a financial contribution is not enough to constitute a subsidy. Whatever financial contribution is provided must also confer a 'benefit' to someone or some entity. There are standards under United States law for determining the existence and amount of benefits conferred under any particular subsidy programme. Moreover, the law makes clear that any such benefit will 'normally be treated as conferred where there is a benefit to the recipient'.

There are four specific examples of the types of activities that would 'normally' be treated as benefits conferred under the law:

❑ Equity infusions (if the equity infusion is 'inconsistent with the usual investment practice of private investors');

❑ Loans (if the recipient pays a different amount for the loan from the rate that could be obtained on the market);

❑ Loan guarantees (if the recipient pays a different amount for the guaranteed loan than would be paid in the market for a non-guaranteed loan); and

❑ The provision or purchase of goods or services (particularly where the amount paid is 'less than adequate' when the government provides goods or services to firms, or 'more than adequate' when the government purchases goods or services from firms).

Suffice it to say that any methodologies used to measure the value of benefits bestowed are complex and critical, and vary by the type and use of the subsidy at issue. Generally, the adequacy of any type of remuneration will be determined based on prevailing open market conditions (price, quality, availability, marketability, and other factors involving 'conditions of purchase or sale'). Moreover, in making these determinations, the Commerce Department is not required to consider the effect of the subsidy in determining whether a subsidy exists (e.g. the effects on prices or outputs from income or price supports).

The Commerce Department has developed a very detailed set of policies that explain how to calculate the value of the benefit from various types of programmes that come up frequently in United States countervailing duty investigations. These policies have been codified in the Commerce Regulations, and can be found at *www.ita.doc.gov*.

Finally, situations where an industry that has previously received a benefit has been 'privatized' pose particular problems. The fact that a previously subsidized industry has been sold at arm's length to a private enterprise does not automatically extinguish any prior subsidies conferred. Indeed, this can be an extremely complex analysis, and is handled on a case-by case basis.

This area represents a current conflict between United States law and WTO law. The Appellate Body in *United States – Imposition of countervailing duties on certain hot-rolled lead and bismuth carbon steel products originating in the United Kingdom* specifically overturned this feature of United States law, and stated that privatization does extinguish subsidies. The United States has been very stubborn in refusing to apply this Appellate Body decision in other cases, however. As a result, various countries have been filing new WTO panel proceedings in other cases where the Commerce Department continues to find subsidies at privatized companies. Presumably these new panel cases will apply the Appellate Body decision. Perhaps in time this conflict will be resolved, and the United States will bring its practice into compliance more generally.

Specificity

A government programme providing a benefit must also be 'specific' to an enterprise or industry. This means that the programme must be targeted to provide benefits only to a specific enterprise, industry, or group, rather than providing some type of benefit generally to the economy as a whole.

The purpose behind the 'specificity' requirement is to ensure that those types of broad-based government assistance programmes or services that most governments normally provide as a routine function of governing are not subject to countervailing duties. For example, items such as public roads and bridges, which generally provide a benefit to anyone that uses them rather than to specific industries, are not 'specific'. Thus, the specificity requirement ensures that duties are not imposed unreasonably on broad government programmes (such as road building) that provide any benefits broadly throughout the economy.

In an effort to simplify the 'specificity' issue, United States law classifies all such government subsidies into one of three broad categories: (1) export subsidies; (2) import substitution subsidies; and (3) domestic subsidies. Export subsidies and import substitution programmes are automatically deemed specific and are always actionable. For purposes of the statute, an 'export subsidy' refers to a subsidy that is contingent on export performance. An 'import substitution subsidy' refers to a subsidy that is 'contingent on the use of domestic goods over imported goods'. These are discussed below.

Export subsidies

As one would expect, export subsidies can take many forms. Annex I of the WTO SCM Agreement provides an illustrative list of common types of export subsidies. In addition to 'direct subsidies' paid to a firm based on export performance, there are several other less obvious types of export promotion tactics that may amount to export subsidies, including: exemption or remission of direct or indirect taxes upon exportation; currency retention schemes that provide a 'bonus' for exports; provision for transport or freight charges on more favourable terms for export than for domestic shipments; and the remission or 'drawback' of import fees or other charges on imported inputs upon exportation.

Whether or not a particular export promotion programme amounts to an 'export subsidy' within the meaning of the statute depends, of course, upon the unique circumstances of each tax rebate or programme. Nevertheless, the law is sufficiently broad to classify a wide variety of export promotion programmes as prohibited export subsidies.

United States law makes clear that a programme can create an export subsidy by being contingent, either in law or in fact, on exports. When a programme makes exports an explicit condition of benefits, the linkage is clear and cannot be contested. Sometimes a programme refers to both export and non-export factors. In those instances, the Commerce Department almost always views the explicit listing of an export factor as tainting the whole programme and making the programme an export subsidy.

The more interesting cases, however, involve so-called *de facto* export conditions. Even when the foreign government law does not specifically discuss export conditions, the Commerce Department is often willing to find *de facto* export conditions in the circumstances of a particular case. For example, is the foreign company's home market so small that a producer would have to export to have commercially viable production levels? Does the foreign company in fact export most of its production? Are companies that export a large portion of their production the only ones that ever seem to qualify for benefits under a programme? All of these details are relevant.

The Commerce Department applies more inclusive standards than the WTO SCM Agreement may contemplate. Under WTO principles, the mere fact that a company exports should not be sufficient reason to find an export subsidy. Although this issue has been raised in a few WTO proceedings, the standards are still very much in the process of being defined and clarified.

Import substitution subsidies

The same types of issues arise with regard to import substitution subsidies. As mentioned above, import substitution subsidies involves subsidies that are contingent on the use of domestic inputs over imported inputs. Typically, such subsidies take the form of a direct payment by the government to the producer to compensate for any price differential between the domestic and imported input. For example, assume a country provides inputs to the steel industry at a price lower than the market price. In this example, the government provides a financial benefit (i.e. below-market price for domestic inputs) to a specific industry.

Assessing the countervailability of such programmes invariably raises several issues, such as the comparability of the substituted products, and documentation of the price differential between the import and domestic input. As with export subsidies, the Commerce Department casts a very wide net to catch import substitution subsidies.

Domestic subsidies

Although both export subsidies and import substitution subsidies are always specific under United States law, and therefore always countervailable, the situation is not so clear with regard to domestic subsidies. Domestic subsidies are those subsidies that are not contingent on export performance. Determination of whether or not a domestic subsidy is specific has been the subject of many previous CVD proceedings.

The statute seeks to resolve this issue by providing two avenues for determining the specificity of domestic subsidies. Domestic subsidies may be determined to be specific either as a matter of fact (*de facto* specificity), or as a matter of law (*de jure* specificity). '*De jure*' specificity means simply that the programme is considered specific because eligibility for the programme is expressly limited *by law* to a company or industry by the specific eligibility terms of the enabling programme.

Even if the terms of the law providing the subsidy do not determine it to be specific, the statute nevertheless permits a finding of specificity 'as a matter of fact'. Such *de facto* specificity means simply that although eligibility for the subsidy has not been limited by the precise eligibility terms of the programme, the actual usage of the programme by a limited number of companies or industries demonstrates that the programme is *in fact* specific.

This issue of *de facto* specificity has generated a long history of intense dispute in countervailing duty cases over the years. This issue has also been frequently taken to the United States courts, which have offered lots of guidance, but much of it has been inconsistent depending on the specific judge making the decision. This murky area was codified into the United States statute in 2001, and Congress thus tried to set forth its view.

A subsidy is *de facto* specific if one of four factors exists as part of the programme. The factors are: (1) whether the use of the subsidy programme is limited to a specific number of enterprises; (2) whether the programme is in fact used only by certain types of enterprises; (3) whether the programme grants a disproportionately large amount only to certain enterprises; or (4) whether the discretion used in granting the particular subsidy favours a specific enterprise or industry.

Even this attempt at codification, however, does not help very much. This issue is inherently fact-specific, and Congress has refused to set any clear guidelines to help companies know in advance what is specific and what is not. Congress believes that leaving the decisions to the Commerce Department on a case-by-case base creates a 'zone of uncertainty' that can serve as a deterrent to those who might come too close to the edge.

To determine whether the number of users is limited, Commerce Department considers the diversity of the overall economy of the jurisdiction providing the subsidy (i.e. if a targeted sector represents a small portion of the jurisdiction's overall economy, the subsidy may be specific even if generally available to all producers within a certain sector). A subsidy may be specific to a 'group' of industries even if the industries have nothing in common other than the receipt of the subsidy.

Clearly, the determination of whether or not a particular domestic subsidy meets the 'specificity' tests outlined above is both complicated and fact-specific, and will proceed on a case-by-case basis. Many domestic financial assistance programmes can be difficult to gauge under this standard, particularly those involving various types of direct equity investments in private corporations, as well as direct government loans made to private companies. As outlined above, resolution of these issues often comes down to a technical decision as to whether or not these decisions or practices are consistent with market decisions.

Finally, domestic subsidies known as regional subsidies are separately addressed under United States law. Regional subsidies are those limited to certain enterprises within a designated geographical region. Generally, such subsidies that are provided by a state or province within that state or province are not specific, and therefore not countervailable. However, such regional subsidies provided by the central government to a specific region or province of the country are deemed specific, and therefore are countervailable.

What is not a subsidy

To further clarify what constitutes a subsidy under the law, it is helpful to understand what is *not* considered a subsidy. Certain provisions or benefits can be provided, yet still not qualify as a subsidy because all the elements of a subsidy have not been met. A few examples will illustrate this principle.

Assume a country provides a line of credit at the market rate to the steel industry. Although in this situation there is a programme established by the government to assist a specific industry, nevertheless there is no countervailable subsidy here within the meaning of United States law because there has been no financial benefit provided to the company. The line of credit is at market rates.

Similarly, assume a private association voluntarily provides information free of charge to its members. Although in this situation a financial benefit has been provided to the members, there has been no government action. The association took this action on its own.

Or assume a country provides a tax holiday to new industries in the country. Is such activity a countervailable subsidy? This depends upon the number of industries that receive the benefit (i.e. lower taxes), and how the government uses its discretion to provide such benefits (i.e. specificity test). If the tax benefit has been applied very widely throughout the economy it is probably not a subsidy.

The underlying theme is that all three elements must be met for there to be a subsidy. Any two elements without the third is not sufficient. Of course, sometimes there will be intense debates during a case about whether, as a factual matter, the element has been met.

When is a subsidy actionable?

Even though certain government-provided programmes or benefits meet the technical definition of a subsidy under United States law as discussed above, this is not the end of the analysis. The WTO SCM Agreement establishes a 'traffic light' analytical framework for determining which subsidies may be countervailed and which may not. Under this system, not all subsidies are countervailable. Rather, only those fitting within the WTO framework as either 'prohibited' red light subsidies or 'actionable' yellow light subsidies may be countervailed under the terms of the WTO.

Although the terminology differs, the basic WTO framework is reflected in United States countervailing duty law. As described below, the United States will always countervail both red light and yellow light subsidies because an affirmative Commission injury determination is required before either can be countervailed. Both the WTO and the United States law previously exempted green light subsidies from countervailing duties, but that is no longer the case.

Red light subsidies

Red light subsidies are subsidies whose very nature makes them intolerable and automatically actionable. Red light subsidies are deemed specific by law and are *per se* prohibited. They include export subsidies and import substitution subsidies. Annex I of the SCM Agreement provides a list of common types of export subsidies, which includes such items as direct subsidies based on export performance, and rebate or remission of direct and indirect taxes. Prohibited import substitution subsidies are subsidies contingent on the use of domestic goods over imported goods (whether solely or as one of several conditions). Both of these types of programmes are considered red light subsidies, which are clearly countervailable by WTO Members. United States law reflects this approach.

Yellow light subsidies

In contrast to the outright prohibited red light subsidies, the WTO SCM Agreement establishes a second tier of actionable subsidies known as yellow light subsidies. These are generally those subsidies that are neither the outright prohibited (i.e. red light) subsidies nor the non-actionable green light subsidies (discussed below). In addition, yellow light subsidies are also generally understood to include four other types of subsidies specifically mentioned in Article 6.1 of the SCM Agreement, being: (1) total subsidization exceeding 5%; (2) subsidies covering the operating losses of an industry; (3) subsidies covering the operating losses of an enterprise; and (4) direct forgiveness of a debt.

Yellow light subsidies are actionable under the SCM Agreement (and under United States law) only if they are found to adversely affect the interests of a WTO Member. Despite this distinction in the SCM Agreement, however, whether or not a particular subsidy amounts to a yellow light subsidy is not a meaningful distinction for United States proceedings. Under United States law any subsidy must injure (i.e. adversely affect) a domestic industry to be actionable. United States law now provides an 'injury test' in all cases brought against WTO Members, and thus requires a Commission determination of injury before imposing duties. Other countries are not entitled to an injury test. (It is theoretically possible for a country to assume equivalent obligations and qualify, but this would be extremely rare.)

Thus, the yellow light distinction is mainly meaningful in a WTO proceeding because adverse effects include the material injury test plus two additional possibilities for finding adverse affects, which are: (1) nullification or impairment of GATT 1994 benefits accruing to a Member; or (2) serious prejudice to the interests of another Member. Other than this distinction, red light and yellow light subsidies are essentially treated the same from the perspective of the United States countervailing duty law.

Green light subsidies

The third type of subsidy under the SCM Agreement is a green light subsidy. Green light subsidies are non-actionable by WTO Members even though they might otherwise be considered countervailable. The most common type of green light or non-actionable subsidies include those provided for research and development, those provided to disadvantaged regions of a country, or those provided to assist environmental concerns.

It is worth noting that the Commerce Department strictly and narrowly interprets what constitutes a green light subsidy to prevent expansion of the green light provision. The United States statute places specific limitations on the scope of these exceptions, and the government providing the subsidy has the burden of proving that these limitations have been met. Any doubts are resolved in favour of the subsidy programme being considered actionable under United States law.

For example, *non-actionable research and development subsidies* are limited to two basic types of subsidies. The first type, 'industrial research' subsidies, are subsidies provided to enhance research aimed at the discovery of new knowledge with the objective of developing new products or significantly improving existing products. The second type is 'pre-competitive development activity', which involves subsidies provided to assist the translation of industrial research into a plan for new and improved products up to the point of the first non-commercial prototype.

United States law imposes further limitations on these subsidies before they are deemed non-actionable. Specifically, to qualify as green light subsidies, they must be limited to funding a very narrow set of expenses, such the cost of research personnel, or costs of instruments, equipment, land and buildings used exclusively and permanently for the research, or related costs of consultancy used exclusively for the research activity. These programmes may also fund certain additional overhead costs or other running costs incurred directly as a result of the research activity. Any such reimbursed costs must not cover more than 75% of the industrial research costs or 50% of the pre-competitive development costs.

United States law similarly restricts the types of subsidies that qualify as non-actionable *disadvantaged regional subsidies*. These are generally defined as those subsidies provided as part of a generally applicable regional development policy. Moreover, strict criteria must be met before even these types of subsidies qualify as non-actionable. First, the subsidy must be designed for a clearly designated, contiguous geographical area with a definable economic and administrative identity. Second, the region receiving the subsidy must be disadvantaged more than temporarily. Third, the assistance provided must be generally available, not targeted to any specific industry. Fourth, eligibility criteria for receiving assistance must be neutral, objective and capable of verification. And, fifth, the overall programme must include ceilings on the subsidy amount available per project.

In addition to these strict criteria, United States law also imposes further limits on the economic circumstances of the disadvantaged region, which must be assessed over a three-year period. The Commerce Department must make this assessment based either on the overall per capita income, household income, or gross domestic product per capita, any of which must not exceed 85% of the average for the territory concerned. Alternatively, the unemployment rate must be at least 110% of the average for the territory as a whole.

There are also strict limits on what qualify as non-actionable *environmental subsidies*. These must involve the adaptation of existing facilities to new environmental requirements imposed by law which result in greater financial burden on firms. To qualify for green light status, the subsidy must be a one-time, non-recurring measure whose total value is limited to 20% of the adaptation cost (if 21% of the cost is subsidized, the entire subsidy is countervailed). Moreover, such subsidies must be directly linked to planned nuisance and pollution reduction and be made available to all firms that can adopt new equipment or production process. Further, the subsidies may be used only to upgrade existing facilities in operation for at least two years at the time the environmental requirements were imposed; and they cannot involve the cost of replacing and operating the actual facility.

Finally the subsidies may only compensate for environmental requirements which are new and unforeseen.

As one can easily see, the United States Congress has been very careful to define strictly and narrowly the programmes that can qualify as non-actionable subsidies. These provisions were reluctantly added to the United States statute to reflect United States obligations under the SCM Agreement.

The irony is that, as a technical matter, the green light subsidies provisions of the SCM Agreement do not currently apply. Under Article 31 of the SCM Agreement, the rules on green light subsidies applied for only five years, after which time the WTO Members were to decide whether or not to extend the rules. By the end of 2002, no formal decision to extend had been made, and the issue was still pending in Geneva.

A similar provision in the United States law calls for the various provisions that declare certain subsidies to be non-actionable to not apply after the five-year period, unless they are specifically extended. Reflecting its desire to keep more control over trade policy, Congress required the Administration to come back to Congress for new authorization to extend these provisions, even if the WTO Members decided to extend them. At this time, therefore, the provisions do not apply.

Note, however, that most of the rules for non-actionable subsidies reflect general principles that would apply anyway, and probably would be sufficient to keep the programme in question from being declared an actionable subsidy. The main difference is that the specific rules provided so-called safe harbours that allowed countries and companies to proceed with more confidence that their actions were not creating actionable subsidies. Now that we are back to the general principles, the 'zone of uncertainty' applies once again.

Agricultural subsidies

Subsidies on agricultural products raise complex questions beyond the scope of this chapter. Foreign companies should note a few general points. First, the Commerce Department has conducted countervailing duty investigations of agricultural products in the past. In principle, the law applies to agricultural products just as it does to manufactured products.

Second, if a subsidy has been listed in Annex I of the WTO Agreement on Agriculture, the subsidy is non-actionable. Since this area involves the interplay of the complex provisions in the Agreement on Agriculture and the provisions of the SCM Agreement, a foreign company facing a countervailing duty investigation involving agricultural products will have a more complex task at hand.

Third, another complexity that arises for agricultural products involves the relationship between the growers and processors. The United States law specifically allows domestic industries to file countervailing duty cases against subsidies to either the raw agricultural product or the downstream processed product. These special rules create yet another level of complexity.

Fourth, agricultural products are usually seasonal, and both the Commerce Department and the International Trade Commission have adapted their rules from time to time to account for the special circumstances raised by seasonal products.

Countervailing duty calculated and collected

Once the necessary findings are made, the United States Government may then impose countervailing duties to offset the impact of the subsidy. The duties are paid by the importer of record in addition to any other customs duties or charges applicable at the time of entry. The theory underlying the law is that by collecting a countervailing duty equal to the net subsidy provided by the foreign government, any unfair advantage is eliminated.

The general rule favours the calculation of individual countervailing duty rates for each exporter or producer investigated. A weighted average 'all others' rate applies to those exporters or producers not individually investigated. The averaging excludes those individual rates found to be *de minimis* or determined wholly on the basis of facts available (formerly called 'best information available'). If exporter-specific rates are too burdensome, Commerce has the discretion to calculate a single countrywide rate.

To calculate the subsidy rate for a particular programme, the Commerce Department divides the value of the subsidy benefit in the period of investigation by the sales in that period that are 'tied' to the benefit from the subsidy programme. This calculation requires the Commerce Department to separately define the numerator and denominator. The numerator is the amount of the subsidy benefit. The denominator is the sales value of the product to which the subsidy is attributed. Commerce then calculates the overall subsidy rate by dividing the numerator by the denominator.

One potential complication in making this calculation is that there are different types of sales denominators. The type of sales denominator used depends on the nature of the underlying subsidy programme. For example, for a domestic subsidy the Commerce Department will use the total sales of all products (domestic and export, subject and non-subject) to calculate the subsidy margin. For an export subsidy, the Commerce Department will use total sales of all exported products (subject and non-subject) to calculate the subsidy margin. The following sample calculations for different types of subsidies will to help clarify the methodology used by the Department to calculate the subsidy margin.

For a *recurring grant linked to a particular product*, assume a pharmaceutical company receives an annual, recurring grant from the government of $1 million to produce a particular drug called GEN. Assume further that the pharmaceutical company's total sales (both home market and exports) amount to $10 million. In this case, the Commerce Department will calculate the subsidy rate by dividing the total amount of the subsidy by total sales of GEN, as shown below:

Subsidy rate: 1,000,000 ÷ 10,000,000 = 0.1, or 10%

The Commerce Department would use a similar approach to calculate the subsidy rate for *tax credits tied to exports*. In this example, assume a steel mill receives a $10 tax credit for every $100 in exports. Assume further that the steel company exported a total of $10,000 during the year, creating a total benefit of $1,000. In this case, the Commerce Department would calculate an overall subsidy rate of 10%, as shown below:

$$\text{Subsidy rate: } 1,000 \div 10,000 = 0.1, \text{ or } 10\%$$

A final example shows the methodology that would be used for *preferential export financing* on a loan for exports to the United States market. In this example, assume the government provides preferential export financing for a company's exports of any product to the United States. The benefit is the difference between the financing cost under the government programme and the financing cost under a market interest rate – assume $500. To calculate the subsidy rate, the Commerce Department would take the value of the company's sales to the United States of all products – assume $15,000 – and divide by the total subsidy amount of $500, yielding an overall subsidy rate of 3.33%, as shown below:

$$\text{Subsidy rate: } 500 \div 15,000 = 0.033, \text{ or } 3.33\%$$

These rules seem easy, but in practice there can be fierce debates over just what goes into the denominator. Depending on how these issues are resolved, the subsidy margin could go up or down by a considerable amount.

Other issues

Non-market economies

Non-market economies have had an interesting history under the countervailing duty law. For a number of years, there was debate about whether it made any sense to apply the law – which is based on the idea of comparing what the government is doing and a market-based benchmark – to a country in which there was no meaningful market-based benchmark. The courts finally ruled that the law could not be applied to non-market economies. The current rule continues to be that the United States countervailing duty law cannot apply to non-market economies.

The factors to be considered in determining whether a country is a non-market economy, as set forth in the statute, are:

❑ The extent to which the currency of the foreign country is convertible into the currency of other countries;

❑ The extent to which wage rates in the foreign country are determined by free bargaining between labour and management;

❑ The extent to which joint ventures or other investments by firms of other foreign countries are permitted in the foreign country;

❑ The extent of government ownership or control of the means of production;

❑ The extent of government control over the allocation of resources and over the price and output decisions of enterprises; and

❑ Such other factors as the administering authority considers appropriate.

Upstream subsidies

There are special rules allowing an investigation of subsidies to an input used in producing the product under investigation ('upstream subsidies'). For example, in an investigation of steel disc wheels from Brazil, the Commerce Department investigated possible subsidies to the Brazilian steel industry – not surprisingly, steel was the single most important input in making steel disc wheels.

These specific rules are beyond the scope of this chapter. From a practical perspective, this issue is most likely to occur when the United States has already conducted a countervailing duty investigation of an industry in a certain country and found subsidies, and then a downstream industry in the same country is subject to a new investigation. In such situations, foreign exporters have a much greater risk of needing to address these special rules.

Developing country rules

Developing countries are entitled to a different rule for *de minimis* countervailing duty margins. For developing countries the threshold is 2%, rather than the 1% that applies to developed countries. Least developed countries benefit from an even more generous 3%, but this special rule was scheduled to expire on 1 January 2003. The United States Trade Representative decides the status of each country, and the status is subject to change depending on the evolving level of the country's development. Least developed normally means a per capita GNP of less than $1,000 per year.

Developing countries in countervailing duty cases also benefit from special rules on 'negligible imports' that are discussed more generally under 'Cumulation of imports' in chapter 11. The thresholds for negligibility for developing countries go up in countervailing duty cases: the 3% threshold for an individual country goes up to 4%; and the 7% threshold for all negligible countries goes up to 9%.

The issue of special rules for developing countries continues to be very much at issue. It was an important part of the discussions leading to both the Seattle WTO Ministerial in December 1999 and the Doha WTO Ministerial in November 2001. Developing countries feel the WTO system has not been sufficiently sensitive to their particular concerns. Although the issue of special and differential treatment continues to be debated as part of the ongoing Doha Round negotiations, as at the end of 2002 no breakthroughs have been made. The focus has been on special and differential treatment in other areas, not in the area of trade remedy laws. It remains to be seen how the Doha Round will decide to address this important issue.

Subsidy library

The Commerce Department maintains on its website (*www.ita.doc.gov*) a library of materials on foreign government programmes that have been previously investigated in countervailing duty cases. The website also provides previous Commerce Department determinations on various issues.

Although these materials are provided to make it easier for United States domestic industries to consider and prepare countervailing duty cases against foreign countries, the materials can also be used by foreign exporters. If you are using, or considering taking advantage of, a programme that has previously been found to be a subsidy, you should be aware of the increased risk you will face in any countervailing duty investigation that might take place.

Countervailing duty procedures and strategies

The procedures applicable in a countervailing duty (CVD) investigation are complex, and strict time limits set out in the statute and regulations must be adhered to. In general, the procedures follow the framework set forth in chapter 2 for both anti-dumping and countervailing duty investigations. A few important differences are highlighted here.

Initiation

Once it receives a petition, the United States Government must decide whether to initiate the CVD investigation. First, within 20 days the Government must decide whether the petition is in the proper form with the necessary allegations and information. Commerce must also determine that the domestic industry supports a countervailing duty petition before it initiates an investigation.

The main difference is that the Commerce Department will not automatically initiate investigations against every programme named in the petition. It is quite common for Commerce to decide there is insufficient evidence that a programme is a subsidy, or that it has in fact been used by any company. If the evidence is insufficient, Commerce will not initiate on that programme. In light of the new WTO standards for the evidence necessary to initiate an investigation, Commerce has become somewhat more careful.

There are no immediate business implications associated with the initiation. Imports can continue without additional deposits or duties. Formal initiation should, however, serve to warn United States importers and overseas exporters of possible CVD duties on future imports of subject merchandise into the United States.

Preliminary injury determination

Forty-five days after the petition is filed, the Commission must make a preliminary determination of whether there is a reasonable indication that causal injury exists. If there is such a reasonable indication, the case continues. The finding has no direct business implication. It simply means the Commission has preliminarily determined that there is a 'reasonable indication' of injury. If there is a negative determination, however, the case ends.

Questionnaires

The Commerce Department sends a questionnaire to the foreign government seeking information regarding subsidization. Unlike anti-dumping cases, in which the foreign company controls its own destiny, in countervailing duty investigations the main focus of the Commerce questionnaire process is on the foreign government and the various foreign government agencies that administer the programmes in question.

The questionnaires request detailed information about the various types of subsidies provided by the government. Although questionnaires vary by country and by industry, they often request detailed information about a range of potentially countervailable programmes, including: tax incentives; duty exemptions; corporate income tax exemptions; tax deductions and value-added tax; various types of subsidy programmes existing in the home market; debt restructuring activities of specific companies; loans and loan guarantees from banks owned, controlled or influenced by the central government; export promotion programmes; other government-sponsored financing programmes; and any specific subsidy programmes known to be provided in the country involved in the proceeding. The foreign government must also obtain relevant information from exporters and submit it to the Commerce Department.

This process moves very quickly. Responses are due within 30–45 days, with little flexibility on extensions. Since the timeline for countervailing duty investigations is shorter than that for anti-dumping investigations, the Commerce Department feels more pressure to move the investigation quickly.

Commerce Department preliminary determination

Eighty-five days after the petition is filed the Commerce Department must make a preliminary determination of whether there is a reasonable indication that a subsidy exists and, if so, the estimated value of the subsidy. The decision is based upon the questionnaire responses of the foreign government and the exporters. Importantly, this is the first decision that directly affects importers. If the Commerce Department makes an affirmative determination, then Customs will suspend liquidation on goods entered on or after publication of preliminary results, and the importer will be required to post a bond equal to the estimated subsidy on all entries made after the publication of the preliminary determination.

Verification

The Commerce Department sends a team to the foreign country to verify the information in the response. The team reviews the books of the companies involved and the foreign government's records to ensure accuracy. If a response is incomplete or its accuracy cannot be verified, the Commerce Department will calculate countervailing duties based on the facts available, which normally means accepting the petitioner's allegations and results in extremely high countervailing duties.

Verification is discussed in depth in chapter 10. Those general principles apply here, but in CVD investigations the involvement of the government raises some special problems. First, the foreign government is sometimes less committed to the defence than the exporters involved. Although the case may be a major issue for the exporters, the foreign government officials usually have numerous other jobs, and simply cannot devote as much time to the investigation. It is particularly important to make sure the team handling the case at the various government agencies understands the magnitude of the task and is committed to spending the time necessary to succeed.

Second, the foreign government often has difficult problems with national laws involving the secrecy of certain types of information. For example, central bank officials are often reluctant or unable to disclose certain types of company-specific information. These secrecy laws can pose real problems for investigations. It is usually possible to work something out, but it can take time, and parties to a countervailing duty investigation are well advised to begin this process early.

Final Commerce Department subsidy determination

Seventy-five days after its preliminary determination, the Commerce Department makes a final determination of subsidization. This decision is based upon the verified information, public hearing, and briefs submitted by counsel involved in the case. The Commerce Department announces the final CVD margin. If there is no subsidy (i.e. in the aggregate less than 1.0% for developed countries or 2.0% for developing countries), the investigation ends. Importers are now required to make cash deposits equal to the countervailing duties on entries made on or after the date of the order. The new cash deposit rate establishes the maximum potential liability on these entries.

If the Commerce Department final determination is negative, the case ends. There is no liability, all cash deposited is refunded, with interest, and any bonds necessary as a result of the preliminary determination are terminated.

There is a special rule for countervailing duty cases. Since there is an upper limit on the time for which provisional measures can be imposed under the WTO rules, an extended Commerce final determination in a countervailing duty case creates a problem, since the preliminary determination comes so early and an extended final goes beyond the 120 days for provisional measures allowed under Article 17.4 of the Agreement on Subsidies and Countervailing Measures. United States law deals with this situation by allowing the liability for duties to lapse during the gap period, and then having liability resume once the final decision is made. This rule is not triggered very often, but when it applies it can create a significant commercial benefit for those importers liable for duties.

Suspension agreement

It is possible to enter into a settlement with the United States Government known as a suspension agreement. Under such an agreement, the foreign government and the exporters undertake certain commitments. In return, the United States Government suspends its investigation and will not require deposits or collection of countervailing duties. Although this can be a worthwhile solution, the United States Government rarely allows suspension agreements. There normally must be political support for such an agreement, particularly in light of the fact that petitioners can be expected to lead the fight against such agreements. Suspension agreements are discussed in more detail under 'Settlement of anti-dumping and countervailing duty cases' in chapter 14.

International Trade Commission final injury determination

Forty-five days after an affirmative Commerce Department final decision, the Commission must make a final injury determination. If this decision is affirmative, the United States Government will issue an order and require cash deposits equal to the estimated net subsidy upon entry of the subject merchandise. If the decision is negative, no duties can be collected even if subsidies were found to exist.

This Commission decision must meet this deadline. If both countervailing duty and anti-dumping duty investigations are proceeding simultaneously, the deadline in the countervailing duty case hits first. Unless the domestic parties agree to align the two cases, and thus push back the CVD deadline, the CVD drives the timing of the Commission investigation and decision. This shorter time frame can pose real problems for the defence effort, if the parties have not anticipated it.

Countervailing duty order

The final phase of the proceeding is the publication of the final CVD order. Subject merchandise entered on or after publication of the CVD order is subject to a cash deposit equal to the estimated subsidy. Typically, the amount of the cash deposit is equal to the calculated CVD rate multiplied by the entered value of the merchandise.

The cash deposit is just an estimate. The final CVD duty assessed is ultimately calculated and levied only after participation in an annual administrative review. There is theoretically *no limit* to the importer's liability on such entries as a result of subsequent reviews. Importers receive a refund with interest for the difference if the review rate is less than the deposit rate, however.

Court appeals

Commission and Commerce Department decisions in CVD investigations and reviews can be appealed to the United States Court of International Trade. Subsequent appeals to the United States Court of Appeals for the Federal Circuit and the United States Supreme Court are possible. Judicial review is discussed in more detail under 'Review in United States courts' in chapter 16.

Administrative review

During the anniversary month of the underlying order, any interested party can request an administrative review of the previous period. If no party requests a review, the entries during the past period are liquidated at the bond rate or cash deposit rate. If a review is requested, the Commerce Department conducts an investigation into the value of the subsidy during the review period.

An administrative review has two purposes. The first is to determine the exact amount of the subsidy provided during the review period. The second is to establish a new CVD deposit rate that will be applied against all imports of subject merchandise in the future. Calculation of the new deposit rate is made in the manner discussed above, using the appropriate numerator and denominator for the review period.

Such annual CVD administrative reviews can be conducted every year until the countervailing duty order is revoked.

Sunset reviews

Five years after a CVD order is issued, the Commission and Commerce Department must determine whether revocation of the order would likely lead to continuation or recurrence of a countervailable subsidy and of material injury. If the Commission or Commerce Department make negative determinations, the order is revoked. Both agencies must make affirmative findings for the order to be continued. Sunset reviews are discussed in more detail under 'Sunset reviews to terminate orders' in chapter 15.

In making its sunset determination, Commerce will not consider company- or industry-specific renunciations of countervailable subsidies, by themselves, as indication that continuation or recurrence is unlikely.

Chapter 7

Section 201: Global restrictions on all imports

United States trade remedy laws are commonly understood to address unfair trade practices that violate international rules of conduct. In the context of import trade, United States anti-dumping and countervailing duty laws are typical examples. Nonetheless, United States trade remedy laws also offer a response to fair trade under certain conditions, the most common of which is an 'escape clause' or 'safeguard' measure to address fairly traded imports. Section 201 of the Trade Act of 1974, as amended, provides the specific authority for imposing such a measure, the result of which can be significant import restraints.

Although Section 201 was considered something of a 'dead letter' for many years, domestic industry interest in filing Section 201 investigations increased in the late 1990s. Foreign companies therefore need to be aware of this law, and how it can affect their commercial interests.

This chapter reviews some background to Section 201, and then explores the various phases of a Section 201 proceeding. The International Trade Commission first decides whether there is injury, and then conducts a separate proceeding to make remedy recommendations to the President. Finally, the President must make the decision what remedy, if any, to impose. This process is quite discretionary, and thus creates a very different decision-making process to the more automatic unfair trade proceedings. Those differences are discussed in this chapter.

General background

Development of Section 201

Escape clause measures were developed to facilitate efforts by the domestic industry to make a positive adjustment to import competition. This positive adjustment to imports could involve industry restructuring to become more internationally competitive, or it could involve some domestic firms deciding to leave the market and focus on other lines of business. In the United States, the measures were born out of an understanding that trade liberalization could be highly disruptive to vulnerable domestic industries. A decision was made that a period of import relief should be available to such industries to adapt to new conditions of competition brought on by new trade concessions. Although this is in apparent contradiction to the purpose of trade liberalization and the efficient reallocation of resources, escape clause or safeguard measures were viewed by many as a necessary political safety valve, in the absence of which a consensus on trade liberalization in the United States could not be achieved.

Section 201 dates back to the Trade Act of 1974, but similar mechanisms have existed since the 1930s and the first statutory procedure and criteria for escape clause or safeguard actions appeared in the Trade Agreement Extension Act of

1951. Although the legislation has been amended a number of times since, the basic tenets are essentially still the same: following an investigation and determination by the United States International Trade Commission (previously the Tariff Commission), the President may impose duties or other restrictions for a limited period of time on increased imports of any article found by the Commission to cause or threaten to cause serious injury to the domestic industry producing the like or directly competitive article.

International disciplines

International rules on escape clause measures developed hand-in-hand with their development in the United States. Indeed, in 1947 the United States insisted on an escape clause provision, modelled on its own, within the General Agreement on Tariffs and Trade (GATT). The United States proposal is embodied in Article XIX of GATT, which remains in force to this day along with important new disciplines under the WTO Safeguards Agreement, which came into force in 1995.

Article XIX established certain steps to be taken before an escape clause measure can be imposed. In early practice, it offered protection against import surges following trade concessions that caused unexpected economic dislocation (i.e. serious injury). In 2001, the WTO reconfirmed the requirement that the serious injury from increased imports must be unforeseen, but over time the need to identify the link between injury and a particular trade concession was discarded. The Safeguards Agreement enhanced the disciplines of Article XIX, most significantly by prohibiting use of the 'grey measures' such as voluntary export restraints (VERs) and orderly marketing agreements that emerged over time outside the scope of Article XIX disciplines. Examples of such 'grey measures' include the United States steel voluntary restraint agreements with various countries in the 1970s, 1980s and early 1990s; its steel trigger price mechanism of the 1970s; and its automotive voluntary restraint agreement with Japan in the 1980s.

Because of the United States role in helping to shape Article XIX, United States domestic law is similar in many respects to the language of Article XIX and the WTO Safeguards Agreement. In key areas, however, there are significant points of tension where United States law either omits wording or differs from Article XIX and the Safeguards Agreement. The result has been a handful of important dispute settlement rulings at the WTO – safeguards involving wheat gluten and lamb meat – finding United States escape clause actions to be inconsistent with its international obligations. Over time, this may lead to amendment of United States law, or a change in practice or procedure, and it remains important for parties involved in Section 201 actions to appreciate how United States law is different and how the United States Government copes with WTO challenges to its practice.

History of Section 201 actions

Between 1974 and the implementation of the WTO Safeguards Agreement in 1995, a total of 63 Section 201 petitions were filed. A little more than half of those petitions led to affirmative injury findings by the Commission. The President declined to take *any* action in more than half of those affirmative findings. Only nine cases resulted in direct trade action within the contemplation of Article XIX. Four other cases led to orderly marketing arrangements or VERs outside the scope of Article XIX. As demonstrated by the numbers, the chance of a domestic industry achieving import relief under Section 201 during the period was a relatively slim one in five, or considerably lower than the success rate under United States anti-dumping (AD) and countervailing duty (CVD) laws.

Since implementation of the WTO Safeguards Agreement, however, domestic industries have achieved a decidedly improved success rate, securing import relief in several cases. Any number of factors may have played a role in this development. Certainly, changing political attitudes on trade, the make-up of the Commission, and the willingness of the White House to grant import relief during this period are among the most important. Another important factor, however, is the prohibition on grey measures imposed by the Safeguards Agreement. By eliminating grey measures as a political outlet and forcing governments to work within the confines of Article XIX and the Safeguards Agreement, the standards for determining the need for import relief, both qualitative and political, may have been adjusted down to accommodate the new environment. Whatever the reason, a law that was once rarely employed because of the limited chance of securing import relief is now finding new popularity.

Comparison to 'unfair' trade laws

It is useful to compare Section 201 to the AD and CVD laws, since both sets of laws address imports and share some of the same procedural concepts. First, as stated above, there is no need under Section 201 to demonstrate that imports are somehow unfair (i.e. dumped or subsidized). There is a distinct requirement, however, that imports be increasing in absolute or relative terms over the period of investigation.

Second, Section 201 may provide more substantial relief from imports than remedies that might otherwise be available under United States AD and CVD laws. Rather than targeting specific countries, Section 201 import relief is generally global and can take the form of duties, quotas, a combination of the two, or other restrictions.

Third, the threshold for demonstrating a need for import relief under Section 201 is generally higher than under AD and CVD laws. In particular, Section 201 concerns itself with 'serious injury' whereas the AD and CVD laws address 'material injury'.

Fourth, any resulting import relief under Section 201 is typically the product of a more intensely political decision subject to far greater external influences. Unlike the imposition of AD or CVD duties, the President is the final arbiter and must be persuaded before import relief can be imposed under Section 201. Moreover, given the involvement of the President in the process, judicial review is limited.

Finally, in another important contrast to the AD and CVD laws, once import relief is secured, the domestic industry will often have to demonstrate that it is making a positive adjustment to import competition, or the relief may be terminated early. Other differences between Section 201 and the AD and CVD laws will also be addressed in this chapter, but these differences are among the most significant.

As an added consideration, as at the end of 2002 important elements of the Section 201 statute, as well as practice and procedure under the statute, have been successfully challenged at the WTO by trading partners of the United States. This creates some uncertainty regarding future practice under United States law, which may be subject to legislative amendment, possible practice and procedure revisions, and probably future WTO challenges, all of which could affect how Section 201 actions are handled.

The mechanics of Section 201

There are two stages to a Section 201 investigation and two main government actors. The first stage of the investigation is known as the injury phase. This includes an investigation by the Commission to determine whether an article is being imported into the United States in such increased quantities as to be a substantial cause of serious injury, or threat thereof, to a domestic industry producing the like or directly competitive article. If the Commission finds serious injury or threat thereof, the process enters the second stage of the investigation, known as the remedy phase. During the remedy phase, the Commission crafts recommendations for action intended to facilitate positive adjustment to import competition for the domestic industry in question. The Commission forwards its affirmative injury finding and remedy recommendation in a report to the President for final consideration and action. The President may take action in the form recommended by the Commission, impose his own remedy, or decline to take any action at all. Each of the relevant steps and issues involved in the process is discussed in greater detail below.

Standing and initiation

There are six separate means by which a Section 201 investigation may be commenced: (1) a petition to the Commission by representatives of the allegedly injured domestic industry; (2) a request of the President; (3) a request of the United States Trade Representative; (4) a request of the House Ways and Means Committee; (5) a request of the Senate Finance Committee; or (6) upon initiation of the Commission itself. All but the first option are exceedingly rare. One of the few limitations on initiation of an investigation is that no investigation will commence, save for good cause shown, with respect to the same subject matter as a previous investigation unless one year has elapsed since the Commission made its report to the President in the prior investigation.

Looking specifically at petitions filed by representatives of the domestic industry, there is virtually no standing requirement to overcome before the Commission will initiate a Section 201 investigation. Unlike the AD and CVD laws, an entity is not required to account for a certain percentage of production (although Commission regulations request an accounting of such production within the petition). The statute merely provides that the Commission shall initiate an investigation upon receipt of a petition from an entity 'representative' of an industry, which might include a trade association, firm, union or group of workers. There are practical limitations to this loose standard, however, and no action should be anticipated if a majority of an industry opposes an investigation.

Industry apathy, however, has been treated somewhat differently. For example, in a Section 201 case involving lamb meat imports, the Commission found injury and recommended import relief based on a petition filed by two trade associations representing lamb feeders and growers, and only a few individual grower, feeder, and meat processing firms. Actual domestic industry participation in the investigation was low. The Commission achieved a questionnaire response rate for the domestic industry of little better than 50% from an extremely narrow cross-section of the industry, ultimately relying on data accounting for only 5% of the domestic lamb slaughter. No adverse inferences were drawn and the investigation eventually led to import relief.

The lamb meat case demonstrates how a minority of relatively motivated interests within an industry can secure import relief under the statute.

There have been only rare instances in which a proceeding was not initiated by a petition from the private sector. Under intense and mounting pressure from the United States steel industry, labour unions and steel state lawmakers, on 22 June 2001 the United States Trade Representative requested the Commission to conduct a Section 201 investigation of steel imports. The action was taken only after the realization that a majority of the Senate Finance

Committee was prepared to make the request itself. Fearing it would lose control of the process and important political leverage on steel and other issues, the Bush Administration elected to take the action.

Whether the steel action will promote greater activism in the Senate Finance Committee and House Ways and Means Committee with respect to requesting Section 201 investigations is uncertain. It proves, however, that government initiation of one variety or another is not beyond the realm of possibility. Taking lessons from the steel case, the situation probably has to be extreme. For example, it took over two years and the collapse of significant portions of the steel industry by 2001 before action was seriously threatened by the Finance Committee and USTR finally made its request. Given the political component of Section 201, any initiation effected by an arm of the government must be considered a significant victory for the domestic industry seeking relief and a major setback for interests opposed to that relief.

The injury phase

Schedule and procedural matters

Normally, the Commission must make its injury determination within 120 days of receipt of a petition or request. If the Commission determines that an investigation is extraordinarily complicated, however, it may extend the deadline up to 30 additional days.

At the beginning of this period, the Commission drafts questionnaires to issue to relevant parties, whether they are domestic producers, foreign producers, exporters, importers or purchasers of the like or directly competitive article at issue. The process is not unlike that seen in AD and CVD investigations, including the opportunity for interested parties to comment on the draft questionnaires before they are distributed. Questionnaire responses often form the core of the Commission's analysis, along with the submissions and testimony of the parties involved in the proceeding.

Upon initiation, the Commission will schedule a hearing for interested parties to present testimony, typically within three months of initiation. Again, the process is not unlike that involved in AD and CVD cases. Questionnaire responses are due before the hearing date and the Commission staff will issue a pre-hearing staff report covering the data collected and research conducted by the staff. The Commission will receive pre-hearing submissions from the interested parties and the Commissioners and Commission staff will appear at the hearing to hear testimony and ask questions of the parties appearing before them. Post-hearing submissions are also made.

All submissions made to the Commission, including the original petition, are eligible for confidential treatment under an administrative protective order (APO).

A final point of similarity is that, as in AD and CVD investigations, a tie vote among the Commissioners on the issue of injury is the same an affirmative finding of injury.

Analytical framework and criteria for determining serious injury or threat thereof

As outlined earlier, Section 201 directs the Commission to conduct an investigation to determine whether an article is being imported into the United States in such increased quantities as to be a substantial cause of serious injury, or threat thereof, to the domestic industry producing an article like or directly competitive with the imported article. Each term in this provision has a distinct meaning under United States statute, with important ties to and potential implications under Article XIX and the WTO Safeguards Agreement.

Increased imports

The first prerequisite under Section 201 is the existence of increased imports. This same requirement is found in Article XIX and is repeated again in the WTO Safeguards Agreement. Under the United States statute or international rules, the increase in imports may be either in absolute terms or relative to domestic production. Less defined is the period over which increased imports are found to exist and the amount of increase required to meet the standard. A five-year window has been the traditional period of investigation for the Commission, although it has made clear that it has the discretion to consider longer or shorter periods as it deems appropriate. Moreover, it has taken the position that no minimum quantity of increase is required. A simple increase is sufficient. The WTO has begun to step in to help better define 'increased imports', particularly with respect to the kind of trends analysis that is acceptable for showing an increase.

Domestic industry and like product

The Commission has to set the scope of its investigation, which is shaped by the nature of the product produced by the allegedly injured domestic industry. Section 201 defines 'domestic industry' as that industry making articles that are 'like' or 'directly competitive' with the imported article. The language is consistent with Article XIX and the WTO Safeguards Agreement, which have identical definitions. The concept of 'like' products is borrowed from AD and CVD practice and essentially means identical articles, but the term 'directly competitive' is unique to safeguards legislation and suggests a more flexible definition. The Commission has used a definition of 'substantially equivalent for commercial purposes', meaning 'adapted to the same uses' and 'essentially interchangeable'. However, United States statutory language also defines 'directly competitive' to potentially encompass products at different stages of processing. This is an important consideration since it theoretically allows the Commission to cobble together an 'industry' from unrelated segments of a production chain.

To illustrate, a producer of semifinished steel might be considered part of the industry producing finished steel in an action against imports of a finished steel product. In reaching such a finding, the Commission could substantially alter the analysis and outcome of a Section 201 investigation depending upon the circumstances.

As at the end of 2002, the Commission has yet to test the bounds of the term 'directly competitive', and it has even rejected arguments using a 'directly competitive' analysis to group products at more attenuated stages of production. More often than not, it has relied on a 'like' product analysis to define the industry and articles involved. The WTO has also yet to examine 'directly competitive' in greater detail, but it has hinted that the term is more expansive – how expansive has yet to be determined in the context of dispute settlement.

Serious injury

'Serious injury' is defined by Section 201 and the WTO Safeguards Agreement as a significant overall impairment in the position of the domestic industry. This is considered to be higher than the 'material injury' standard under United States AD and CVD law. It is noteworthy that in recent years, however, the Commission appears to have recalculated the standard depending on the political climate and the make-up of the Commission. For example, in the

1990s the United States carbon steel wire rod industry filed successive AD and CVD petitions only to be turned away by the Commission, which found no material injury or threat thereof by reason of imports. Nonetheless, in a somewhat remarkable turnaround, the Commission found serious injury by reason of imports in the context of a Section 201 case following the AD and CVD actions. At a minimum, the wire rod cases illustrate that the calculus of serious injury (and also causation) is not always very precise.

There are two prongs to the injury analysis, one focused on current serious injury and the other focused on threat of serious injury (i.e. injury which is 'clearly imminent'). A finding under either prong is sufficient for purposes of an action. In making its determinations, the Commission will consider all economic factors that it deems relevant. With respect to current injury, the Commission is directed to consider the following, non-exclusive set of factors: (1) the significant idling of productive facilities in the domestic industry; (2) the inability of a significant number of firms to carry out domestic production operations at a reasonable level of profit; and (3) significant unemployment or underemployment.

Regarding threat of serious injury, another non-exclusive set of factors is considered, including: (1) a decline in sales or market share, a higher and growing inventory (whether maintained by domestic producers, importers, wholesalers or retailers), and a downward trend in production, profits, wages, productivity, or employment (or increasing underemployment) in the domestic industry; (2) the extent to which firms in the domestic industry are unable to generate adequate capital to finance the modernization of their domestic plants and equipment, or are unable to maintain existing levels of expenditures for research and development; and (3) the extent to which the United States market is the focal point for the diversion of exports of the article concerned by reason of restraints on exports of such article to, or on imports of such article into, third country markets.

Causation

For an industry to achieve import relief under Section 201, imports have to be a 'substantial cause' of the industry's serious injury or threat thereof. United States statute defines 'substantial cause' as one that is important and not less than any other cause. The interplay between this language and the provisions of Article XIX and the WTO Safeguards Agreement is a source of some controversy and confusion. Article XIX and the Agreement merely state that imports must cause or threaten to cause serious injury. In recent dispute settlement cases, WTO panels and the Appellate Body have interpreted the Agreement language to require the demonstration of 'a genuine and substantial relationship of cause and effect' between imports and the injury suffered by the industry. This somewhat nebulous standard has been used to strike down Commission causation methodology and the 'substantial cause' standard.

The WTO rulings are based primarily on a requirement of non-attribution. That is, the competent authorities administering safeguard actions must ensure that other causes of injury are isolated and do not infect the analysis of injury caused by imports. According to the WTO Appellate Body, the 'substantial cause' standard, by weighing the relative causal importance of each factor of injury, does not meet the 'genuine and substantial relationship' standard. The Appellate Body has specified that the Commission must illuminate the process by which it has separated causes, examined each causal factor individually, and ensured that independent causes do not infect the injury cased by imports. Part of this process includes examining all relevant factors of injury raised during the course of the investigation. The battle over causation is probably far from over. At the time of this writing we have yet to see how the Commission intends to adjust its practice.

Unforeseen developments

The issue of unforeseen developments is not addressed under Section 201, but is an important element of Article XIX and the WTO Safeguards Agreement. In the last year, the WTO Appellate Body has reaffirmed the requirement that competent authorities administering safeguard actions must demonstrate, as a matter of fact, that serious injury to a domestic industry by reason of imports was the result of unforeseen developments. Failure to do so compromises the action, and at least one United States action has been declared invalid as a result. Under the circumstances, industries in long-term decline through periods of lower and higher imports, for example, may not be eligible for an action. As with the issue of causation, the Commission has yet to reveal how it will fully implement this WTO requirement.

Limitations on investigations

Except for good cause shown, the Commission will decline to conduct an investigation under Section 201 with respect to the same subject matter as a previous investigation, unless one year has elapsed since the time of the last investigation. Moreover, no investigation will be conducted where the domestic industry in question received import relief as the result of a prior action under Section 201; the moratorium on future investigations is measured roughly by the duration of the previous action.

The remedy phase

Industry adjustment plan

Under Section 201 the domestic industry seeking relief is not required, but is strongly encouraged, to submit an industry adjustment plan detailing how the industry intends to adjust to import competition. While this suggests discretion, failure to submit a plan could compromise the effort and few would consider pursing Section 201 import relief without preparing some sort of adjustment proposal. Under the statute, a formal plan should be submitted to the Commission and the United States Trade Representative at the time of the petition filing, or at any time up to 120 days after the date of the filing of the petition. There is some opportunity for the industry to consult with the United States Trade Representative on its proposal, particularly as it relates to United States international obligations.

Whether or not the industry submits an adjustment plan, the Commission is likely to inquire about adjustment efforts through the questionnaire process. Moreover, if the Commission finds in the affirmative on the issue of serious injury, any entity representative of the industry may submit to the Commission commitments regarding actions such entities intend to take to facilitate positive adjustment to import competition. All of these proposals and commitments will be factored into the Commission's separate recommendations on an appropriate remedy and the President's decision to impose a remedy.

Commission proceedings, remedy recommendations

The Commission must submit a report to the President containing its findings on injury and recommendations on relief for the domestic industry no later than 180 days after the date on which the petition was filed. This gives the Commission 30–60 days to consider the issue of relief after making its injury determinations (depending on whether the Commission considered the case 'complex' and extended the injury decision deadline to 150 days). This means yet another hearing at the Commission, with submissions and testimony offered by parties in favour and in opposition to the action. The purpose of the proceeding is to arrive at recommendations for relief that provide 'greater economic and social benefits than costs'.

In crafting the Commission's remedy recommendations, only those Commissioners who voted in the affirmative on injury can propose recommendations. As a result, there is a strong incentive for Commissioners who would otherwise find no injury to find injury in cases where a final affirmative determination is assured (i.e. cases split 3–3 or better). This allows those Commissioners to play some role in the remedy phase. Commissioners are authorized to recommend a number of different relief actions, including: (1) an increase in, or the imposition of, any duty on the imported article; (2) a tariff rate quota on the article; (3) a modification or imposition of any quantitative restriction on the importation of the article into the United States; (4) one or more appropriate adjustment measures, including the provision of trade adjustment assistance (effectively domestic support subsidies for firms and employees); or (5) any combination of the first four actions described.

In addition to these recommendations, the Commission may also recommend that the President initiate international negotiations to address the underlying cause of the increase in imports of the article or otherwise to alleviate the injury or threat. It may also recommend any other action otherwise authorized under law that is likely to facilitate positive adjustment to import competition.

While Commissioners will vote on a final recommended remedy, there is no requirement that the recommendation receive unanimous or even majority support among the Commissioners before being sent to the President. Indeed, multiple recommendations, representing the views of different Commissioners, may be included in the final report sent to the President.

Presidential determination and remedy implementation

After receiving the Commission's report, the President is tasked with taking all appropriate actions within his power to facilitate the efforts of the domestic industry to make a positive adjustment to import competition. His powers are entirely discretionary, however, and it is at this point in the process that all the political pressures surrounding the issue come to the forefront. To the extent that parties with an interest in the investigation have invested time and resources in convincing political power bases within the United States Government of their positions (e.g. Congress or relevant Executive Branch agencies), these forces will play out in the remedy decision. Lawmakers will lobby the White House and an interagency body representing various interests within the Executive Branch, headed by the United States Trade Representative, will debate the merits of the case.

Ultimately, the President makes the final decision on relief. In doing so, he will take into account the positions of various lawmakers, the findings of his own interagency debate, and also the findings and recommendations of the Commission. Like the recommendations of the Commission, his decision is to be based upon implementing relief that provides greater economic and social benefits than costs, with a host of additional, related factors to be weighed. As specified by statute, these additional factors include: (1) the adjustment efforts made and to be implemented by the domestic industry; (2) the probable effectiveness of any import relief actions to facilitate positive industry adjustment; (3) other factors related to the national economic interest of the United States; (4) the extent to which there is a diversion of foreign exports to the United States marked by reason of foreign restraints; (5) the potential circumvention of any import action taken; and (6) the national security interests of the United States. All actions within the realm of recommendation by the Commission are at his disposal.

Under the statute, the President shall take action in response to an affirmative Commission report within 60 days of its receipt. Underscoring the depth of the President's discretion, however, the 60-day deadline has not proven to be a binding requirement. Notwithstanding the explicit direction of the statute, the President has delayed decisions in response to an affirmative Commission report for well beyond the 60-day period. For example, in a recent Section 201 action on carbon steel wire rod, the Clinton Administration received the report of the Commission in July 1999, yet the President did not act to impose import relief until February 2000. The timing of the action was as much political as it was anything else, intended to capitalize on prevailing political winds.

It is important to stress that it is of little or no use to challenge the President through United States courts on the issue of delay, as litigation might only antagonize rather than benefit the situation. The President must still issue his decision, and a court challenge is unlikely to create a more favourable result.

Once a decision is made to take action, the President will publish his decision in the *Federal Register*. On the day that action is taken, the White House will also transmit to Congress a document describing the reasons for taking the action. If the President's action is different from the Commission recommendations, including a decision to take no action, the document shall set forth the reasons for the difference. Congress, in turn, may pass a joint resolution demanding implementation of the Commission-recommended relief within the 90-day period beginning on the date on which the document setting forth the reasons for the President's actions was transmitted to Congress.

Scope of relief and limitations

NAFTA exception

For purposes of its investigation, the Commission is bound by United States statute instituted as a result of the North American Free Trade Agreement (NAFTA) which requires a separate injury analysis with respect to articles imported from Mexico and Canada. Under this separate analysis, the Commission must determine whether imports from Mexico or Canada, by themselves, result in serious injury to the domestic industry. Only if the Commission investigation results in an affirmative serious injury finding (or threat of serious injury in the case of Mexico) on this point may a trade remedy be applied against imports from Mexico or Canada.

The provision is the source of great controversy as it allows the Commission to aggregate imports from Mexico and Canada with other imports as part of its overall analysis of serious injury to the domestic industry under Section 201, then carves out an exception with respect to the two countries. The WTO has found the provision inconsistent with United States international obligations, and particularly the most favoured nation principle. Treatment under the provision is necessarily unequal. While it is still too early to tell how the United States will respond to the WTO finding, early indications are that the Commission will qualify its injury analysis by determining whether increased imports, except for those imports from Mexico and Canada, are a source of serious injury or threat thereof. Whether or not this complies with WTO disciplines will likely be the subject of future dispute settlement.

Other limitations on scope and duration of relief

Import relief under Section 201 is not without end, and there are a number of limitations placed on the scope and duration involved. With respect to scope, import relief should be available only to the extent necessary to prevent or remedy serious injury. This limitation ends up being a major point of debate during the remedy proceedings at the Commission and again once the Commission's report is in the hands of the President. Beyond this basic principle, no action may be taken which would increase a rate of duty to more than 50% *ad valorem* above the rate existing at the time the action is taken.

Finally, any quantitative restriction imposed shall permit the importation of a quantity or value of the article which is not less than the average quantity of such article imported into the United States in the most recent three years that are representative of imports of such article and for which data are available, unless the President finds that the importation of a different quantity or value is clearly justified in order to prevent or remedy the serious injury. Any relief effective for a period of more than one year is to be phased down at regular intervals during the period in which the action is in effect.

Regarding duration, no action taken by the President shall exceed four years, unless it is determined that the action continues to be necessary to prevent or remedy serious injury and there is evidence that the domestic industry is making a positive adjustment to import competition. Such a decision takes place within the context of an extension investigation conducted by the Commission (discussed later in this chapter). In the aggregate, however, the effective period of any action taken by the President under Section 201 may not last longer than eight years.

Provisional relief for agricultural products/critical circumstances

Section 201 contains certain provisions that circumvent the normal schedule involved in an injury investigation and jumpstart the application of trade measures where warranted.

Perishable agricultural products

Representatives of an industry producing perishable agricultural products may petition the Commission for provisional relief, provided that such product has been the subject of import monitoring by the Commission for at least 90 days prior to the request for provisional relief. The United States Trade Representative administers such requests for monitoring and is authorized to request the Commission to commence such monitoring.

Once a petition for provisional relief is received by the Commission, it has 21 days in which to determine whether increased imports of the perishable agricultural good in question are a substantial cause of serious injury or threat thereof to the domestic industry. Part of this determination involves an assessment of whether the serious injury would be difficult to repair after or could not be prevented during a full 180-day investigation as envisioned under normal procedures. An affirmative determination and recommendations on relief are forwarded to the President, who has seven days in which to consider the matter and provide any provisional relief. The provision relief remains in effect for the duration of the Commission's full investigation. The full investigation moves forward whether the Commission makes an affirmative or negative finding on provision relief.

Critical circumstances

A petitioner may allege in its petition that critical circumstances exist. As with the perishable agricultural product provision, the issue for the Commission is to determine whether any delay in relief would result in undue damage to the domestic industry in question.

Under the statute, critical circumstances are considered to exist if: (1) there is clear evidence that increased imports of the article are a substantial cause of serious injury, or threat thereof, to the domestic industry; and (2) delay in taking action would cause damage that would be difficult to repair.

Within 60 days of receiving a critical circumstances allegation, the Commission is required to make its determination and forward any affirmative finding in a report to the President along with recommendations for appropriate provisional relief. The President has 30 days upon receipt of the Commission report containing its determination and recommendations to determine whether any provisional relief is warranted. Typically, any relief would be in the form of a tariff.

Regardless of the critical circumstances determination, the Commission continues its full investigation, but its timetable for the injury phase begins only after it has completed its critical circumstances investigation and determination. Any provisional relief terminates when:

❑ The Commission reaches a negative final determination on injury;

❑ The President takes more permanent action in response to a final affirmative finding on injury;

❑ The President declines to take permanent action; or

❑ The President determines that the provisional relief is no longer warranted as a result of changed circumstances.

Provisional relief may not exceed 200 days.

Related proceedings

Mid-term monitoring investigation

Section 201 includes some checks on the domestic industries that have successfully secured relief. There is at least some degree of oversight of industry efforts to make a positive adjustment to import competition, with the risk of losing relief before the full term of relief is completed.

In any investigation that results in action exceeding three years, the Commission is required to conduct a mid-term review of the action to investigate and report to the White House on the developments related to the domestic industry and the industry's efforts to make a positive adjustment to import competition. A similar review takes place if an extension of the action is granted beyond three years. The report is due not later than the mid-point of the initial period in which the action is in effect, and of each such extension during which the action is in effect. Upon the request of the President, the Commission shall also advise the President of its judgement on the probable economic effect on the industry concerned of any reduction, modification, or termination of the action which is under consideration.

For practical purposes, a mid-term review is always conducted, as it has been the practice of the White House to grant initial relief for a period of three years and one day. The review itself is not unlike an original Section 201 investigation in that the Commission will issue questionnaires and a staff report, hold a hearing and entertain submissions and testimony from interested parties. The Commission recently instituted APO procedures for mid-term reviews, allowing counsel access to confidential information.

Upon receipt of the Commission mid-term review report, the President may reduce, modify or terminate the action. His decision may be based on changed circumstances related to domestic industry adjustment efforts (or lack thereof) or other developments that have rendered the action ineffective. Likewise, a majority of the representatives can petition the President for reduction, modification or termination.

The mid-term review process under existing United States law has a limited history. There is some indication that the degree of scrutiny applied by the Commission is limited, and the review perfunctory. Until June 2001, relief had been terminated early as a result of a mid-term review in only one instance, and only after the domestic industry involved failed to even participate in the proceeding. This may change over time, but in the handful of actions reviewed the outcome has been continued relief even when significant doubts were raised about the continued efficacy of the action. For parties opposing continued relief, any effort made during the mid-term review is often viewed as an investment toward blocking any extension of the action when the initial relief expires.

Extension investigation

As stated earlier, any initial action taken under Section 201 can last no longer than four years. To extend the period, an interested party must petition the Commission or convince the President to make the request himself. In response to the petition or request, the Commission shall investigate whether the action continues to be necessary to prevent or remedy serious injury and whether there is evidence that the industry is making a positive adjustment to import competition. The petition or request must take place within nine months of and no later than six months before the date of the original action under Section 201 is scheduled to terminate. The Commission, in turn, must issue a report regarding the investigation no later than 60 days before the original action is set to expire. Once again, the process involves a hearing, with the Commission affording interested parties an opportunity to appear, present testimony and offer other submissions. Based on the report findings, the President has the authority to extend the action for a period not to exceed eight years in the aggregate from the date of the original action.

Judicial review

Judicial review is extremely limited in the context of Section 201 cases. While procedural irregularities at the Commission might be a basis for challenge, where the President is involved the courts have historically shown extreme deference. Since there is no explicit statutory authorization to appeal, it is unlikely a court would agree to hear the case or reverse a Presidential decision.

Safeguard restrictions on steel

Although the focus of this book is to provide more a general explanation of United States law and practice, an important recent development merits some additional discussion. In March 2002, President Bush decided to impose wide-ranging restrictions on steel imports pursuant to the United States safeguard law, Section 201 of the Trade Act of 1974. This decision, and the ongoing foreign reactions to it, could have far-reaching consequences for future safeguard proceedings.

This section provides a brief summary of the background that led to this decision and the various stages in the proceeding, followed by a brief summary of the foreign reactions to date. Please note that, as this book goes to publication, this trade dispute is still evolving and will continue to evolve over the next few years.

The decision to begin the case

In the late 1990s the United States steel industry once again began to seek special protection. (The United States steel industry has a history of more than three decades of requesting various types of import protection.) Following what was perceived to be a surge of steel imports in 1998, the industry, the union, and the Steel Caucus in Congress made several efforts to persuade the Clinton Administration to self-initiate a Section 201 case to address the so-called import problem. But these efforts were successfully blocked.

From 2000, economic conditions have worsened. In the second half of 2000, the manufacturing sector of the United States economy began to suffer and United States demand for steel fell sharply. By 2001, several high-profile steel companies had begun to threaten or declare bankruptcy. With weak demand and substantial new domestic capacity, domestic steel prices were at record lows.

More importantly, the political dynamics changed and forces emerged that pushed for a congressionally initiated Section 201 case against steel imports. The White House announced in June 2001 that President Bush would request the Section 201 investigation.

The Commission injury investigation

The Commission began its injury investigation in July 2001. Under United States law, all Section 201 cases must include a factual investigation into whether the domestic industry is suffering serious injury, and whether increased imports are a substantial cause of that serious injury. But this particular case involved a number of unusual issues.

The first novel issue involved the scope of the investigation. The President's request included virtually all types of steel products. The Commission's first task was to figure out how to organize its product-by-product analysis. The union argued for a single like product: all steel. The domestic steel mills argued for four broad like products: flat-rolled carbon steel; long products; pipe and tube; and stainless and tool steel products. The foreign respondents argued that the Commission should follow its traditional like product categories from prior trade cases, and divide steel into a variety of specific products. For example, carbon flat-rolled steel would be divided into slab, plate, hot-rolled, cold-rolled, corrosion resistant, and other specific products. After some initial argumentation back and forth, the Commission decided to collect data for both narrowly defined and broadly defined like products, so that it could decide the issue later. Consequently, the Commission collected complete data for 33 different steel product categories. This meant, effectively, that the Commission's investigation consisted of 33 cases in one.

The second novel issue was the inclusion of slab in the investigation. There had been a fierce battle in the industry discussions with the Administration about whether to include iron ore, and whether to include slab. Both of these products, which are feedstock for the production of finished steel products, were imported by a small group of United States finished steel producers. In the end, the Administration decided not to include iron ore, but to include slab. This decision set the stage for a rare split among the domestic mills – a battle between those mills that imported slab to roll into downstream products, and those mills that primarily produced their own slab. The unique status of slab, as the one product imported in large quantities by the domestic mills themselves, continued throughout the case.

The third novel issue was the pace of the investigation. This case was enormously complicated, with more different products and more different issues than any other recent Section 201 case. The foreign respondents wanted more time to prepare their defence. But the domestic industry and its allies knew that a quick investigation would work to their advantage. So they generated strong pressure on the Commission not to extend the case. In the end, although the statute arguably allowed it to do so, the Commission decided not to extend the case, and instead pushed ahead on a normal schedule.

The fourth novel issue was the extent of economic argumentation. In light of the recent Appellate Body jurisprudence on the need to separate and distinguish the various causes of injury, respondents decided to make a major effort to document and quantify the alternative causes. They hired economic experts to prepare various statistical and econometric analyses. The domestic industry also hired economic experts. Much more than in any other Section 201 cases, there were extensive and detailed economic and econometric arguments about what truly was causing the difficulties of the domestic industry.

The fifth novel issue was the fact that many of the imported steel products – and virtually all the sensitive flat-rolled products – were already subject to anti-dumping and countervailing duty (anti-subsidy) cases. It was rather unusual for the United States Government to seek an extra layer of protection when it was obvious that the anti-dumping and subsidy cases had already begun to restrain imports of steel.

In October 2001, the Commission found 'serious injury' caused by imports for most of the products covered by the President's request, including the large flat rolled category. The details of what each Commissioner found varied, but the main elements of the decision were as follows:

❑ On *like product*, most Commissioners adopted a broad definition of flat-rolled steel – including both slab and the various finished flat-rolled products. For the other categories, the Commissioners tended to adopt narrower categories of like products.

❑ On *serious injury*, the Commission found most segments of the domestic industry to have been injured. Although the decision went through all the various statutory factors, the key element appears to have been financial losses. If the segment of the domestic industry had been suffering negative operating losses, the Commission found serious injury. The only segments for which the Commission did not find serious injury were those with positive operating income.

❑ On *increased imports*, the Commission generally found this requirement to have been met. In its finding, the Commission followed United States law, which allows an increase of any size to meet the statutory requirement. Thus, as long as the absolute level of imports was higher in 2000 than in 1996, the Commission found an increase.

❑ On *causation*, the Commission generally found that imports were the most important cause.

The Commission therefore made affirmative injury findings for about half of the different like products, but those findings covered about 70% of the steel being imported into the United States. None of the commercially significant products escaped.

The Commission remedy investigation

The Commission then turned to its remedy investigation. Under United States law, if the Commission finds serious injury in the initial phase, it then begins a separate proceeding to prepare recommendations to the President about what remedy to impose.

At this stage, more end-users became involved. Typically end-users are slow to organize, and this case was no exception. Although there was some end-user participation in the injury phase, in general users were reluctant to become involved.

The domestic industry argued generally for 40% tariffs. The industry goal was to shut as much imported steel out of the market as possible. Such high tariffs, on top of other anti-dumping and countervailing duties already in place, would largely block imports from the market. The domestic industry theme was consistently that only strong measures would give the United States industry the 'time out' necessary to restructure and recover.

The foreign industries argued for either no restrictions or more modest restrictions. The Europeans most strenuously argued for no restrictions at all. Other major steel exporting countries, such as Brazil, Japan and the Republic of Korea, argued for no restrictions, but then also argued in the alternative for less restrictive alternatives such as quotas or tariff rate quotas at historical levels. Rather than blocking imports completely, such quantitative limits would allow some imports to continue in the market, but would prevent any future surges from injuring the industry.

The problem with the foreign industry argument, however, was that import levels had already fallen dramatically. The various unfair trade cases had largely shut out many steel products, so 2001 import levels were already considerably lower than import levels in 2000 or prior years. The various quota recommendations would therefore not be binding: any reasonable approach to historical import volumes would set the quota level higher than current import levels. This approach to remedy, while economically sensible, would be politically unacceptable, since it did not provide for any further roll-back of import volumes.

In the end, the majority of the Commission recommended 20% tariffs on most products. The individual Commissioners split. One Commissioner opted for tariff rate quotas. Two Commissioners agreed with the domestic industry demand for 40% tariffs. But the three remaining Commissioners agreed on 20% tariffs on flat-rolled steel, and somewhat lower tariffs on some other products.

Interestingly, slab was treated differently. Although slab had been considered part of the single flat-rolled like product in the injury determination, the Commission recognized that slab was different from other finished flat-rolled products. So the remedy recommendation was for a tariff rate quota, with the 20% tariff applying only after a certain tonnage had been imported.

The Commission then released its written report. Under United States practice, the Commission does not describe in detail its injury findings or remedy recommendations until after both phases are finished. The three-volume report contains 560 pages of determinations by the various Commissioners on the various products and issues, and an equivalent amount of tables and data from the staff.

The USTR remedy phase

The proceedings then turned to the USTR remedy phase. Under United States law, the Commission recommends some form of relief on the products for which it makes affirmative injury findings, but the President then has discretion to make whatever decision he would like. Given this flexibility, the President typically has his own staff conduct its own investigation to collect information, study the markets, and assess how different constituencies feel about the proposed actions.

Both sides held repeated meetings with USTR officials and representatives of the interagency committee that helps to advise the President (known as the Trade Policy Staff Committee or TPSC). Many agencies in the United States Government weigh in on such trade policy issues, and working level officials from each of these agencies were given the chance to attend hearings at which interested parties made presentations. Beyond these formal meetings, both sides also had repeated informal meetings with various agency officials. All of this reflected normal practice for high-profile, politically contentious safeguard investigations.

At this stage, the efforts to obtain targeted product exclusions intensified. Although the Commission has been reluctant to address the exclusion issues directly, the USTR process focused very much on exclusions. USTR invited formal applications for exclusions, and made the arguments for and against exclusions a major part of this stage of the proceedings.

The President's decision

After all the 'legal proceedings' had finished, President Bush had to make a decision. The Commission process and the USTR process had generated lots of data and set up various options, but the President had to decide. Under the law it was up to him whether to accept the Commission recommendation, reject it completely and impose no remedy, or devise his own remedy.

The economic advisers recommended that the President take no action. The various economic arguments were quite strong that although the domestic industry was suffering, the role of imports in causing those difficulties was limited at best. Moreover, the economic advisers were concerned about two other major issues. First, import protection probably would impose more harm on downstream user industries than it would benefit the domestic steel industry. Second, such a blatant act of protectionism would send the wrong signal to trading partners. At a time when the United States was trying to lead countries to liberalize trade as part of the Doha Round, imposing protection for the steel industry would trigger backsliding by other countries.

The political advisers, however, recommended strong action to restrict imports. Steel workers were concentrated in politically key states, and were very active. Although the number of steel workers had shrunk, there were many more retirees and dependents who relied on the flow of retirement and health care benefits provided by the steel mills. The domestic steel industry had commissioned many polls and analyses of the political impact of protecting the steel industry, and argued this point forcefully.

President Bush decided to impose 30% tariffs on most steel products. Some smaller volume products received lower tariff rates, but the large quantity flat-rolled carbon steel products were subject to a uniform 30% tariff. (Slab was the only exception, and was subjected to a tariff rate quota, with a 30% duty on the amount in excess of the quota.) This decision was surprising, in that the President adopted more severe import restrictions than recommended by the majority of the Commission.

President Bush moderated the decision in two ways. First, he excluded developing countries from the restrictions. Second, he also excluded certain specific products from the scope of the remedy, and announced that future exclusions might be forthcoming. Although a lot of effort had gone into the exclusions process, the sheer number of exclusions clogged the system, and only a fraction of them were acted upon in the initial decision. But by opening the door to future exclusions, the Administration kept its political options open and maintained some influence over how the process would unfold.

Foreign reactions

The initial reaction was largely shock at both the decision and the nature of the remedy. The number of products restricted and the magnitude of the restrictions surprised many.

As the details emerged, many countries expressed dissatisfaction with the process and the outcome. In their view the process had made clear that imports were not really the problem. Indeed, import levels had been falling since 1998, not increasing.

What is evident from reviewing the President's decision is that the burden of the safeguard measures is not spread equally among suppliers to the United States market. Much of the burden is imposed on suppliers in the Republic of Korea, Japan, and the European Union. For example, in carbon steel flat products (a category which includes slab, plate, hot-rolled flat products, cold-rolled flat products, and corrosion-resistant flat products), of the five largest traditional suppliers to the United States market only the Republic of Korea and Japan are significantly affected by the import relief. Canada and Mexico, both countries which shipped high volumes of flat products in every year from 1996 to 2000, are completely excluded from the relief. This differential treatment becomes even clearer when one takes into account the developing countries that the United States excluded from the import restraints. Looking at carbon and alloy flat-rolled steel, for example, in absolute volume, the increase from excluded developing countries over 1996–2000 was eight times the increase from countries subject to the relief.

Foreign countries responded in several ways. First, many countries began to impose their own restrictions on steel imports. Citing the likely shift of export volumes to their own markets, many countries imposed various forms of monitoring and steel restrictions of their own. By 30 June 2002, according to press reports, the following countries had reacted in some way:

Country	Action
Algeria	Tariffs on welded and seamless tubes have been provisionally raised from 15% to 63% to protect local producers.
Argentina	Producers asked the Government to hike steel tariffs to 30% from 5%–20%.
Bolivia	Tariff increases of up to 35% were under consideration, over the concern that Section 201 restraints could divert up to 15 million tons of steel to Latin America.
Brazil	Under the steel monitoring system implemented on 21 February, the Brazilian customs authority heightened its scrutiny of steel imports from Japan, the Republic of Korea, Taiwan Province (China), and Malaysia, as 'a defensive measure to protect Brazilian steel' from imports deflected from the United States market by import restraints imposed under Section 201. Each import shipment must gain a licence from the Government.
Canada	The Canadian Government initiated a steel safeguards investigation into 10 steel products on 22 March and made affirmative findings on some of these products.

Country	Action
Chile	*Prompted by the threat of imports displaced by Section 201 restraints, Chilean producers initiated a safeguards action requesting duties of up to 35%. After Chilean regulators rejected this request on 11 April, the lower house of the Chilean Congress unanimously voted to ask President Ricardo Lagos to impose temporary safeguard measures against steel imports.*
China	*China imposed anti-dumping duties of 20%–32% on cold-rolled steel imports from the Republic of Korea, Taiwan Province (China), the Russian Federation, Ukraine and Kazakhstan, and the trade press suggested that the tariffs were partly in response to the United States steel safeguard measure. The Chinese Government was to impose tariffs of 7%–26% on nine steel products in retaliation for the United States safeguard measures.*
Colombia	*Colombian producers requested a doubling of duties on steel imports. In anticipation of the imposition of safeguard measures, the Colombian Government requested permission from the Andean Community, a customs union, to increase its steel tariffs.*
European Union	*On 27 March, the EU initiated a safeguards investigation and adopted provisional safeguard measures on steel imports on the grounds that the European steel industry was threatened by the 15 million tons of steel imports diverted by the United States steel safeguard measures. The action imposed tariff rate quotas on the same 15 steel products covered by the United States measures, with the quota for each product equal to the 2001 import volume plus limited growth and out-of-quota tariffs of 14.9%–26%.*
Hungary	*Hungary was to impose provisional safeguard measures beginning 3 June in the form of tariff-rate quotas on 15 steel products. The quotas were to be based on average import levels during the 1998–2000 period plus 10%, and out-of-quota tariffs would be either 20% or 25%.*
Indonesia	*The Indonesian Government planned to hike duties on hot-rolled and cold-rolled steel by 15%.*
Republic of Korea	*The Republic of Korea entered into 'intensive discussions' with Malaysia, Thailand, Indonesia, and Taiwan Province (China) to prevent any market disruptions following import restraints imposed under Section 201.*
Malaysia	*The Malaysian Government doubled steel tariffs to as high as 50%, retroactive to 15 March.*
Mexico	*In a 'clear response' to the threat of Section 201 action, Mexico increased import duties on 39 steel products to 35%, from 13%–18%, on imports from all but 31 countries with which it has free trade agreements.*
Peru	*Tariff increases of up to 35% were under consideration.*
Poland	*Poland was to impose provisional safeguard measures on steel imports in late June or early July.*
Thailand	*Thailand imposed temporary import surcharges of 25% on hot-rolled and cold-rolled steel, 5% on galvanized steel, and 15% on stainless steel, effective for six months.*
Venezuela	*After completing a safeguards investigation initiated in September 2001, the Venezuelan Government imposed safeguard tariffs of 20%–35% on steel imports.*

Second, many countries also decided to challenge the United States actions in the WTO. The EU filed the first case (DS248), and was quickly followed by Japan (DS249), the Republic of Korea (DS251), China (DS252), Switzerland

(DS253), Norway (DS254), New Zealand (DS258), and Brazil (DS259). These cases are all moving forward in a single consolidated panel.

The EU and Japan also began to explore the feasibility of immediate compensation for the damage their industries had suffered. Under Article 8.3 of the Safeguards Agreement, Members agree to suspend for three years their right to compensation for safeguard actions taken by another Member, but only if the Member imposing safeguards has followed the Safeguards Agreement, and only if there has been an absolute increase in import levels. The EU and Japan believe that the United States did not act in conformity with the Agreement, including the increased imports requirements, and therefore took procedural steps to assert their right to immediate compensation. The United States insists that it found absolute increases and was otherwise in compliance with the Agreement, and argued that the EU and Japan must wait for the WTO dispute settlement process to unfold before acting.

In the end the United States decided to exclude enough EU and Japanese products from the scope of the Section 201 remedy that both the EU and Japan decided not to push this issue. Both the EU and Japan decided not to push ahead with their demands for immediate compensation, and decided instead to wait for the WTO process to run its normal course. Clarification of the meaning of Article 8.3 will have to wait for a future case.

As this process unfolded, the Administration made clear that future exclusions would be intertwined with actions by foreign countries.

These issues are still very much evolving. As this book goes to press, many of them are still pending. But however these specific issues are resolved, the various trade disputes over steel will shape the future direction of both the steel trade and the administration of safeguard measures.

Chapter 8
Section 337: Protecting intellectual property

Section 337 of the Tariff Act of 1930 provides a potential trade remedy for domestic producers to use against certain specified unfair acts and practices involving imported merchandise. Specifically, the statute prohibits unfair methods of competition and unfair acts involving the importation of merchandise, including primarily the infringement of a valid and enforceable United States patent, copyright, registered trademark or mask works.

This distinctive provision of United States law creates a special forum for these actions with expedited, specially tailored procedures, and a limited but powerful remedy. If a violation of Section 337 is found, infringing products and downstream products containing infringing articles may be excluded from entry into the United States. Given the rather draconian sanction, foreign companies need to be particularly sensitive to possible problems with this law.

Legal requirements

Section 337 is a specialized remedy that dates back to 1922 and is intended to protect United States industries. Several requirements must be satisfied before a company can bring a Section 337 action. First, there must be an unfair act or practice. In most cases, this means that the company filing the complaint must be the owner or exclusive licensee of a valid and enforceable United States patent, copyright, registered trademark or mask work. The company must also be able to show that the patent, copyright or other intellectual property is being infringed by imported merchandise.

Another requirement under Section 337 concerns the domestic industry. Because the law was written to protect domestic industries, a Section 337 complainant must show that there is a domestic industry in the United States relating to the articles that are protected by the patent, copyright, trademark or other intellectual property. (This is known as the economic prong of the domestic industry test.) In general, it is not difficult to make this showing. The statute specifies that an industry in the United States will be considered to exist if there is in the United States with respect to the articles concerned: (a) significant investment in plant and equipment; (b) significant employment of labour or capital; or (c) substantial investment in its exploitation, including engineering, research and development, or licensing.

It is not sufficient, however, to merely show that a domestic industry exists. A Section 337 complainant must also show that the domestic industry is exploiting the intellectual property at issue. (This is known as the technical prong of the domestic industry test.) For example, where the allegation of an unfair act involves patent infringement, the complainant must show that the patent is practised in the United States and that there is significant activity exploiting the patent. Thus, if the entire manufacturing, packaging, and quality control of the patented product occurs outside of the United States, the technical prong of the United States industry requirement may not be satisfied. If the patents cover the elements of an article and those elements are considered essential to the finished product, however, the Commission has found that the assembly of the elements into the finished article in the United States is sufficient to satisfy the technical prong of the domestic industry test.

Prior to 1988, it was not sufficient to simply show that a domestic industry existed and that the industry exploited the intellectual property in question. To be entitled to relief under Section 337, the complainant also had to show that the domestic industry was being injured as a result of the infringing imports. Growing concern about lost sales attributed to foreign counterfeiting and infringement of United States intellectual property rights, however, led to the elimination of the injury requirement in the Omnibus Trade and Competitiveness Act of 1988 for alleged unfair practices involving intellectual property rights. If other unfair methods of competition and/or unfair acts involving imported merchandise are alleged, the complainant must show that the threat or effect of the imports is to: (a) destroy or substantially injure an industry in the United States; (b) prevent the establishment of such an industry; or (c) restrain or monopolize trade and commerce in the United States.

Limitations

Along with the special benefits it provides for qualified domestic parties, the statute also imposes certain limitations. First, the only remedies provided (discussed in greater detail below) are equitable in nature – general or specific exclusion orders or cease and desist orders. The Commission cannot award monetary damages.

Second, although respondents are permitted to raise any counterclaim at the Commission, the statute requires respondents to immediately remove any counterclaim to the appropriate United States district court. Consequently respondents' ability to raise issues and claims that are not directly related to the original complaint are limited.

This limitation on counterclaims does not, however, affect respondents' ability to raise legal or equitable defences in the Section 337 proceeding. Respondents can and do routinely challenge the patent's validity, asserting waiver, estoppel, implied licence, anticipation, obviousness, inequitable conduct, and other issues.

The Section 337 forum

Section 337 is administered by the United States International Trade Commission, an independent, quasi-judicial agency, whose six Commissioners serve nine-year terms. No more than three Commissioners may be members of the same political party. Unlike federal courts, the Commission can hear any and all Section 337 cases; that is, it has nationwide jurisdiction based on the allegedly infringing articles and the subject matter (the alleged infringement). There are no other venue or personal jurisdictional requirements (other than service of process). Appeals of the Commission's determinations under Section 337 are taken directly to the United States Court of Appeals for the Federal Circuit.

In Section 337 proceedings, an administrative law judge (ALJ) conducts the investigation, supervises discovery, holds trial-like hearings, and makes the initial determination. ALJs are career civil servants who function like federal district court judges in civil cases, but there is no jury. The ALJs at the Commission are hired exclusively to deal with Section 337 proceedings. Because almost all cases involve intellectual property, the ALJs develop specialized expertise in this area.

The ALJs are assisted in Section 337 proceedings by a staff attorney assigned from the Commission's General Counsel's Office. The role of the Commission's investigative attorney is unique. The staff attorney is a full party to the proceeding and his or her role is to protect the public interest. As a result, although essentially neutral, the staff attorney assists in the administrative adjudication process and can initiate discovery, examine witnesses, and elicit facts and evidence to clarify contested issues and help to assure the development of a full and complete record.

The procedures for Section 337 investigations

As indicated above, Section 337 investigations are administrative, not judicial, proceedings. The advantage of these administrative proceedings is that they are narrowly focused and highly condensed. In general, Section 337 investigations are completed within 12–18 months from the date of initiation.

The proceedings are normally initiated by the filing of a complaint by a qualified domestic entity with the Commission's Office of Unfair Import Investigations. Although the Commission has the authority to self-initiate a Section 337 investigation, it has never done so.

The complaint must meet certain minimum requirements, which are detailed and extensive. Because the proceedings move at such a rapid pace, the requirements are designed so that the complaint itself establishes a *prima facie* case that would warrant relief under the statute. When the complaint is filed, the Commission has 30 days to review the complaint to determine whether it satisfies the regulatory requirements or whether it should be discarded as frivolous, premature, or incomplete. During this period, the staff may request additional information to cure technical deficiencies, and the complaint may be amended without constraint.

Once the staff is convinced that the complaint is in order and has been properly filed, the case will be initiated. Once it is initiated, the Commission has 45 days to establish a target date for completion. Discovery may commence immediately after initiation. The investigations conducted by the Commission require formal evidentiary hearings in accordance with the Administrative Procedure Act. The rules of evidence and procedures that are employed are very similar to the Federal Rules of Civil Procedure, though not as strict.

The proceedings in a Section 337 investigation roll out under a very compressed time frame. The response to the complaint is due 20 days from the date of service. A preliminary conference to structure discovery and discuss issues is usually held 1–2 months from the date of initiation. The hearing is usually held 7–8 months from the date of initiation, unless it is a complicated case.

The initial proceedings and hearing are held before an ALJ. Following the initial proceedings, the ALJ issues an initial determination on all issues related to violations of Section 337 (generally 9–10 months from the date of initiation) and a recommended determination on issues related to the applicable remedy (usually within 14 days of the initial determination). The Commissioners may review and modify the initial determination (usually done within 3 months). If the Commission does not review the initial determination, it becomes the Commission's decision.

Another interesting aspect of Section 337 proceedings is that the Commission determinations are subject to Presidential review. As a result, if the Commission determines that there is a violation of Section 337 and issues an affirmative finding and a remedy, the agency's determination may not become final for 60 days. During that period, the President receives a copy of the Commission's determination and may review the decision. The President can disapprove the determination for policy reasons. If the President disapproves the determination, the Commission's decision will have no force or effect. The President may also approve the determination, in which case it will take effect on the date the Commission is notified of the President's approval.

Remedies and penalties for violation of Section 337

The reason Section 337 proceedings are so attractive to domestic producers and so threatening to United States importers and foreign producers is the severe remedies that can be obtained. If the Commission finds a violation of Section 337, it will issue either orders excluding the products from entry into the United States (exclusion orders) or orders directing United States parties to cease and desist from selling the articles (cease and desist orders), or both.

If an exclusion order is issued, the United States Customs Service becomes the enforcement agent. The Customs Service will monitor imports at all ports of entry, 24 hours a day, at no cost to the domestic producer and will exclude from entry into the United States all articles that the Commission has found to infringe the intellectual property right in question. In addition, the exclusion orders may prohibit the entry of products that contain the infringing product.

Exclusion orders are used to reach the foreign suppliers and/or importers of the infringing merchandise. Such orders may be 'limited' or 'general'. A general exclusion order prohibits the entry of all infringing merchandise, regardless of the country of origin and regardless of the manufacturer. As a result, unsuspecting third parties can be affected as well as the foreign respondents in the case. A limited exclusion order, on the other hand, applies only to infringing articles that originate from the particular foreign respondent in the case.

Cease and desist orders are used to reach United States parties that have already purchased the infringing merchandise. For example, a foreign supplier may have a network of distributors in the United States, and these distributors may maintain significant inventories of the infringing product. If the only available remedy to United States producers were an exclusion order, the distributors could 'stock up' on the infringing articles during the Section 337 investigation and continue to sell the products even after the Commission had found them to be infringing. Cease and desist orders are routinely issued to protect against such continuing infringement.

Once an exclusion order or a cease and desist order has been issued, those that violate the order may be liable for civil penalties of up to $100,000 a day or twice the value of the imported articles.

If the Section 337 proceeding involves articles that are used as materials, parts or components in other merchandise, the exclusion order may cover these downstream products as well.

The Commission has authority to issue exclusion orders covering downstream products to prevent circumvention and to provide the aggrieved party complete relief and full protection of the patent rights involved. In deciding whether to include downstream products within the scope of an exclusion order and which downstream products to include, the Commission balances the complainant's interest in obtaining complete protection from all infringing imports by means of exclusion of downstream products against the inherent potential of such an exclusion to disrupt legitimate trade.

In applying this balancing test, the Commission generally considers the following factors:

❑ The value of the infringing articles compared to the value of the downstream products in which they are incorporated;

❑ The identity of the manufacturer of the downstream products, i.e. whether it can be determined that the downstream products are manufactured by the respondent or by a third party;

❑ The incremental value to complainants of the exclusion of downstream products;

❑ The incremental detriment to respondents of such exclusion;

❑ The burdens imposed on third parties resulting from exclusion of downstream products;

❑ The availability of alternative downstream products that do not contain the infringing articles;

❑ The likelihood that imported downstream products actually contain the infringing articles and are thereby subject to exclusion;

❑ The opportunity for evasion of an exclusion order that does not include downstream products; and

❑ The enforceability by Customs of an order covering downstream products; and any other factors the Commission determines to be relevant.

This list of factors is not exclusive, however, and the Commission may identify and take into account any other factors which it believes bear on the question of whether to extend the remedial exclusion.

In one case, the Commission was considering the issuance of an exclusion order prohibiting the entry into the United States of certain flash memory circuits and *all* the products in which they were contained, whether those downstream products were made by the respondent or some other company that simply used these memory chips in the manufacture of its product. Had such an order been issued, it potentially would have excluded computers, digital cameras, and a wide variety of other electronic goods with memory capability simply because one of the chips inside was found to violate a valid and enforceable United States patent.

In addition to the long-term relief requested, complainants may also request temporary relief pending final resolution of the case. Temporary relief can consist of a temporary exclusion order or a cease and desist order. The ALJ considers motions for temporary relief in the first instance. To order temporary relief, it must consider: (1) the likelihood of success on the merits; (2) whether there is a threat of irreparable harm to the domestic industry if no relief is granted; (3) harm to respondents if temporary relief is granted; and (4) the public interest. In fact, temporary relief is difficult to obtain because it is difficult to show that the domestic industry will suffer irreparable harm during the proceedings of the Section 337 investigation.

The importance of monitoring of Section 337 investigations

The increasing number of Section 337 investigations and affirmative determinations by the Commission and the possibility that downstream products will be included indicate that foreign producers and importers should monitor Section 337 proceedings to keep informed of potential disruptions to trade that may result if it is determined that an important part or component infringes a United States patent. Unfortunately, exporters and importers often learn of pending Section 337 investigations too late to participate in the proceeding and never know whether the Commission will grant relief covering downstream products until after the Commission issues its determination.

If the Commission issues an exclusion order covering a downstream product that catches foreign suppliers unaware, considerable cost and effort can be required to design around the infringing article or replace it with a part or component from another supplier. Companies may be willing to incur this expense, however, to avoid the greater expense caused by the disruption that would result from an order excluding downstream products from the United States market altogether. These potential business costs make it advisable to monitor Section 337 cases to determine whether they might cover a product that a foreign or domestic manufacturer includes in its final product line.

Decisions to design around a part or component or to obtain an article from an alternative source in face of infringement allegations also can provide incentive for the supplier of the allegedly infringing article to reach a settlement or licensing agreement with the United States patent holder earlier than would otherwise be the case.

Section 337 cases can have adverse consequences even for foreign suppliers of goods that do not contain infringing articles. When there is a question as to whether an imported product contains an infringing article, United States Customs often imposes a certification procedure. Under this procedure, the exporter and importer must certify that the article does not contain the infringing article. Although this sounds simple enough, in fact, it means that importers and exporters must incur the cost of investigating the source of the product and/or its components and demonstrating that the product does not contain the infringing article in question.

Chapter 9

Section 301: Market access and trade policy issues

The final frequently invoked United States trade remedy is Section 301. This trade remedy is famous around the world – foreign businesspeople who may know nothing else about trade remedies will generally have heard of Section 301.

Section 301 provides the legal mechanism through which the United States Trade Representative pursues a variety of United States trade policy objectives. If the United States wants to pursue a market access issue with some foreign country, or wishes to complain about the lax enforcement of intellectual property rights, Section 301 and the related procedures are often the way the issue will be pursued.

This legal provision also provides a formal way for United States domestic industries to petition for some issue to be put on the trade policy agenda. If informal consultations with USTR do not succeed, United States domestic interests can use Section 301 to politicize the issue, and try to pressure USTR to take their interests more seriously.

Section 301 has a long history. This chapter briefly introduces Section 301 and describes how the proceedings work. Since 2000 WTO decision made clear that sanctions pursuant to Section 301 almost certainly would violate WTO obligations, the future use of Section 301 is less certain. The ability of the United States to use this law as the basis for making a credible threat to invoke sanctions has been limited. But there have been various proposals to make changes to Section 301 to find ways to impose effective sanctions in spite of the WTO finding, and by doing so to restore the credibility of Section 301 as a trade remedy.

Nature of Section 301

Fundamentally, Section 301 proceedings involve political pressure and policy objectives more than law and facts. United States companies pursue Section 301 cases when they want the United States Government – through the use of threatened sanctions – to help the company or industry achieve some objective in relation to foreign rivals. Not surprisingly, foreign countries have balked at this approach. Section 301 has therefore emerged as one of the most controversial and politically sensitive weapons in the arsenal of United States trade remedies.

The intensely political nature of what is commonly referred to as Section 301 emerged over time. Congress initially enacted it as part of the 1974 Trade Act. Originally intended to provide United States industries with a mechanism to enforce United States rights under international agreements, over the years Section 301 has been transformed by Congress from a narrow legal tool for raising issues under international agreements into a much broader policy weapon for United States industry to wield. Congress has expanded the reasons for invoking Section 301 and has intensified the political pressure on the Administration to act.

Some perceive Section 301 as being targeted at developed countries and areas such as the EU and Japan. Although there certainly have been Section 301 cases against developed countries, there have also been numerous cases against developing countries. These cases have involved a wide range of United States complaints against its trading partners.

Table 6	**Developing country Section 301 cases since 1974, in chronological order**	
Country	*Product/issue*	*Allegation*
Guatemala	*Cargo preference*	*Discriminatory shipping practice*
China	*Major home appliances*	*Confiscatory tariff levels*
Brazil, Republic of Korea and China	*Thrown silk*	*Preventing entry of imports*
Argentina	*Marine insurance*	*Requirement that marine insurance be placed with Argentine firm*
Republic of Korea	*Insurance*	*Failure to issue a licence*
Argentina	*Hides*	*Export controls on hides*
Brazil	*Non-rubber footwear*	*Import restrictions*
Republic of Korea	*Steel wire rope*	*Subsidization of export of Korean steel wire rope*
Brazil	*Soybean oil and meal*	*Export and production subsidies and quantitative restrictions*
Taiwan Province (China)	*Rice*	*Subsidization of exports*
Argentina	*Air couriers*	*Exclusive control over the air transportation of commercial documents*
Taiwan Province (China)	*Films*	*Discrimination against foreign film distributors*
Brazil	*Informatics*	*Investment restrictions, subsidies, and import restrictions*
Republic of Korea	*Insurance*	*Restriction of the ability of United States insurers to provide insurance services*
Republic of Korea	*Intellectual property rights*	*Lack of effective protection*
Argentina	*Soybeans and soybean products*	*Differential in export taxes*
Taiwan Province (China)	*Customs valuation*	*Duty paying system to calculate customs duties*
Taiwan Province (China)	*Beer, wine and tobacco*	*Policies and practices regarding distribution*
India	*Almonds*	*Licensing requirements and steep tariffs*
Brazil	*Pharmaceuticals*	*Lack of process and patent protection*
Republic of Korea	*Cigarettes*	*Unreasonable denial of access*

Table 6 (cont'd)

Country	Product/issue	Allegation
Republic of Korea	*Beef*	*Restrictive licensing system on imports of all bovine meat*
Republic of Korea	*Wine*	*Unreasonable denial of access*
Argentina	*Pharmaceuticals*	*Denial of product patent protection*
Brazil	*Import licensing*	*Certain import restrictions*
India	*Investment*	*Trade-restricting measures on foreign investors*
India	*Insurance*	*Barriers to foreign insurance providers*
Thailand	*Copyright enforcement*	*Inadequate enforcement*
Thailand	*Pharmaceuticals*	*Denial of adequate and effective patent protection*
India	*Intellectual property protection*	*Denial of adequate and effective protection*
China	*Intellectual property protection*	*Denial of adequate and effective protection, equitable market access*
Indonesia	*Pencil slats*	*Enhancement of export to third-country markets*
Brazil	*Intellectual property rights*	*Denial of adequate and effective protection*
Republic of Korea	*Agricultural market access restrictions*	*Practices regarding importation*
Colombia	*Bananas*	*Practices regarding exportation of bananas*
Pakistan	*Pharmaceutical and agricultural chemicals*	*Denial of patents, and exclusive marketing rights*
Turkey	*Tax on box office revenues*	*Discriminatory treatment of United States films*
India	*Pharmaceuticals and agricultural chemicals*	*Denial of patents and exclusive marketing rights*
Argentina	*Apparel, textiles, footwear*	*Specific duties, statistical tax and labelling requirement*
Indonesia	*Promotion of motor vehicle sector*	*Grant of conditional tax and tariff benefits*
Brazil	*Trade and investment in auto sector*	*Export performance and domestic content requirements*
Republic of Korea	*Auto imports*	*Barriers to imports*
Honduras	*Intellectual property rights*	*Inadequate protection*
Paraguay	*Intellectual property laws and practices*	*Denial of adequate and effective protection*
Mexico	*High fructose corn syrup*	*Agreement between Mexican sugar growers and bottlers*

As table 6 shows, a wide range of countries and a wide variety of practices have been challenged under Section 301.

Procedures

Section 301 provides a rather simple procedural framework. If a private interest files a Section 301 petition, USTR may accept or reject the petition. It is rare for a party to submit a Section 301 petition without pre-filing consultations with USTR, and so USTR rarely rejects petitions. More importantly, the question of whether USTR accepts a Section 301 petition and how vigorously it pursues the petition now also depends on the petitioner's ability to generate political support for its case.

In theory, USTR can self-initiate a Section 301 case. The statute authorizes this, but in practice USTR rarely takes such action. This reluctance reflects two concerns. First, if no private party cares enough about the issue to file a petition, USTR doubts that the issue should be a United States Government priority.

Second, reacting to a petition allows the United States Government to deflect foreign country anger at the United States action. The Administration can shift the blame to Congress for creating the private right of action.

Although called an 'investigation', a Section 301 proceeding involves only limited fact-finding. The proceeding is more about deciding on United States objectives and how best to achieve them than about traditional fact-finding. In theory, USTR undertakes fact-finding and conducts an investigation. In practice, USTR does little more than rely on submissions made by the parties and presume that the United States party must be correct. This limited approach makes complete sense from USTR's perspective: why would it undertake fact-finding that might well undermine or destroy its negotiating leverage during the dispute?

Section 301 provides two avenues for a complaining United States company. Under the 'mandatory' first procedure the United States Government must retaliate against countries that violate trade agreements. Under the mandatory procedure, a United States company alleges that a foreign competitor is engaged in unfair trade practices that either (1) violate or are inconsistent with trade agreements; (2) nullify or impair benefits granted under a trade agreement; or (3) are unjustifiable and burden or restrict United States commerce. The statute does not define the term 'unjustifiable', so it has been defined on a case-by-case basis. The phrase 'burden or restrict' implies an injury-type finding, but again the statute does not provide a definition so USTR has wide discretion.

The term 'mandatory' under this provision is somewhat misleading. The 'mandatory' procedure is not really mandatory. Several broad statutory exceptions excuse the need for action. Moreover, this procedure seems to require the United States to go through WTO dispute settlement before imposing sanctions. In 1979, Congress amended Section 301 to require the United States to consult under the General Agreement on Tariffs and Trade (GATT) before imposing sanctions. Because GATT had no means to enforce its decisions at that time, this amendment meant little as a practical matter. In 1994, the international community adopted the WTO Dispute Settlement Understanding (DSU), and created binding dispute settlements. At United States insistence, the DSU's procedures track the timeline for Section 301 mandatory action, giving parties 18 months to settle their disputes. This parallel timetable suggests that the United States must go to the WTO before it can impose retaliatory sanctions under Section 301.

The second procedure available under Section 301 is 'discretionary'. Under this procedure, a United States company alleges that a foreign country has engaged in 'unreasonable or discriminatory' trade practices which may not technically violate United States legal rights under trade agreements, but are nonetheless 'unfair and unreasonable' and a 'burden or restriction on United States commerce'. If USTR concurs with the allegations, action can be taken if USTR deems it appropriate.

Within the proceeding, the statute imposes few rules on how USTR should proceed. USTR must react to a petition within 45 days. It must decide within 6–18 months depending on the circumstances; most cases fall under a 12-month deadline. The statute provides neither guidance about the investigative process, nor guidance on what the vague standards really mean. The lack of specificity gives USTR broad flexibility.

Although USTR leads and coordinates Section 301 cases, the decisions emerge from an interagency process. The Section 301 Committee has representatives from the Departments of State, Treasury, Commerce, Agriculture, Labour, Justice, the Interior, Defense, and Transportation, and the Council of Economic Advisers, the Office of Management and Budget, the National Economic Council, the National Security Council, and the International Trade Commission. Depending on the issue, various agencies play different roles. For most key trade policy decisions, USTR, State, Treasury, and Commerce play the leading roles in shaping the interagency debate.

Opposition to Section 301

As Section 301 evolved, foreign government opposition to its use grew. United States trading partners perceive Section 301 as United States hypocrisy at its worse: the United States pursues multilateral options when they serve United States interests, but then reverts to 'aggressive' unilateralism whenever doing so better serves its interests. The EU and Japan have both been particularly vocal critics of Section 301, but so have developing countries.

This foreign criticism intensified after the Uruguay Round. Many United States trading partners believe that Article 23 of the DSU and Article XVI of the Marrakesh Agreement prohibit the use of Section 301. The United States does not share this view, and believes that the amendments made in 1994 brought Section 301 into compliance with WTO obligations. The WTO may impose a penalty on the United States as the price for using Section 301, but the United States still retains that option.

A recent WTO panel largely resolved this debate. The panel found that Section 301 does not violate WTO obligations on its face, but would violate WTO obligations if sanctions were ever imposed before all formalities under the DSU had been completed. The panel decision provided a clear and unambiguous advisory opinion about how it would have judged any United States use of Section 301 sanctions. This decision was not appealed to the Appellate Body, however, so we do not yet have the final word on this issue.

Chapter 10
Conducting verification

A crucial part of every anti-dumping and countervailing duty investigation is the 'verification' of the foreign company's response. Prior to the Trade Agreements Act of 1979, United States law did not require foreign producers to substantiate any of the information submitted to the Treasury Department in unfair trade investigations. Concerned that foreign companies might take advantage of this situation, the United States Congress changed the law to require that all information used in anti-dumping investigations be verified as accurate.

When the Commerce Department first took over responsibility from the Treasury Department in the early 1980s, no one was sure how to conduct verifications. The initial uncertainty about what constitutes a verification has been resolved. Over the past decade, the Commerce Department has developed a well-settled theory and policy concerning what a verification represents and how a verification should be conducted. In practice, however, verifications can differ greatly.

This chapter reviews both the theory and practice of verification. The first section presents the theory of verification, including the standard of proof and the verification methodologies used by the Commerce Department. Submitting an inaccurate response greatly increases the risk that the foreign company may fail verification and receive margins based on the punitive 'facts available'. The second section then summarizes various strategies for a successful verification, including a list of specific actions to avoid. These strategies and suggestions should help foreign companies pass verification.

The theory and practice of verification

The standard of proof

The fundamental purpose of verification for the foreign company is to prove the accuracy of the responses it has submitted. One of the most difficult aspects of verification is understanding the methodology used by the Commerce Department to measure accuracy. The Commerce Department does not check every number in the response; to do so would be impossible. Rather, it selects certain transactions as examples. If those examples are verifiable and accurate, and if no problems surface, the Commerce Department assumes that the remainder of the response is also accurate. A few minor mistakes (for example, transcribing the wrong number or arithmetic mistakes) are inevitable. The greater the number of mistakes, however, the greater the risk that the Commerce Department will reject all or part of the response.

It is important to remember that this 'spot check' standard of proof has both subjective and objective aspects. The particular Commerce Department staff person conducting the verification must be satisfied that each element of the response has been adequately verified. Obviously, different people apply somewhat different and subjective standards of proof. Depending on personal attitudes and prior experiences, different Commerce Department staff might be satisfied by different levels of proof.

In addition to being personally satisfied, the Commerce Department staff person must also have sufficient objective information to write a report that will satisfy his or her superiors in Washington DC that the verification was complete and successful.

Is it better for the foreign company to have an inexperienced Commerce Department verifier visit the company? The answer is not as obvious as it appears. On the one hand, a verifier who is not familiar with accounting systems may be more likely to perform a superficial verification that overlooks questionable aspects of the response. A less experienced verifier is also more likely to concentrate on trivial points and to neglect the fundamental portions of the response. If these parts of the response are problematic, then the foreign company might benefit from a verifier who 'cannot see the forest for the trees'.

Nevertheless, because the Commerce Department's verifiers must prepare a detailed report about the verification, a foreign company is often better off with an experienced Commerce Department staff person at the verification. Although the verification itself may be more difficult – the experienced person may have a higher standard – at least at the end of the verification the company will know what was adequately verified and what issues may raise problems. The judgements of inexperienced or lenient staff people are sometimes reversed or ignored by the supervisory staff in Washington. In addition, the verification must ultimately withstand scrutiny by the lawyers for the United States domestic industry, and possibly by the Court of International Trade. A verification by an experienced staff person is more likely to survive this scrutiny.

The level of detail required in a verification is often difficult for a foreign company to understand. For example, the verifiers sometimes ask for individual employee time cards to substantiate labour costs, or daily production records to support the total output recorded in a company's accounting records. Verifiers also often ask for proof, such as bank statements or receipts, that the company paid particular invoices for expenses. The purpose of such inquiries is to reach the most basic accounting records that a company maintains, the records that are least likely to be forged or altered.

Often the requests for underlying source documents seem silly. Often the requests *are* silly, and provide the Commerce Department staff person with little, if any, useful information. Many companies justifiably ask why, if a company maintains a regularly audited accounting system, the Commerce Department is so suspicious and reluctant to accept the results shown in the normal accounting records and the audited financial statements. It is important for company officials to remember that the verifier may have only a vague idea how accounting systems are structured. Rather than try to educate the verifier, it is usually best just to respond to the request, no matter how pointless, unless the request requires an unreasonable amount of work. Unfortunately, the subjective aspects of the standard of proof are very important, and so foreign companies have little choice but to make good faith efforts to comply with every request.

Legal framework

The anti-dumping law incorporates two basic principles concerning the importance of accuracy. First, the statute requires that the Commerce Department verify the accuracy of all information submitted during an anti-dumping investigation.

Second, if the necessary information either is not submitted or cannot be verified, the statute authorizes the Commerce Department to use the 'facts available' (previously known as 'best information available') instead of the missing or inaccurate information.

The terms 'facts available' and 'best information available' are somewhat misleading. In fact, the statutory provision authorizes the Commerce Department to use the worst possible information, at least from the perspective of the foreign company. Most often, the 'facts' available are simply the allegations made by the petitioner. In other cases, the information may be adverse inferences drawn by the Commerce Department to inflate the dumping margins. There have been a number of court cases in which foreign companies have challenged the Commerce Department's use of the facts available provision in harsh ways to punish foreign companies. The United States courts have generally upheld the Commerce Department's discretion to use the 'facts available' provision as punishment, provided the Commerce Department has in fact requested the necessary information and given the foreign company an adequate opportunity to respond. The courts have held that the United States Congress intended the Commerce Department to use the provision to force foreign companies to cooperate with the investigations, and to force them to provide accurate information.

Although the statute sets forth these basic principles, neither the statute nor the regulations define in any detail what is meant by 'verification'. The Commerce Department, rather than codify its practice in regulations, has consciously chosen instead to develop its policies about verification on a case-by-case basis, reacting to the particular facts of each case. The Commerce Department's policies have therefore emerged rather slowly, as the various cases have been decided.

The importance of accuracy

In recent years, it has become increasingly important for companies involved in anti-dumping and countervailing duty investigations to submit accurate responses to the Commerce Department. In the early years of administering the anti-dumping law, the Commerce Department was sometimes lax in requiring accuracy. This attitude has completely changed, and foreign companies are now at great risk if they submit inaccurate or incomplete responses. The most important step in a successful verification is therefore to submit an accurate response.

Verification methodologies

During the verification the Commerce Department uses two basic methodologies – known as 'up' and 'down'. First, beginning with the information in the response, the Commerce Department traces various items 'up' to the company's financial statement. If the aggregate information is consistent with an audited financial statement, the Commerce Department believes it can more reasonably rely on the accuracy and reliability of the information.

A company will not have a specific line item on its financial statement for all categories of information submitted to the Commerce Department. The verifier usually understands that companies do not design their financial statements to simplify the process of verification. A company must, however, *reconcile* the information submitted in the response to the audited financial statement.

For example, a first worksheet might show how the individual inland freight reported in the response can be reconciled to the amount of total inland freight for that particular product reported in the general ledger. Then, reconciling the information in the response 'up' to the financials is an exercise in showing that the particular figure in question is included in successively more aggregated accounting entries. The company must have these reconciliations prepared beforehand in the form of worksheets. If the financial statement has a line item for total inland freight for all products, a worksheet might show the breakdown of inland freight by product line (supported by entries from the general ledger).

The second methodology is to trace various items 'down' to the basic supporting documents and accounting records. Again, the starting point is the information in the response. Using inland freight as an example again, the verifiers might trace inland freight charges to individual invoices from the companies supplying the services, to payment records showing that the invoices were actually paid, and to the accounting records showing both the receipt of the invoice and the payment of the invoice. The verifier sometimes even insists on seeing external proof of payment (for example, a cancelled cheque or a debit on a bank account statement) to establish the reliability of the payment records in the company's accounting system. The verifier may also want to check the allocation of the individual charges to particular models using worksheets, evidence of the validity of the allocation factors, and model-by-model records of shipments included in the allocation.

This process of verifying 'up' to the financial statement, and 'down' to the source accounting records is a standard part of every verification. Different Commerce Department staff members, however, apply these two methodologies with different degrees of rigour. Some insist on using both methodologies for every single item in the response, even though it may seem redundant to trace those items specifically linked to the financial statement to source accounting documents as well. Others accept short cuts as long as they are satisfied that the information is correct and there are no serious distortions or errors. The most common short cut is to trace up only to the general ledger once the company has established that this record traces reliably to the financials.

The role of documents

Source documents are extremely important in a verification. The Commerce Department is reluctant to accept testimonial evidence on any point; it wants to see documentary evidence. The particular documents used in individual verifications can vary considerably. The following documents, however, are used in most verifications:

❑ *Financial statements* – Foreign companies normally use both the audited annual financial statement and any semi-annual reports.

❑ *Management report/internal profit and loss accounts* – These documents are useful for identifying monthly expenses. They also sometimes provide more detailed reporting of expenses than do the financial statements. For example, companies often keep separate, unaudited records by product line prior to aggregating them in the financials.

❑ *Trial balance* – The trial balance reconciles the general ledger to the financial statement, but, unlike the general ledger, the trial balance is usually aggregated. At times when the company does not want the verifiers to examine the detail in the general ledger, the trial balance may serve the same purpose without revealing the detail.

❑ *General ledger* – This document is usually the crucial link between the other accounting records of the company and the financial statements. A thorough verifier will trace every figure being verified to the general ledger.

❑ *Sales journal* – The sales journal is used to show that the response included all of the appropriate sales. Using this document may be a problem because some companies do not incorporate the sales journal into their audited accounting system; instead, they use it as a management tool. When that is the case, the company will have to prepare documentation that reconciles the response, the sales journal and the general ledger.

❑ *Accounts receivable aging report* – The verifier will use this document to check the dates of sale and payment for all the individual sales chosen for verification. Receivable periods on individual sales will also be compared to the average receivable period reported in the response (on which the direct credit expense is calculated) to determine whether there are any large variations that call into question the use of an average.

❑ *Cash receipts journal* – The verifier will trace sales receipts to this journal to see whether they are properly entering the company's accounting system. Commerce believes that unreported discounts and rebates can be detected in this way.

❑ *Cash disbursements journal* – The verifier will trace disbursements for expenses to this journal to check whether expenses claimed in the response are properly reported. This journal is also considered by Commerce a potential location of unreported rebates.

❑ *Loan ledger* – Some of the information reported for the direct credit and inventory 'imputed interest' expenses will be traced to the loan ledger. For many companies the loan ledger is simply part of the general ledger.

❑ *Sales documents* – Each sale in the United States or other market must have a corresponding purchase order and sales invoice. For export transactions, there are usually a number of other documents (such as bills of lading, letters of credit, shipping documents and export licence documents) that the verifier reviews.

❑ *Payment records* – The verifier usually asks to see some documentary proof that the price shown on the invoice is the actual price the company received. This demonstration often involves matching total invoice amounts with cancelled cheques or with the bank statements showing the appropriate amounts being credited to the company's account.

If the investigation involves cost of production, numerous cost accounting records also have to be available for review. The particular documents needed vary depending on the type of cost accounting system maintained by the company. These are discussed in more detail in the chapters on cost and constructed value investigations.

Countervailing duty verifications involve many of the same documents, particularly the financial statements and the basic accounting records. The Commerce Department staff wants to be able to trace through a company's accounting system any subsidies being received. In addition, depending on the types of programmes being investigated, different documents might be necessary. For example, verification of an export loan programme would involve careful review of bank borrowings to establish benchmark interest rates. Verification of a tax benefit would involve careful review of the tax returns for all relevant years, including those going back a number of years if the programme involves carry-forward issues. Verification of a government equity infusion would require careful review of all studies and reports that discuss the commercial viability of the company and its future prospects.

The Commerce Department insists on copying some of the source documents reviewed during the verification. The purpose of copying is twofold. First, copying the source documents eliminates the need to take detailed notes during the verification; the Commerce Department staff can refer to the documents themselves when they write the verification reports. Second, the documents become part of the administrative record that the Commerce Department (and the parties, including those representatives of the domestic industry with APO access) can use later, in any court appeal, to support its decisions. Because of this Commerce Department practice, the foreign company should plan for copying to take place. If any special permission will be needed to release any of the documents or records to the Commerce Department, or to make copies of certain company records, the company should obtain that permission before the verification starts.

Building an administrative record

Many anti-dumping decisions are eventually reviewed by the Court of International Trade (CIT). CIT bases its review on the various documents and arguments submitted to the Commerce Department, known as the 'administrative record'. Except in extreme circumstances, CIT must limit its review to the information that has become part of the administrative record. It is therefore very important for a foreign company to make sure that the administrative record supports its positions in the anti-dumping investigation.

The foreign company and its lawyers should monitor both what is included in the administrative record and what is not included.

It is important to include any documents necessary to establish the truth and accuracy of any claim made by the foreign company during the investigation. Then if the Commerce Department uses the wrong price, or denies an adjustment, the company and its lawyers will have the factual basis on which to urge the CIT to overturn the Commerce Department decision. It is also important to exclude any documents that could prove embarrassing, or that could undermine arguments that the company hopes to make during the investigation. Although a foreign company does not have complete control over the documents that are included or excluded during the verification, it should strive to maintain as much control as possible by following the various suggestions set forth below.

Major topics in a price verification

Every verification involves the price response submitted by the foreign company. Although each verification is different, the following topics are always important:

❑ *Completeness check* – In every verification, the Commerce Department needs to establish that all relevant sales (United States sales, home market sales, or third country sales) have been reported. This step usually involves tracing the sales figures reported in the response to the sales journal, or some similar document listing all of the sales, to the financial statement, thus demonstrating that all sales have been reported. This is a more difficult exercise than it appears. As mentioned previously, there may be no regularly kept company book that records sales for only the product under investigation. Even if there is, such a book – like the sales journal – may not be part of the company's audited accounting system. It is essential in these situations that, beginning from the time that they help prepare the response, the company accountants keep systematic worksheets that trace every step from the figures reported in the response to the audited accounts. The Commerce Department will also select random sales documents that are viewed at verification and ask to see whether the transactions have been included in the response's sales listing. The Commerce Department then selects a transaction from the sales listing, and asks to see where it was reported in the response.

❑ *Date-of-sale methodology* – The Commerce Department checks the method used to establish the date of sale to make sure the company has not inappropriately shifted sales either inside or outside the period of investigation. Depending on the prices for the transactions included or excluded, the dumping margins could be significantly affected. The degree of scrutiny depends on the Commerce Department staff assigned to the case. The Commerce Department will examine the entire documentation for at least one sale to determine whether the material terms of sale, especially price and quantity, were fixed when the company reports they were fixed.

❑ *Relationship of the parties* – To make sure that the foreign company has appropriately classified sales as either 'export price' or 'constructed export price' transactions, the Commerce Department investigates the relationship between the foreign exporter and its United States customers. Again, the degree of scrutiny depends on the Commerce Department staff assigned to the case.

❑ *Product comparisons* – There may be some controversy concerning the products that are being compared to the products sold in the United States, for example whether they are sufficiently similar to be compared. In that case the verifier will scrutinize the physical examples and will examine any other information relevant to the Commerce Department's standards for 'such or similar' merchandise. These can include records of manufacturing costs, schematic diagrams, product design records and so forth.

❑ *Accuracy of prices* – The Commerce Department normally demands not only sales documents, for example purchase orders and invoices, but also detailed proof of payment, including external documents (such as bank statements). The verifier will trace these documents into the company's sales journal and into such accounts as the accounts receivable aging report and general ledger to check whether the foreign company received the amount claimed for each sale.

❑ *Accuracy of adjustments* – The verifier will trace to the accounting records any expenses that are the basis for significant adjustments to the price. The Commerce Department also inquires into the allocation of expenses among various products, to make sure that expenses have been properly allocated to the product under investigation. Adjustments that typically receive detailed scrutiny include: rebates and discounts; credit expenses; indirect selling expenses; difference-in-merchandise adjustments; and any large adjustments.

In every verification, there are also particular issues that are specific to that investigation. These issues are usually identified in the Commerce Department's verification outline, which is given to the foreign company prior to the verification.

Major topics in a cost verification

If the anti-dumping investigation also involves cost of production, the verification is even more time consuming and difficult. The Commerce Department usually sends an accountant (either an employee of the Commerce

Department or an outside consultant from an accounting firm under contract to the Commerce Department) to conduct the cost verification. The accountant concentrates on several general issues:

❑ *Have all of the costs of producing the merchandise have been included in the response?* – Many of the requests made at a cost verification, such as an examination of the engineering drawings for a product and a factory tour, are intended to discover whether all of the costs have been included. If the Commerce Department finds some component listed on the engineering drawing that has not been included in the cost, it expects an explanation.

❑ *Have the costs been properly allocated to the individual products or models under investigation?* – The Commerce Department must ensure that costs have not been allocated to other products that are not under investigation, as this would understate the costs of the products that are under investigation. The Commerce Department is especially careful when examining factory overhead expenses, which are relatively easy to reallocate to products not under investigation.

❑ *Have all of the appropriate costs been included in the period of investigation?* – The Commerce Department must also ensure that costs have not been allocated outside the period of investigation. For example, it usually examines whether an appropriate allocation of research and development costs has been included, even if those costs were incurred prior to the period of investigation. Unfortunately, the Commerce Department's policy with regard to R&D costs has not been consistent. This problem is discussed further in chapter 3.

❑ *Have the costs been properly allocated among the various categories used by the Commerce Department?* – The Commerce Department knows that companies try to shift costs among the various categories to lower the total costs. For example, shifting overhead expenses into general and administrative expenses can reduce the total cost, and thus reduce the dumping margins. The Commerce Department tries to prevent such shifts. (GSA is usually expressed as a percentage of cost of manufacture, including overhead; switching an expense from overhead to GSA will often create only a very small increase in the GSA percentage while reducing per-unit cost of manufacture significantly. In addition, in constructed value cases when GSA is less than the statutory minimum 10%, adding to GSA up to the minimum is an obvious tactic used by respondents.)

❑ *Have all financial statement costs been attributed to the product under investigation?* – Cost accounting systems often adjust costs between the finished goods cost of the product and cost of goods sold in the audited financial statement. When the finished goods cost is lower, respondents often attempt to report this as the cost of production. Commerce Department accountants therefore always trace to the cost of goods sold account in the audited financials even when the product under investigation has its own profit and loss statement.

❑ *Does the company's cost accounting system have any internal flaws that result in underreporting of costs?* – All cost accounting systems are *not* created equal. Commerce Department accountants often concentrate – to the respondent's surprise – on seemingly academic cost accounting issues if they believe there is a flaw in the company's system. For example, in one case Commerce Department cost accountants determined that a respondent's work-in-process system inaccurately expressed work-in-process quantities. The cost accountants completely recalculated the quantities on the grounds that they had not been adjusted to a 'completed-unit' basis. Be prepared to explain any idiosyncratic aspects of the company's system.

Unfortunately, companies usually do not have accounting systems that are specifically designed to answer the questions posed by the Commerce Department. The preparation for a cost verification is thus often very difficult and time consuming.

The best preparation for a cost verification is to anticipate possible Commerce Department questions. Often foreign cost accountants have not thought very carefully about their cost accounting system; they simply follow the system. As part of the preparations, the lawyers and cost accountants should think about the possible weaknesses in the system, and prepare defences of those weaknesses. If a company is prepared to show that a particular distortion is insignificant in calculating the total cost of the products under investigation, the Commerce Department usually pays much less attention to the distortion.

Major issues in a countervailing duty verification

Countervailing duty verifications are much less predictable than dumping verifications. As noted earlier, the scope of the verification needs to adjust to consider the specific programmes at issue. Loan programmes are very different from tax programmes, and equity infusions have little to do with either loan programmes or tax programmes.

One issue common to all countervailing duty verifications, however, is the need to show 'non-utilization'. In a typical countervailing duty petition, the domestic industry will make a wide range of allegations, in the hopes that some of the allegations will be applicable. It is therefore quite common for individual companies not to have used many of the programmes alleged to exist. If the programmes in fact exist, but the company simple did not use the programmes, the company will need to demonstrate that fact at verification. For some programmes – such as tax benefits – demonstrating non-utilization is easy. By showing a tax return that did not make the claim, the company can demonstrate the lack of utilization. For other programmes, proving the negative – that the programme was never used – can be more challenging. For example, an alleged government grant for some purpose may have been recorded on accounting records in a creative way, or may have gone to a subsidiary rather than the parent company. The foreign company must consider each instance of non-utilization on its own.

The most important difference for countervailing duty verifications is the two-stage process: the Commerce Department verifies both the foreign company and the foreign government. Unlike dumping cases, which involve only the foreign company, a major part of the countervailing duty investigation involves the foreign government. This aspect introduces another complication, since the foreign company has no control over the government verification. The government's failure to 'pass verification' could result in the foreign company being penalized in the investigation.

The role of lawyers

The outside lawyers assisting the foreign company have an important role to play, both before and during the verification. The lawyers should be actively involved. Too often lawyers are only passive participants in the process, letting the Commerce Department staff completely control the verification. Lawyers who watch passively during the verification are not serving their clients' interests.

The lawyers should ensure that the verification preparations are thorough and complete. They should review all of the documents prepared by the company, advise as to what additional materials should be prepared, and suggest how to present sensitive topics. Often the company has several alternative ways to verify the same information; the lawyers can help decide on the best approach. To uncover any problem areas or weak points in the company's preparations, the lawyers should be even more demanding and suspicious than Commerce Department staff will be during the actual verification. Although this approach may seem harsh and burdensome, it is more likely to ensure a successful verification.

Once the verification begins, the lawyer's role changes. The Commerce Department is usually suspicious if the lawyer makes all of the presentations at a verification. The lawyer and the company officials must therefore decide in advance who should present what portion of the verification. This balance between lawyer and client is part of the overall planning for the verification. This planning should also include consideration of what must be proved during the verification, and what topics should be avoided. This planning continues even during the verification, with the company and lawyers consulting regularly on the progress of the verification, and about changes that might be necessary in the strategy for the verification.

The lawyers can also help during the verification by steering the Commerce Department staff away from sensitive topics. In some cases, where it is impossible to avoid the topic, the lawyers may choose to make the presentation directly. Non-native speakers of English sometimes convey the wrong impression and encourage the Commerce Department to pursue the topic. Presentations by the lawyers in English, which avoid the need for translations, can sometimes avoid such problems.

Strategies and suggestions for verification

There are several strategies that a company can follow to minimize problems during the verification. Underlying all of these strategies is a common theme: to the extent possible, the foreign company and its lawyers should try to control the verification. Obviously, the Commerce Department staff tries to resist this control. The challenge of the verification is to maintain control – of both the information released and the timing – without antagonizing the Commerce Department staff. The most successful verifications are those in which the Commerce Department staff members think that they have been in control, but in fact have seen nothing that the company did not want them to see.

Prepare as thoroughly as possible

The importance of preparing thoroughly for the verification cannot be overemphasized. The first step in the preparations is to anticipate the need for verification at the same time that the response is being prepared, so that the company staff save and organize the important information. Advance planning when preparing the response can save enormous amounts of time later when preparing for the verification.

The second step is to review carefully the verification outline. The Commerce Department usually issues an outline of the verification topics at least a week prior to the verification.

This verification outline may specify certain transactions and items about which the Commerce Department wants very detailed information. This information must be prepared in advance. Unfortunately, the outlines prepared by the Commerce Department are often very brief and do not provide much guidance to a company deciding what to prepare for the verification. The lawyer representing the foreign company usually has to prepare the company for the verification based on his or her past experience in similar verifications.

The third step is to prepare some materials in advance, based on the verification outline and the lawyer's experience. A company need not prepare detailed information about every transaction and every piece of information in the response. Samples showing the methodology used and the types of accounting records available to substantiate the information should be prepared for each category of information, however. The number of examples necessary depends on the nature and importance of the item. Adjustments that are the same for both United States price and foreign market value – and thus have little effect on the net dumping margin – usually receive less scrutiny than adjustments based on large home market expenses. The advance preparation should reflect the relative importance of the various topics.

The fourth step is to anticipate possible follow-up questions by the Commerce Department staff, and prepare the necessary materials. Since the Commerce Department usually selects additional examples to check during the verification, the company needs to have the other documentation readily available. For example, the company prepares a detailed packet for one month, and the Commerce Department then asks for the same information for another month randomly selected during the verification. The documents needed to meet such requests should be readily available.

The last step is to solve the logistical problems of the verification. It is helpful to have a copier available for exclusive use during the verification. Because of the number of documents that need to be available, companies often reserve several large conference rooms for the entire period of the verification. One of the rooms can be used as the site of the verification. The other rooms can be used for storing additional documents and for private meetings between the company staff and the lawyers during the verification.

The amount of time necessary for these preparations varies depending on the circumstances of the case. A simple case involving only an investigation of prices at a company with a well-organized accounting system could be adequately prepared in as few as three or four days. A complex case involving both price and cost investigations could take as long as two or three weeks to prepare adequately. Other factors that affect the amount of time needed include the number of corporate entities involved in the investigation, the complexity of the issues, and the amount of time the Commerce Department expects to spend at the verification. Most typically, the Commerce Department allows one week to conduct a price verification and another week if the verification also involves cost.

Organize the verification materials in advance

Given the amount of detail that the Commerce Department expects, a week is a short time within which to finish a verification. A foreign company must therefore organize its materials to help the verification go as smoothly and efficiently as possible.

Wasting time during the verification trying to locate the necessary documents increases the risk that the Commerce Department will find that the foreign company has failed verification.

Our experience has been that the best way to organize materials for a verification is to copy all of the relevant documents in advance, and place all the documents relating to a particular topic into a labelled folder. Where a particular topic involves several transactions, each transaction should have a separate folder. This method of organizing materials has two advantages. First, it organizes all of the documents in an easily understood and flexible system. If the order of the verification changes, the documents can be presented in the new order very easily. Since the Commerce Department staff will take back to Washington D.C. large numbers of documents as verification exhibits, such a system also makes it much easier for the Commerce Department staff person to collect the necessary exhibits for the verification report.

Second, and more important, preparing the documents in advance forces the company staff and the lawyers to review carefully every document to be used during the verification. It is crucial to review all of the documents before the verification. Any problems should be discovered so that they can be solved. Every company has minor discrepancies in its accounting system. As long as the discrepancies are explained persuasively, they generally do not create a problem at the verification. Unexplained discrepancies, however, can be a disaster. It often takes some time to resolve discrepancies, so the sooner they are discovered, the easier it will be to deal with them in a satisfactory manner.

Decide on the order of the presentation

The Commerce Department usually gives the foreign company some flexibility in deciding on the order for presenting the various topics at the verification. In exercising this flexibility, the company and its lawyers should rely on several basic principles. First, the order of the presentation should be logical. The basic information about the company's accounting system and distribution system should be discussed early in the verification so that the Commerce Department staff can better understand the specific topics that arise later in the verification. If two topics are closely related, they probably should be presented together. The Commerce Department might become suspicious if related topics are discussed at separate times without any explanation.

Second, the foreign company generally should present its strongest points early in the verification. During the verification, the foreign company must persuade the Commerce Department to believe in the accounting system of the company, and in the reliability of the information that has been submitted. To win this trust, it is usually advisable to present those topics with the best supporting documentation early in the verification. The Commerce Department thus begins the verification with a good impression of the company and its accounting system.

Third, the foreign company should think carefully about the weak points in its verification presentation, and when best to present those points. At every verification, no matter how thoroughly the company prepares, there will be some weak points – topics where the supporting documentation is weak (or non-existent), or where careful scrutiny by the Commerce Department could lead to a rejection of a key argument that the company needs to win.

It is difficult to say when the best time is to present these difficult topics. Sometimes companies save such topics for the end of the day, when the Commerce Department staff members are tired. The risk, however, is that the Commerce Department staff members might decide to resume the same topic the next morning when they are rested and more alert. Sometimes companies save such topics for late in the verification, when the Commerce Department staff may not have much time to probe very carefully. The risk here is that the Commerce Department staff might decide that the topic cannot be verified in the time remaining and consider the verification to be a failure. The judgement about how best to present a weak point in a verification has to be made based on the circumstances of a particular case, and the particular Commerce Department staff assigned to the verification.

Solve any staffing problems

Foreign companies involved in anti-dumping investigations face a variety of potential staffing problems. First, companies involved in an investigation involving both price and cost have to anticipate the need to defend two verifications. The Commerce Department often sends two teams to a company to conduct simultaneous verifications of the price response and the cost response. If the foreign company has used the same staff people to prepare both responses (which is quite common since the price response and cost response are usually due at different times during the investigation), there is often a scheduling conflict. The same person may be needed simultaneously in both the price and cost verifications.

Such conflicts can usually be resolved, but they require some advance planning. Sometimes the Commerce Department agrees to schedule sequential verifications – the price verification is held first, and then the cost verification. Other times the Commerce Department agrees to rearrange the order of verification topics so that the necessary company officials can be present at both verifications.

Second, companies need to anticipate a splitting of the Commerce Department team. An increasingly common Commerce Department practice is to divide the two- or three-person verification team into two or three independent points of verification. Such a division makes it more difficult for the company officials and the lawyers to control the verification. The company should anticipate such a problem and have a contingency plan in place: which company officials can meet with the Commerce Department staff alone, without the assistance of the lawyers; and more important, what topics can be treated separately and with little risk? Answering these questions in advance, in consultation with the lawyers, helps prevent major problems from developing at the verification.

Third, companies should make arrangements to free key staff members from their other responsibilities during the verification. Too often companies require key staff to assist in the verification and continue to perform their other jobs at the same time. Such an arrangement almost always leads to a less effective performance at the verification.

A fourth staffing problem relates to the number of clerical workers necessary for a verification. It is important that the company assign enough clerical staff to finish all of the work that is necessary during a verification. An enormous amount of copying takes place during the verification.

Numerous calculations are also necessary – for example, totalling all of the invoices for inland freight charges during a particular month to prove that the total matches the figures reported in the company's accounting records. It is a waste of resources to have the outside lawyers or the company's professional staff performing these clerical tasks.

A final staffing problem relates to language skills. The Commerce Department staff members rarely speak the language of the foreign company that they are verifying. The Commerce Department verification team usually brings a translator, but there are limits to what this single translator can do during the verification. It is therefore vital for most of the important verification documents to be translated prior to the beginning of the verification. Some companies can prepare adequate translations using company staff. Other companies prefer to use outside translators to prepare more official translations. Beyond these translations prepared in advance, the company should be ready to prepare additional translations, on very short notice, of other documents that become relevant during the verification.

Establish good relations with the Commerce Department staff

As noted above, a significant part of the verification is subjective – whether or not the Commerce Department staff believes in the accuracy and reliability of the company's accounting system. Because of this subjective element, it is important to develop a good working relationship with the Commerce Department staff members and win their trust. The foreign company should begin developing this relationship early in the investigation. At the verification, developing this relationship becomes even more crucial.

It is impossible to set forth comprehensive guidelines for establishing a good working relationship with every type of Commerce Department staff. Like every organization, the Commerce Department has both good and bad professional staff. A foreign company should learn as much as possible about the particular staff people assigned to the investigation, and their reputation. Sometimes the outside lawyer will have had experience working with the same staff people on other anti-dumping investigations.

Regardless of the person, it is always helpful to have a pleasant, comfortable work environment for the verification. In general, the company should make the verification as smooth and as pleasant an experience as possible for the Commerce Department staff. The Commerce Department staff members are people, and cannot help but react (even if only on a subconscious level) to the environment of the verification. A clean, well-lit room is a must. Because verifications usually last a week or more, it is not difficult to understand that those conducted in rooms with natural light and plenty of windows have a better chance of maintaining the good humour of Commerce and company officials till the end.

The topic of gifts, meals, and gratuities is important, but also somewhat delicate. The official Commerce Department position is that staff should accept nothing of value from the company. As a practical matter, however, most Commerce Department staff members accept modest lunch-time meals, especially if the company has the meals brought to the premises. Most staff recognize that simple catered meals (usually sandwiches) facilitate the verification.

More extravagant dinner-time meals present more of a dilemma for companies. Some staff members accept invitations to dinner. It is usually safe for a company to make one offer, and simply accept the initial response. It is a mistake to pressure a Commerce Department staff member to accept a dinner invitation.

Provide any post-verification assistance requested by the Commerce Department

Once the verification is finished, the Commerce Department staff members begin to draft the verification reports. During this period, the outside lawyers and the foreign company can often be of assistance to the Commerce Department staff in Washington DC. Sometimes the Commerce Department staff members forget the explanations of certain accounting documents. Other times the Commerce Department staff members remember having seen a certain document, but not making a copy of it. Providing the requested explanations and documents helps with the preparation of the verification reports. A foreign company should try to cooperate as fully as possible with such post-verification requests. A failure to do so creates a serious risk that the staff may draft the verification report in a way unfavourable to the company.

Once the verification report has been drafted, the Commerce Department often gives a copy of the draft to the lawyers for the foreign company. The official purpose of this review is to check for confidential information that should be excluded from the non-confidential version of the verification report. It is sometimes possible, however, to suggest changes in the text of the report to the Commerce Department staff. If the Commerce Department staff members have misunderstood an important point from the verification, or have left out an important topic, it is sometimes possible to persuade them to make the corrections before issuing the final version of the report. Commerce Department policy on such changes has become more strict in recent years – officially, no substantive changes are to be made to the draft verification reports – but, depending on the particular staff member, it is sometimes still possible to suggest changes.

It is usually possible for the lawyers to send a copy of the draft report to the foreign company for review. However, the Commerce Department generally gives the lawyers only 24 hours to make any comments, so the company therefore has at most one business day to review the draft and send comments back to the lawyers. If the company wishes to comment on the draft report, it is important to prepare in advance. The draft reports are often 40 to 60 pages long, so it is necessary to have staff with a thorough knowledge of English ready to review the report; there is usually no time for translations.

Of course, once the final version of the report is officially issued, the foreign company still has an opportunity to comment. One of the principle purposes of the pre-hearing and post-hearing briefs is to provide the parties with a chance to comment on the verification reports and clarify any points with which they disagree. Companies therefore frequently prepare translations of the verification reports that can be circulated to the company's accountants (if they do not read English very well). The time available for translation and review is sometimes quite limited. It is not unusual for the Commerce Department to finish the verification reports only days before the pre-hearing briefs are due. Sometimes the verification reports are delayed until after the hearing itself. In such situations, however, the Commerce Department usually accepts written comments about the verification reports after the due dates for the pre-hearing and post-hearing briefs.

Actions that should be avoided

In addition to the positive suggestions made above, there are a number of actions that should be avoided in verifications.

Never make a false statement

It is important to distinguish a limited answer – one that answers only part of a question – from a false answer. A limited answer is consistent with the company's right to defend itself vigorously. A false answer can destroy the company's credibility and result in the company failing verification. If the Commerce Department does not ask direct and specific questions, the company is under no obligation to volunteer damaging information.

Never submit a false or forged document

Although it may be tempting to solve a difficult verification problem by submitting a fabricated document, it should never be done. If such an action were discovered, the company's credibility would be permanently destroyed and the company might never again pass verification. Moreover, submitting false documents might even be a criminal offence in certain circumstances.

Never submit a document that has not been carefully reviewed

It is crucial that every document submitted to the Commerce Department be carefully reviewed. Headings on the document, or seemingly innocent notations, could be very damaging. In addition, all discrepancies should be uncovered before the document is submitted, so that the company and lawyers can develop the best possible explanations.

Never allow a company official to speak with the Commerce Department without preparation

Like documents that have not been reviewed, people who have not been prepared can sometimes create serious problems in the verification. Company officials should understand what is happening in the verification, and what positions the company is trying to take. Without preparation, an innocent comment could destroy the company's credibility and overall strategy.

Never volunteer information that might damage the company's credibility

Companies sometimes make questionable payments in developing countries, or become involved in judicial or administrative proceedings that cast doubt on their honesty or credibility. Company officials should never volunteer such information, even in a joking way. Any topic reflecting negatively on a company's credibility should come only in response to a direct and specific question.

Never guess about the answer to a question

If company officials do not know the answer to a question, they should not answer. Mistaken guesses, and the impressions they leave, are difficult to correct later in the verification. It is better to delay the answer for a while, but to make sure it is correct. A company has the right to present itself in the best possible light. Officials who are unsure about whether a particular way of answering a question is good or bad should check with their lawyer. Most of this checking can be done before the sessions with the Commerce Department staff. Even during the verification, however, it is usually possible to make arrangements for a brief, informal consultation.

Never directly refuse to give a document to the Commerce Department

A refusal to provide a document – even an unimportant document – creates a serious risk that the Commerce Department will use 'facts available'. It may be possible, however, to avoid providing a particular document. For example, suggesting an alternative document that can serve the same purpose is often successful. If the company delays, the Commerce Department staff member sometimes forgets about the particular document or topic. If the Commerce Department persists, however, a company has little choice but to cooperate, or risk the adverse consequences of not cooperating.

Chapter 11

Injury determinations

The International Trade Commission determines whether unfair trade investigations proceed or not. Under both United States and international law, the Commission must determine whether the imports under investigation are causing or threaten to cause 'material injury' to the domestic industry. A determination that there is no material injury, at either the preliminary or the final injury determination, terminates the anti-dumping or countervailing duty investigation.

The Commission injury determinations are the most important part of the overall defence effort. If the determinations are negative, the case ends without any need for burdensome follow up 'administrative reviews' of the anti-dumping order each year. And, more importantly, the likelihood of success at the Commission is greater than the likelihood of success at the Commerce Department. In about 15% of preliminary investigations and about 30%–40% of final investigations, the Commission makes negative determinations. These success rates compare quite favourably to the very rare case in which the Commerce Department does not find dumping margins.

Although very important, the Commission injury determinations are much less predictable than the Department of Commerce determinations. The Commission must make the difficult qualitative judgement of whether the domestic industry is suffering material injury. Even more difficult is the qualitative and somewhat subjective determination of whether the injury is caused by the imported merchandise, or by some other factor. Because of these inherently subjective judgements, it is extremely difficult to predict the outcome of a Commission injury analysis. The outcome is also difficult to predict because new Commissioners are appointed and bring new perspectives to this subjective process.

It is important for foreign companies to understand the process and the key issues involved in injury investigations. The company staff members need to explain to senior management what is happening during the anti-dumping investigation. They also need to supply information to the lawyers as part of the defence. Most importantly, however, foreign companies can sometimes adjust their behaviour in the marketplace to reduce the risk of an affirmative finding of injury. If a company is sensitive to the issues involved in an injury investigation, it has a much better chance of adjusting its behaviour.

This chapter provides an overview of the issues that arise in injury investigations. Chapter 2 has already described the procedural framework of the Commission's preliminary and final determinations. This chapter reviews the four substantive questions that the Commission must answer in each injury investigation:

❑ Which products produced in the United States are 'like' the imported products subject to investigation?

❑ Which companies make up the domestic industry producing the like products?

❑ Is this particular domestic industry 'materially' injured?

❑ Did imports 'cause' the injury being suffered by this industry?

This chapter briefly explains the Commission's conceptual framework for answering each of the questions. Note that these issues are basically the same in both anti-dumping and countervailing duty investigations. Chapters 12 and 13 then go into more detail on preliminary and final injury investigations.

Defining the 'like' product

General considerations

In each of its injury investigations, the Commission must define the scope of its investigation. United States law defines the domestic industry as those companies that produce a 'like product' – that domestically produced product which most closely resembles the imported product under investigation. Defining the like product is not always easy, and the parties sometimes argue a great deal about the proper definition.

The definition of the like product can have a significant impact on the injury analysis. The parties therefore argue for the most favourable definition. The petitioner attempts to define it to include the domestic industry's weakest sector and to exclude the strongest sector, to maximize the appearance of injury. For example, if an industry contains sectors A, B and C – with sector A badly injured and sectors B and C thriving – the petitioner may argue to isolate sector A's product as the like product. If sectors B and C were included, they might compensate for the conditions of sector A to such a point that the Commission would find no material injury.

The foreign company may seek the opposite result in such situations, but the company's strategy depends on its position in the market. Combining thriving sectors with injured sectors usually reduces the risk of an affirmative finding of injury. Of course, if the company happens to produce a product in a sector not suffering injury, it may want to isolate that sector. For example, if the domestic industry sells merchandise assembled from certain components, and the foreign company exports only components, the company might argue that two like products (the assembled products and the components) are present.

Factors to consider

In determining what products are included as the 'like product', the Commission traditionally looks to whether the products have:

❑ Interchangeable uses;

❑ Similar physical appearances;

❑ Common manufacturing and distribution;

❑ Similar prices;

❑ Similar customer perceptions.

No one of these factors is determinative, and some of the factors overlap. The foreign company should structure its like product arguments according to these five characteristics.

Arguments about the like product inevitably become a balancing of each of these factors. These arguments are extremely fact-specific, and it is difficult to anticipate how the Commission will define the scope of a particular like product. Because of this flexibility, the foreign company should define the like product in the most favourable way during the preliminary injury investigation. Even if the effort is unsuccessful at the preliminary determination stage, the company will have framed the debate in its favour and the Commission may accept the argument in the final determination.

There is one important exception to this general rule of defining the like product in the most favourable way during the preliminary investigation. If the defence team believes there is a realistic chance of winning the case at the preliminary stage, then it sometimes makes sense not to contest the like product. The simple reality is that a challenge to the petitioner's definition of the like product at the preliminary stage virtually guarantees an affirmative preliminary determination. Since the Commission will not have the necessary data to make a decision based on the alternative like product – the questionnaires collecting data in the preliminary stage almost always adopt the like product suggested by the petitioners – the Commission has no choice but to make an affirmative preliminary determination and then collect the necessary information during the final investigation.

Interchangeability of use

The Commission investigates whether the two products being considered have the same or similar uses. Take, for example, a steel nail, an iron nail and an aluminium nail. Although they are similar in a sense, they all have somewhat different applications. If a product is wholly 'dedicated' to a specific use and cannot be adapted to another use, one can argue that it constitutes a distinct like product from merchandise wholly dedicated to a different use. Such a situation is an easy case, and the Commission finds two separate like products.

Where a product may be adapted to various uses, the Commission must undertake the difficult task of deciding whether the products are similar enough. The Commission considers the cost of adapting the product to a particular use, and the probability of so adapting the product. If the final user of a product is a household consumer, the Commission may find that the cost of adapting a given product to a new use, even if low, distinguishes the products into two separate like product categories. On the other hand, if the final user is an industry, the Commission may well find that the cost of adaptation, if not higher than the cost of purchasing the merchandise requiring no adaptation, is not prohibitive, and the two products may be found to be the same 'like' product.

Physical characteristics

The Commission also considers the physical characteristics of the product. The more physically similar the two products, the more likely the Commission is to find a single like product. In its analysis, the Commission looks to that part of the product representing the majority of the product's value. Unessential attachments that change the appearance of a product do not create a separate like product. Rather, if the most important elements of two products are physically similar, the two products are probably 'like' for purposes of the Commission analysis. This essential element, however, cannot be defined so broadly as to create an over-inclusive category.

Common manufacturing

The Commission also examines the methods of producing the product. The more similar the methods, the more likely the Commission is to find a single like product. Similar production employees and manufacturing facilities alone do not determine that two products are 'like'. These factors could, however, influence the outcome in a close case. For example, consider two chemical compounds serving exactly the same purpose, but of vastly different quality. If the chemicals share common manufacturing facilities and are produced by the same group of employees, these factors could tip the balance and lead the Commission to find that the two chemicals are a single like product.

Common distribution

The Commission also considers common distribution channels. If two products are sold through common distribution channels, by the same people, to the same customers, then the Commission is more likely to find the products to be 'like'.

Price

Price is a partial gauge of consumer perception and can be used to distinguish between two products, if the price differential is great enough. Price alone is not a determining factor for like product determinations, but rather serves as a proxy for other determining factors – such as interchangeability, quality, and consumer perceptions. The greater the price differential, the greater the difference in some other, more determinative factor.

Consumer perceptions

Consumer perceptions also reinforce the other factors that serve to differentiate products. Even if consumers think that two products are different, if the uses and composition of the products are the same, the Commission will probably find a single like product. In a close case, however, this factor could tip the balance, especially if the evidence of differing consumer perceptions is compelling enough. Since it is difficult to collect reliable data on this issue – other than differences in the prices people are willing to pay – its importance is often limited in Commission investigations.

Defining the domestic industry

Beyond defining the product under investigation, the Commission must also define the industry to be examined. Generally, the first step is to identify all the domestic producers of the like product. The Commission must then decide whether to exclude any of the United States companies producing the like products from the domestic industry. The Commission must also consider whether to base its analysis on a single national industry, or a more narrowly defined regional industry.

Excluding a company from the domestic industry

The anti-dumping law is designed to protect United States industries, not companies that just happen to be located in the United States. The increasing globalization of United States industries has created situations where a company that appears to be part of the domestic industry may in fact be more foreign than American. If the Commission finds that a company's true interests lie with importing, not domestic production, the Commission has the discretion to exclude that company from the domestic industry.

The foreign company may be able to argue that at least part of the petitioning domestic industry should be excluded. This strategy can be an effective way to exclude some companies that have been experiencing problems, and thus have the domestic industry show better performance. When the foreign company first learns of the petition, it can use its own information on the production and sourcing practices of its United States competition to evaluate whether some members of the petitioning domestic industry should be eliminated.

The Commission decides to exclude companies from the domestic industry based on several factors:

❑ *Capital investment* – The extent and source of a firm's capital investment is an important consideration. If most of the capital investment comes from foreign sources, the Commission may consider the company not to be a member of the United States industry. Another important consideration is whether the importer is related to the foreign producer.

❑ *Technical expertise* – The technical expertise involved in United States production is another major consideration. Mere assembly operations in the United States may not qualify as United States companies, if the technically sophisticated operations take place overseas.

❑ *Employment* – Since one of the underlying purposes of the United States anti-dumping law is to protect United States jobs, the Commission investigates how many United States based jobs are involved in the production. The more United States jobs, the more likely the Commission is to find the company to be part of the United States industry.

❑ *Sourcing of parts* – The quantity and types of parts sourced in the United States, which reflects the economic importance of the operation to the United States, is another important consideration.

❑ *Value added* – Underlying the various items above is the general notion of value added. The more value added in the United States, the more likely the Commission is to consider the company part of the United States industry.

❑ *Other costs* – The Commission also considers any other costs or activities in the United States that relate to domestic production of the like product.

The final decision to exclude a company is subject to the Commission's discretion, not a strict legal standard. The Commission staff collects information on these factors, but only if one of the parties raises the issue. It is important, therefore, for the foreign company and its lawyers to evaluate this issue early in the investigation, and decide whether there is a strong enough basis to raise the issue with the Commission.

Even if there is a factual basis for excluding certain companies, it may not be in the best interests of the foreign company to make this argument. If a domestically based manufacturer benefits from lower priced imports, it may well be more profitable than the other domestic companies. Including such a company could reduce the appearance of injury. The foreign company and its lawyers therefore may argue that the related party does not conduct its operations differently from any other United States based industry, and should be considered part of the United States domestic industry. Of course, the domestic industry is likely to make the opposite argument. As is so often true in Commission investigations, companies can find themselves on different sides of an issue, depending on the circumstances.

Regional industries

To isolate the impact of imports and to maximize their effect on the domestic industry, the petitioner may try to limit the injury investigation to a 'regional industry'. By doing so, the petitioner can avoid an analysis of the effect of the imports on the entire United States market, where the effect may be somewhat diluted. To establish a regional industry, the Commission must find that:

❑ The domestic producers sell 'all or almost all' of their production of the like product to customers within the regional market, and not to a national market;

❑ Customers within the regional market do not buy a significant amount of the like product from domestic producers outside the region; and

❑ The imports under investigation are concentrated within the region.

Even though the Commission must determine that 'all or almost all' of the producers are materially injured – as opposed to a finding that a 'majority' is injured – it is usually easier for the Commission to find injury when the impact of the imports is concentrated into a single region.

The foreign company normally attempts to prove that no regional industry exists. To win this argument, the company need only establish that its imports do not all arrive at a single point of entry, or that the 'region' claimed by the petitioner is not isolated from other sections of the United States market. With the trend toward broad product distribution creating larger and larger markets, the foreign company should usually be able to refute a petitioner's claim for a regional industry. Ultimately, however, the outcome depends on the particular facts.

Regional industries are quite unusual in anti-dumping cases. As a practical matter, most markets in the United States are national, and rarely are the costs of transportation relative to the total price of the product significant enough to create regional markets. Indeed, although petitioners sometimes argue for regional markets, since the adverse impact of imports may be felt more sharply in one region, the Commission usually finds national markets. In addition, anti-dumping orders based on regional markets are harder to administer, as the Commerce Department is supposed to apply duties, as much as possible, only to those imports going into the region for which the Commission found injury. For both these reasons, the United States rarely imposes dumping duties only for a regional industry.

Condition of the domestic industry

General considerations

The foreign company and its advisers should develop factual information showing whether the domestic industry is suffering 'material injury'. Obviously, the degree of detail varies for the preliminary injury determination and the final injury determination. Some information comes from the questionnaire responses themselves, which the Commission now releases to the lawyers for the foreign company. Other information comes from independent sources, such as 10K reports submitted to the United States Securities and Exchange Commission, and newspaper articles. The Commission staff will also often make telephone calls to members of the industry in search of information.

To determine whether the industry has been materially injured, the Commission normally looks at industry trends over a three-year period ending with the initiation of the investigation. The Commission considers a wide variety of economic factors in three broad categories: (1) the volume of imports; (2) the prices of imports; and (3) the impact of the imports on the domestic industry. When looking at the condition of the domestic market, the Commission pays special attention to:

❑ Domestic consumption;

❑ Domestic production;

❑ Capacity and capacity utilization;

❑ Shipments and inventories;

❑ Employment levels;

❑ Profitability;

❑ Ability to raise capital; and

❑ Expenditures on research and development.

No single factor is determinative, so it is difficult to predict the Commission's decision in any particular case.

Most of this information is drawn from the questionnaire responses prepared by the domestic industry. Note that while the Commission tries to collect this information for the particular product under investigation, sometimes it is not possible to do so. The Commission is authorized to collect this data on a broader product-line basis, including the particular product under investigation, if that is the only information maintained by the United States companies.

Factors to consider

Domestic market share

If domestic consumption is rising while the domestic industry's market share is deteriorating, there is a strong possibility that imports are replacing sales by the United States industry. The Commission will probably find that the domestic industry is suffering material injury. A decrease in domestic consumption of the like product, however, could mean that there is an independent cause for the domestic industry's difficulties – obsolescence, changing taste, or shifting demand. In such a case, the Commission is less likely to find material injury. Whether consumption is rising or falling, the key factor is the domestic industry's market share. Falling market share is a strong indication of material injury.

Domestic production

The Commission examines domestic production figures to understand the industry trends over the period of investigation. The Commission also relates the production figures to other factors. For example, if the domestic industry decreased production without a tangible, market-based reason, this unilateral action would explain a decrease in capacity utilization, shipments, and employment and the Commission would be less likely to find material injury. If the domestic industry cuts production because of surging imports, the Commission is more likely to find material injury.

Capacity and capacity utilization

The Commission examines capacity and capacity utilization to determine the rate at which the industry is operating. If capacity remains unchanged while capacity utilization drops dramatically, this factor indicates deterioration in the condition of the domestic industry. If the domestic industry has overexpanded its capacity, however, the Commission may interpret low capacity utilization differently. The problems would result from the industry's own actions, not from material injury caused by imports.

Shipments and inventories

Shipment levels and inventory levels are related. When a company stops shipping, and begins to build up inventory, the Commission considers this shift to be evidence of material injury. The number of shipments made by the domestic industry, and especially the trend in shipments, is a sign of an industry's health. Conversely, a build-up of inventory would show that the industry is suffering.

Employment levels

A decrease in employment, like a drop in capacity utilization, shows the Commission that the domestic industry is not operating at full strength. Unemployment – measured both in number of workers employed and total number of hours worked – is considered by the Commission as strong evidence of material injury. Given the protectionist nature of the dumping law, and political significance of employment levels, it is not surprising that the United States law and the Commission's practice place a great deal of emphasis on this factor.

Profitability

The Commission examines the effects of any price suppression on the profitability of the domestic industry. A drop in profitability is a sign of material injury. Profitability also affects many of the other factors that the Commission considers. Falling profitability (especially losses) often causes domestic companies to lay off workers, and to reduce R&D expenditures. Historically, profitability has been one of the most important factors the Commission considers.

Ability to raise capital

If an industry is suffering, lenders usually are more reluctant to make funds available to it. The Commission thus looks to the judgement of these lenders in assessing the condition of the domestic industry. Companies that have trouble borrowing money are more likely to be considered materially injured.

Expenditures on research and development

The Commission must also examine the domestic industry's expenditures on R&D in assessing the condition of the domestic industry. Although this is not a central factor of the analysis, a need to decrease R&D spending is an indication that the domestic industry is suffering injury. In investigations of high-tech products, this factor takes on more importance.

Causation

Beyond finding that the United States industry is materially injured, the Commission must also determine that this injury was caused by less-than-fair-value imports. Historically, individual Commissioners have used different methods of linking causation and injury. In the past, some Commissioners first examined the condition of the domestic industry and then studied the issue of causation. The more common approach since the 1990s has been to look at injury and causation as intertwined questions. Instead of separating the issues, the Commission follows the statutory outline of looking at volume effects, price effects, and adverse impact.

The Commission looks to various factors to determine causation. Among other things, the Commission considers: (1) whether the volume of imports, or the increase in volume, is significant; (2) whether the imported products have undersold the domestic products; (3) whether the domestic industry has lost sales to imported products; and (4) whether domestic prices have been either depressed or prevented from increasing in an economically reasonable manner. The Commission analyses these factors over the three-year period preceding the petition to discern the trends during that period. If imports have been increasing and prices have either decreased or failed to increase reasonably, the Commission is more likely to find causation.

The foreign company should understand the limited standard that must be met. The United States law is clear that the Commission should not weigh alternative causes of injury. The imports need not be the only cause of injury, or even the major cause of injury. The Commission need only find that imports are a cause of injury. Even if imports are the least significant cause, the Commission may find causation.

Because of this standard, it is difficult to disprove causation. If the domestic industry is suffering injury, the Commission is likely to find that imports at least contributed to that injury, and are thus a legal cause of the injury. Nevertheless, the Commission has made negative findings of causation in numerous cases. Indeed, when the Commission makes a negative determination, the reason is often the lack of a sufficient causal link between imports and the problems of the domestic industry. To the extent possible, the foreign company should develop evidence showing other causes for the domestic industry's troubles.

The Commission injury determinations are the most important part of the overall defence effort. If the determinations are negative, the case ends without any need for burdensome follow up 'administrative reviews' of the anti-dumping order each year. More importantly, the likelihood of success at the Commission is greater than the likelihood of success at the Commerce Department. In about 15% of preliminary investigations and 30%–40% of final investigations, the Commission makes negative determinations. These success rates compare quite favourably to the very rare case in which the Commerce Department does not find dumping margins.

Other topics relating to injury determinations

Cumulation of imports

If the petitioner complains about imports from several countries, the Commission may cumulate (combine) the imports from these various sources in assessing whether the United States industry has been materially injured. Although the Commission has always had the discretion to cumulate imports, the United States Congress made cumulation mandatory in 1984.

The Commission cumulates imports from various countries if the following conditions are met: (1) they are all subject to investigation under either the anti-dumping or the countervailing duty law; (2) they compete with each other and with the domestic like product; and (3) their marketing is reasonably coincident. If the products from the various countries are all grouped within a single class or kind of merchandise, it is very likely that these criteria have all been met.

Battles over cumulation usually involve the second element, whether there is a sufficient overlap of competition with other imports and with the domestic product. The United States courts have made clear that there need only be a 'reasonable overlap' of competition, which is a pretty low standard. During the Uruguay Round negotiations, one proposal called for a 20% overlap to meet this standard, but the United States felt such a test would be too strict and insisted that this wording be deleted. In practice, the Commission rarely considers an argument against cumulation unless the foreign country can demonstrate a degree of overlap below 5%. Note that this limited overlap can be either with other imports or with the domestic industry. Under the United States statute both elements must be present, so if the foreign company can show the absence of either element, cumulation is not allowed.

When assessing the degree of overlap, the Commission has traditionally considered the following basic factors:

❑ *Degree of fungibility* – This factor involves the degree to which the various products can be substituted for each other. The Commission asks customers to indicate whether they believe the various products can be used interchangeably. The more interchangeable the products, the more likely the Commission is to find cumulation.

❑ *Geographic markets* – The Commission generally examines the regional pattern of sales, looking at imports into various ports in the United States. If all products are present in all geographic markets (even in very small quantities), the Commission is more likely to cumulate the imports.

❑ *Common distribution channels* – This factor relates to the degree of competitive overlaps; products in different and distinct distribution channels do not really compete with each other. The more overlap, the more likely the Commission is to cumulate.

❑ *Simultaneously present* – Finally, the Commission considers the timing of imports over the three-year period being investigated. If various imports and domestic products are all being sold throughout the period, the Commission is more likely to cumulate.

Where possible, the foreign company should argue against cumulation. The more imports that are grouped together, the greater the impact on the domestic industry, and the more likely that the Commission will find material injury from the imports. It is very difficult, however, to avoid cumulation. The 1984 changes to the law expanded the scope of cumulation, and made clear that the Commission should apply cumulation broadly.

Since then, the Commission has expanded the doctrine of cumulation to include almost every possible scenario.

The one exception to this expansion of cumulation is the doctrine of 'negligible' imports. If the foreign company has few imports into the United States during the period of investigation, it can argue to exclude its imports from the cumulation of other imports. Reflecting the changes mandated by the Uruguay Round, United States law applies the numerical thresholds set forth in the Anti-Dumping Agreement. If imports from a country account for less than 3% of the volume of all imports over the most recent 12-month period for which information is available preceding the filing of the petition, that country will be deemed negligible and the investigation for that country will be terminate. But if all negligible countries together account for more than 7% of the volume of imports, all of those negligible countries can be recaptured and included in the analysis.

These rules have triggered some intense debates. When the import levels for a particular country are low enough, the foreign countries have often tried to argue to shrink the numerator and increase the denominator enough to fall just below the 3% threshold. There have been several cases in which domestic petitioners thought a country would be above 3%, only to discover that the country was able to escape by make detailed arguments about the precise products that should be included or excluded.

The United States law also provides several specific exceptions to cumulation. First, the Commission cannot cumulate a country for which it has made a negative determination of dumping or subsidies. Second, the Commission cannot cumulate if for any reason the investigation with respect to that country has been terminated, for example because the petitioner may have withdrawn the petition and effectively 'settled' the case. Third, the Commission cannot cumulate countries that are designated beneficiaries under the Caribbean Basin Economic Recovery Act. Depending on the particular circumstances of a case, one of these exceptions might apply.

Threat of material injury

Even if the foreign company is successful in disproving the presence of material injury, the Commission may find that the domestic industry is threatened with potential material injury by the foreign company. The Commission analyses threat by considering the foreign company's intentions and potential to export to the United States market in the future. In determining whether imports threaten future injury, the Commission looks at:

❑ The foreign company's excess capacity for producing the imported merchandise;

❑ Recent and sudden increases in the market share of the imported merchandise;

❑ Substantial increases in United States inventories of the imported merchandise; and

❑ Possible price suppressing effects of the imported merchandise, either because of a large market share or because of the general condition of the domestic industry.

The Commission must find that these factors provide evidence that the threat of material injury is real and that actual injury is 'imminent'. An affirmative finding of threat of injury can not be based on mere conjecture or supposition of injury.

The Commission is most likely to find that the foreign company poses a threat if it has expanded capacity and has no other market. If another substantial market exists – either in the exporter's home market or in some other country – it is harder for the domestic industry to show that the excess capacity will lead to a flood of exports to the United States market. The Commission may perhaps be more reluctant to find threat of injury if the imported merchandise is covered by some multilateral, bilateral, or voluntary export restraint agreement. Such agreements put an indisputable cap on potential exports and refute arguments that unused capacity could be directed at the United States.

Note that there is a special rule for cumulation in threat cases. Unlike cases involving material injury, in which cumulation is mandatory, in cases involving only threat of injury, cumulation is still discretionary. In exercising its discretion, the Commission normally examines the trends in various import sources. If all the trends are similar – particularly the rate of increase in import levels – the Commission is likely to cumulate. In cases where the trends diverge – such as some import sources increasing, but other sources decreasing – the Commission can decide and has decided in some cases not to cumulate.

Material retardation

United States law allows a finding of injury if imports prevent the United States domestic industry from being established. This theory is called 'material retardation' – the notion that the United States industry is being materially retarded in its efforts to establish itself. This approach to injury is less common than either 'material injury' or 'threat of injury'. The Commission usually makes its decision on other grounds, and often does not even reach the issue of material retardation. There have been very few cases in which the Commission has found material retardation.

Critical circumstances

If the Commission finds that the domestic industry is suffering material injury, the domestic industry may argue that 'critical circumstances' exist and that anti-dumping duties should be imposed retroactively. Recall that anti-dumping duties are normally assessed only after the Commerce Department's preliminary determination. A finding of critical circumstances allows the assessment of duties to be retroactive to 90 days prior to the preliminary determination.

Both the Commerce Department and the Commission must find that critical circumstances exist. The Commerce Department examines whether there has been a sudden surge in exports, and whether the foreign company should have known the sales were at unfair prices. The Commission examines whether the foreign company has increased its exports after the petition is filed in an attempt to avoid the effect of the anti-dumping investigation by entering the merchandise into the United States market before the Commerce Department's preliminary determination. If the Commission determines that such imports will prolong or cause a recurrence of material injury to the domestic industry, anti-dumping duties may be imposed retrospectively.

As a practical matter, the Commission rarely finds critical circumstances. Although the Commerce Department applies mechanical rules, and is quite willing to find critical circumstances, the Commission has been much more sceptical. Still, if the issue is at stake, the foreign company needs to present complete arguments to avoid being subject to retroactive duties.

Chapter 12

Defending the Commission's preliminary investigation

The preliminary injury determination by the International Trade Commission is the first chance the foreign company has to disprove the allegations of dumping or subsidies. If this determination is negative, the anti-dumping investigation ends, and the company suffers little disruption of its business. If the determination is affirmative, the company must undergo a lengthy investigation by the Department of Commerce. Any company that has been through such an investigation knows the burden and frustration involved, and does everything possible to avoid repeating the experience.

This chapter reviews various considerations involved in defending a Commission preliminary injury investigation. The first section reviews the basic procedures for the preliminary injury investigation, and describes the conduct of the investigation. This section expands on the brief overview provided in chapter 2. The second section then discusses various issues that a foreign company should consider as part of its defence. The particular arguments to make in each case will depend on the facts of that case. The general approach to the defence, however, applies to every preliminary injury investigation.

Procedures for the preliminary injury determination

Timing of investigation

The Commission's preliminary injury investigation proceeds very quickly. The preliminary injury determination must be made within 45 days after the petition is filed, with no possibility of an extension. Because of this strict statutory requirement, the work at this stage is quite rushed. The Commission staff begins work immediately after the petition is filed, and decides on a work schedule within one or two days.

The staff must first ensure that the petition meets the various legal requirements. During the first week after the petition is filed, the Commission staff consults with the Commerce Department staff, who examine the petition for adequacy. As a practical matter, the petition is always adequate, because petitioners usually consult with the Commerce Department and sometimes the Commission before filing their petition. Both agencies encourage this informal contact before the petition is filed.

If the petition meets the regulatory requirements, the Commission publishes a notice initiating the investigation in the *Federal Register*. This notice also sets forth the schedule for the preliminary injury investigation.

Nature of investigation

Even before the formal notice is published, the Commission begins its investigation. The Commission staff assembles a team to handle the case, including an investigator, an economist, an accountant, an industry analyst and a staff lawyer. The Commission staff then gathers data through questionnaires sent to domestic producers, foreign producers and importers of the merchandise under investigation, as well as meetings and telephone conversations with representatives of the United States industry and other industry experts.

The quality of the information collected at this stage can vary dramatically. If the petition involves an industry that the Commission has considered in the past and the particular investigators have personal experience with this industry, the quality can be quite high. The Commission may already have an extensive database with which to work and prior experience so it can understand the industry. If the petition involves a new industry, and especially if the industry structure is complex and changing, the quality of the information can be quite poor. The fault lies not with the staff, but with the severe time constraints for conducting a preliminary injury investigation.

Questionnaires

The Commission's main source of information about an industry is questionnaire responses. Separate questionnaires are sent to importers, domestic producers and foreign exporters. At the preliminary stage, these questionnaires are mailed within two to four business days after the petition has been filed. These questionnaires are mailed before the Commission has decided anything, including the key issue of the product under investigation. For this reason, questionnaires at the preliminary stage tend to follow the domestic industry's suggestions.

Although companies should be careful in how they complete these questionnaire responses, the Commission is not as careful in its scrutiny of the data as the Commerce Department. The Commerce Department always conducts a verification of the information submitted by foreign companies. The Commission, however, does not have enough time to conduct verifications. Although the Commission has the legal authority to verify information, it rarely uses this authority.

Importers' questionnaire

Part I of the importer's questionnaire contains general questions. The main purpose of this section of the questionnaire is to obtain information about the structure of the industry, and the relationships among the various parties. The Commission staff wants to ensure that it has identified all the appropriate companies, and that everyone has received appropriate questionnaires.

Part II asks about trade and related information. This part asks the importer to provide data about imports, shipments and inventory levels. The Commission staff normally requests data for the three most recent calendar years, and year-to-date information for the current year and the immediately preceding year. It is important to provide the data on a calendar-year basis, even if the company's accounting records are kept on a different basis. The Commission staff will ultimately aggregate the data from individual importers to obtain total imports from the foreign country. If importers present data on different bases, the Commission staff cannot accurately aggregate the data.

Part III asks about pricing and related information. In many ways, this is the most important part of the questionnaire. First, the Commission staff must study the relationship of import prices to prices charged by the domestic industry. If there is evidence of underpricing, the Commission is more likely to find a reasonable indication of material injury. The trends in price data are particularly important. The Commission tries to understand the dynamics of competition in the market, and therefore places a great deal of emphasis on the trends in relative prices over time. If the trend in prices is down, the Commission is more likely to find injury.

Second, the pricing section of the questionnaire is also important because of its difficulty. It is often difficult to provide data that allow for an appropriate comparison of prices, since different companies base their prices on different assumptions. When the Commission staff has incomplete or misleading data, the Commission is more likely to make an affirmative determination and to allow the investigation to continue. It is important, therefore, for companies to spend the time to develop and present this information carefully.

Companies should view the questionnaire as an opportunity to persuade the Commission staff, and ultimately the Commissioners themselves. Often companies are overly defensive, and try to hide information from the staff. Our experience has been that complete questionnaire responses are more persuasive, and more likely to succeed, than incomplete questionnaire responses.

Foreign exporters' questionnaire

The questionnaire submitted to foreign exporters is much less detailed. The Commission staff asks about production levels and shipments to various markets, and also about production capacity and inventory levels. The questionnaire is usually only several pages.

Information from exporters is most important for determining threat of injury. The Commission staff is looking for evidence that foreign exporters have excess capacity, and that they will increase their shipments to the United States. Evidence of significant markets other than the United States (and prior sales to those markets) is therefore very helpful. If the United States is the only major market, and the exporters have excess capacity, the Commission is more likely to find threat of injury.

Producers' questionnaire

United States domestic producers must also complete a questionnaire response. The questionnaire asks for information indicating whether the domestic industry is suffering injury because of imports. As discussed in chapter 9, a number of factors are considered by the Commission. The most important of them include:

❑ Market share of the United States domestic industry;

❑ Capacity utilization levels;

❑ Employment levels;

❑ Profitability;

❑ Price trends; and

❑ Allegations of lost sales.

These producers' questionnaires are very important, since they provide the data on which the Commission is to make its determination.

An individual company can file a petition, using estimates of what is happening to other companies in the domestic industry. Before making its determination, however, the Commission will try to obtain questionnaire responses from all the members of the domestic industry, not just the petitioner.

Any United States based producer can receive a questionnaire, whether the producer is owned by United States or foreign parties. All United States based producers are expected to complete the questionnaire. In some cases, however, the Commission has the authority to exclude certain producers from the domestic industry if the United States producers are related to the foreign producers who are the target of the investigation.

Other investigative techniques

Although the Commission relies primarily on questionnaire responses, it does use other investigative techniques. The most commonly used technique is a telephone interview. The Commission staff will usually call as many customers as possible, in an effort to explore in more detail why they made certain purchase decisions. The Commission staff is particularly interested in the reasons for buying imported products, and the role of price in the purchase decision. In addition, depending on the time available, and the professional commitment of individual staff assigned to a case, the staff may collect varying amounts of publicly available data from various sources.

Treatment of confidential information

The treatment of confidential information before the Commission has changed over the years. Prior to 1988, the Commission refused to release any confidential information to the lawyers for the domestic petitioners and foreign respondents. In 1988, however, Congress amended the law to require the Commission to begin releasing confidential data to the lawyers for the various parties under administrative protective orders. The lawyers are under strict obligations to protect the confidentiality of the information, and the Commission has been strict in enforcing these obligations.

Access to the confidential information of the other side has significantly changed the nature of arguments before the Commission. The lawyers now have reasonably complete data about the other side's arguments and factual information, and can respond more effectively.

Staff conference

As part of the investigation, the staff schedules an informal conference at which the parties may present their views to the Commission staff. The Commissioners do not attend this conference; its purpose is to help the staff understand the issues of the case. The domestic industry and the foreign respondents are each usually given one hour to present their arguments. Each side may present witnesses, but there is no opportunity to cross-examine witnesses presented by the other party. Both during and after the formal presentations, the Commission staff asks questions of both sides, to clarify the various issues involved in the investigation.

It is usually better to have businesspeople – either company officials or customers, or both – testify as witnesses. The staff wants to understand how the industry works.

Businesspeople are more credible witnesses to discuss the industry, but sometimes if the time is very limited, or there are no appropriate company witnesses, the lawyers or other advisers make the presentation themselves. Because of the short time involved, it is often difficult to find and persuade appropriate witnesses for the staff conference.

Although the conference is the first opportunity for the foreign company to present its views, the company is at a great disadvantage. Although the domestic industry has been planning its presentation for months, the foreign company has only two or three weeks to prepare its presentation. Since it sometimes takes two or three weeks just to choose a lawyer, there is often very little time to prepare.

Post-conference submissions

After the conference, parties may file post-conference briefs containing additional arguments and information. These briefs should frame the issues clearly for the Commission staff, and should explain why the available evidence supports the particular conclusions urged by the party. These briefs are usually due one week after the conference.

Informal consultations with staff

After the formal submissions, there is often an opportunity for informal consultations with the staff, who may have questions about the various questionnaire responses. Foreign companies should make every effort to cooperate and help the staff resolve any open questions. Open questions are an excuse for the Commission to make an affirmative determination and thus continue the investigation to find the answers to the open questions.

Post-conference staff report

The staff reviews the briefs, collects all the available information, and prepares a preliminary report to the Commissioners. This report presents a first attempt by the staff to define the crucial issues in the investigation. It discusses the merchandise under investigation, the trends in imports and in the domestic market, and the condition of the domestic industry. This report is presented to the Commissioners and forms the basis for the preliminary injury decision. Note that the staff only presents data, and does not make any explicit recommendations about how the Commissioners should decide the various issues.

Decision by Commission

The Commissioners make their decision soon after receiving the staff report. Roughly 4 days after receiving the staff report, or about 10 days before the end of the 45-day period, the Commission votes to determine whether there is a reasonable indication of injury. Tie votes (when fully staffed the Commission has six Commissioners) are considered affirmative determinations. Based on this vote the staff drafts, and the Commissioners revise, an opinion explaining the views of the Commission. Eventually a formal notice is published in the *Federal Register* announcing the results.

As explained in chapter 2, the standard of proof at the preliminary stage is quite low. The Commission must decide only whether a 'reasonable indication' exists that the imports under investigation are causing or threatening to cause material injury. This low standard for finding material injury means that the Commission makes a negative preliminary injury determination only if: (1) there is convincing evidence that no material injury or threat of material injury exists; and (2) there is no likelihood of contrary evidence arising in a final investigation.

Although in theory the Commission can find that imports are not the cause of injury, it is unusual for the Commission to make a negative preliminary injury determination based on causation. In most cases the evidence about causation available at the preliminary stage is so limited that the Commission has no basis for a determination. Because the standard of proof is so low, it is difficult for foreign companies to win negative preliminary injury determinations.

Considerations in defending the investigation

In preparing its defence of the preliminary injury investigation, a foreign company must consider a number of issues. This section addresses the questions that most commonly arise when a company is deciding whether and how to defend the investigation. The focus is on the general approach to defending the investigation.

Should the company defend the case?

Foreign companies sometimes wonder whether they should even bother to defend a preliminary injury investigation. Since the burden of proof at this stage is so low, the domestic petitioner almost always wins. Under these circumstances, why incur the cost of a defence?

There are two important reasons to defend the Commission's preliminary injury determination, even though the likelihood of success is limited. First, the company might win. Although the percentage of victories at this stage is small, some foreign companies have been successful. Statistics for the current Commission show that about 15% of investigations are terminated at the preliminary stage. More broadly over time, the rate of negative determinations at the preliminary stage has varied from 10% to 20%.

Since a victory at the preliminary determination means the investigation comes to an immediate end, it is worth the effort to try. The cost of defending the preliminary determination is small compared to the cost of defending the rest of the anti-dumping investigation.

Second, the Commission preliminary is a chance to define the arguments that might be crucial at the Commission final. If the foreign company does not participate in the preliminary investigation, the domestic industry is free to define the key issues however it wishes. With the investigation framed in the wrong terms, the Commission may not collect the data that the foreign company requires to prove its key arguments. It is therefore important to participate in shaping the form of the investigation.

Who should defend the case?

The company must assemble an effective defence team. Once the right team is assembled, most of the defence work can be handled by the team. Unlike the Commerce Department phases of the anti-dumping investigation, the injury investigations usually do not require a great deal of work by the foreign company. Most of the burden falls on the customers in the United States – whether related or unrelated – who import the merchandise under investigation. Those customers must complete detailed importers' questionnaires.

The foreign company must decide whether it will participate actively in the case itself, or leave this task to its United States subsidiary or importers. All injury investigations focus on imports into the United States market, their competition with the domestic products, and the condition of the United States industry. In most cases, United States subsidiaries (or unrelated importers if there are no subsidiaries) have more data and information with which to formulate arguments regarding the situation in the United States market and the condition of the domestic industry. Thus it is common for foreign companies to allow a subsidiary or importer to assume principal responsibility for the defence of the Commission case. Of course, such a decision assumes the foreign company has confidence in the subsidiary or importer and the team of professional advisers with whom they expect to work on the defence effort.

What is the role of outside advisers?

A defence before the Commission relies much more heavily on outside professional advisers than does the defence before the Commerce Department. Company accountants and staff do not need to collect large amount of data. The Commission itself collects most of the information in the form of questionnaires to domestic producers, importers and foreign producers. Based on this information, and any other information collected from public sources by the parties, the professional advisers prepare the best possible arguments that the United States industry is not suffering any injury because of the imports.

Companies generally use two types of professional advisers. First, lawyers usually coordinate the defence effort. Since the Commission applies legal standards to decide whether or not there is injury, lawyers play an active role in this process. Moreover, because the Commission decisions often result in court appeals, and only lawyers are allowed to argue before the Court of International Trade, companies usually find it more efficient to have a lawyer involved from the beginning of the process. Usually the same lawyer handles both the Commission and Commerce Department phases of the defence, but companies sometimes use a different lawyer for each phase.

Second, economists often assist in the defence effort. Although the Commission applies legal standards, it applies these standards to economic facts. The Commission team handling the case always includes an investigator, a lawyer, and an economist. The team defending the foreign company should have the same expertise. Moreover, the role of the economist on the team has been expanding in recent years, as some Commissioners (many of whom are not lawyers) apply increasingly sophisticated economic analysis in their decision-making process. Under these circumstances, more and more foreign companies are adding an economist to their team of professional advisers.

Typically the lawyers handling the case interview and hire an economist or an economic consulting firm, and assign them specific projects relating to the overall defence. Depending on the issues involved in the case, different types of economic analysis might be necessary. The lawyer must find an economist with expertise in the appropriate areas. The lawyer must also choose between an economist with an academic reputation, and an economist affiliated with a consulting firm. The former may have a better academic reputation, but the later may have more experience in handling Commission investigations.

In some cases, the economist actually supervises the defence of the Commission case. Sometimes lawyers without a great deal of experience before the Commission hire an economic consulting firm with much more experience; soon the economist is handling the overall defence. The Commission has no rules requiring the use of lawyers, so foreign companies may use economists or any other adviser that they wish. It is only when the outcome of the Commission case is challenged in court that lawyers must be used.

Should the company cooperate with the other companies involved?

Another important issue is whether the foreign company should coordinate and cooperate with the other companies and countries involved in the investigation. There are several considerations in favour of cooperation. First, cooperation ensures consistency among the arguments made by the various respondents. Second, cooperation can decrease the cost of hiring an economist, since several or all of the respondents can share the expense. Third, the lawyers representing the various parties can divide the work among themselves to avoid repetition, and thus reduce the cost of the defence to individual companies. Fourth, foreign companies generally prefer to maintain harmonious relations with their foreign competitors, especially when fighting a common battle.

As a practical matter, all the foreign industries targeted by an unfair trade case are going to either succeed or fail together. The Commission's overall determination will apply to a country unless that country can: (1) argue that its imports are 'negligible' and thus cannot be cumulated with other countries subject to the investigation; (2) argue that its imports do not have a 'reasonable overlap' of competition with other import sources or domestic sales, and thus cannot be cumulated with other countries; or (3) otherwise qualify for some exception to cumulation (such as certain Caribbean countries).

Although countries sometimes organize combined defences to minimize costs, more often each country has its own lawyer during Commission proceedings.

Within a country, individual companies sometimes share the same lawyer and sometimes hire individual lawyers. As a practical matter, the countrywide defence at the Commission will be the same. Unlike individual countries, which might have special issues to consider or arguments to make, individual companies within a country face the same legal challenge. Since injury determinations are for countries, not companies, the defence must be countrywide.

It often happens, however, that individual companies decide to hire their own lawyers for a Commerce Department defence, and then have those lawyers handle the Commission phase as well. In such a case, it is imperative that the companies and their counsel cooperate. It makes sense for the foreign industry to designate one of the lawyers to take the role of coordinating the defence, and for the other lawyers to cooperate with the joint defence.

Chapter 13

Defending the Commission final investigation

The final injury determination by the International Trade Commission is the last, and perhaps best, chance for the foreign company to end the anti-dumping or countervailing duty investigation. Because the legal standard changes, and the domestic industry must now actually prove that imports have caused the domestic industry's problems, the chance of success improves substantially from the preliminary phase. Consequently, most foreign companies devote a substantial effort to defending this stage of the proceeding.

This chapter first reviews the relevant procedures, highlighting differences at the final stage compared to the preliminary stage. It then offers some practical suggestions for how foreign companies can organize a more effective defence in this critically important stage in the process.

Procedures for the Commission final

The deadline for the Commission to complete its final injury investigation depends upon the Commerce Department's preliminary determination. If the Commerce Department makes a negative preliminary determination, but then finds less-than-fair-value sales in its final determination, the Commission must make its final determination within 75 days of the Commerce Department's final determination. If the Commerce Department's preliminary determination is affirmative, the Commission must make its final determination by the later of: (1) 120 days after the Commerce Department's preliminary determination; or (2) 45 days after the Commerce Department's affirmative final determination.

The final injury determination consists of several stages. First, the Commission begins collecting information. After an affirmative preliminary less-than-fair-value determination, the Commission formally initiates its final injury investigation. If they are available, the staff members from the preliminary stage might be reassigned to the final stage. The Commission thus begins its investigation even before it knows what the Commerce Department's final less-than-fair-value determination will be. The staff prepares questionnaires to send to the various members of the domestic industry, the foreign producers exporting the merchandise, and the companies (both related and unrelated) that have been importing the merchandise under investigation. The Commission staff usually allows the lawyers for the various parties to review draft questionnaires, if the parties express an interest in doing so. As discussed below, foreign companies and their advisers should participate actively in this process.

Collecting information

Draft questionnaires

Unlike the preliminary stage, the final stage of the investigation allows the Commission enough time to be more deliberate in its investigation. The

Commission staff prepares draft questionnaires, and then allows all the parties to the investigation to comment on those draft questionnaires. This process allows foreign respondents a chance to shape the fact-gathering process to develop certain arguments that may be helpful.

The staff is particularly interested in questions that help address specific issues identified by the Commissioners themselves in the preliminary determination.

This process is particularly import for the questionnaire that goes to customers. Again unlike the preliminary stage, the final stage allows enough time for the Commission to gather information from customers. (The Commission staff uses the information about the largest customers of each producer that was collected as part of the preliminary investigation stage.) Customers often have a critically important perspective on the market, which can differ significantly from domestic producers, foreign producers, and importers. Commenting on the customer questionnaire, and ensuring that it obtains the necessary information, can be particularly a critical part of the defence.

Evaluating final questionnaire

Once the questionnaire has been finalized, the foreign respondent must then assess the information that will be gathered and decide whether it will be sufficient. The Commission staff never accepts all of the changes requested by any party. It is quite possible that the foreign respondent will believe that some important factual issue is not going to be adequately developed by the Commission questionnaires. In that case, the foreign respondent needs to develop some alternative strategy for gathering the necessary information.

Responding to questionnaires

All the parties receive questionnaires from the Commission, including both foreign producers and importers. These questionnaire responses are important, and should be drafted carefully.

Parties make several mistakes in completing the questionnaire responses. First, foreign producers often misunderstand the Commission concept of 'practical capacity', and over-report their capacity. The Commission questionnaire does not ask for theoretical capacity – which foreign producers often report. Rather, the questionnaire requests practical capacity – how much can be made assuming normal down time, normal production levels, and normal product mix. In most instances, practical capacity is lower than theoretical capacity.

Second, both foreign producers and importers often provide too little information in their responses. Businesspeople are busy. They look for ways to avoid answering questions, and ways to provide less information rather than more information. In fact, what parties should be doing is using the questionnaire as a chance to put evidence on the record. Information provided in questionnaire responses is considered 'factual information', and has more credibility than arguments submitted later by lawyers and consultants. Sometimes supplemental information provided in questionnaire responses is picked up by the staff and included in the staff report that is provided to the Commission.

Third, sometimes parties simply refuse to answer the questionnaire. Although the Commission has the legal authority to compel answers, it rarely exercises this authority. If a party does not respond, the Commission staff will usually ignore the missing questionnaire unless the party is very important to the investigation. These unanswered questionnaires, however, usually disadvantage the foreign respondents. The domestic industry seeking protection usually provides complete responses, and lots of data and answers that are unfavourable. A limited response on the other side undermines the credibility of the alternative data and answers. The more responses by importers and customers, the better. To the extent that foreign interests can urge others – particularly customers – to provide answers to questionnaires, they should do so. Sometimes this requires urging customers who may not have received questionnaires in the first instance to call up and request a questionnaire.

Evaluating information

Once the questionnaires have been completed, the Commission and the parties begin an intense process of evaluating that information and making arguments on various issues. This process is well defined, and quite intense. Since this process will determine to a large extent the outcome of the case – whether the Commission finds injury or not – foreign companies are well advised to focus their best efforts at this critical stage.

Pre-hearing staff report

The Commission staff collects all the questionnaire responses, and summarizes the data in the pre-hearing 'staff report'. This report reflects the quantitative data collected through the questionnaires, some standard analytic exercises conducted by the staff, and some discussion of the key issues identified by the parties.

The quality of this 'pre-hearing staff report' can vary from case to case. If the Commission has had recent experience with an industry, the staff report is usually higher quality, reflecting this prior experience. If the Commission staff members assigned to a case are particularly dedicated, the staff report will reflect the extent of their effort. Finally, if the Commission staff members are not overwhelmed with other investigations at the same time, they can produce a higher quality report. In many cases, however, these ideal situations do not occur, and the pre-hearing staff report can be disappointing and incomplete.

Pre-hearing briefs

One week after the pre-hearing staff report, the parties usually submit their pre-hearing briefs. (At the time of the formal initiation of the final investigation, the Commission publishes in the *Federal Register* a notice that sets forth all of the applicable deadlines for that particular investigation.)

These lengthy written submissions present the parties' arguments, drawing on the pre-hearing staff report, other information on the administrative record, and any public information that helps the case. Any information that has not already been submitted to the Commission can be included with or attached to the pre-hearing brief.

Public hearing

A week after the pre-hearing briefs, the Commission holds a public hearing. Unlike the staff conference held in the preliminary stage, the public hearing includes the Commissioners themselves, many of the Commissioners' private staff, and the Commission staff. Each side presents its case, and the Commissioners and staff then ask questions of the parties.

As part of their case, parties usually present witnesses. Industry witnesses generally have more credibility than the interested parties in the case, who make rather predictable statements. Customers – particularly those that buy from both domestic and foreign suppliers – are particularly credible as sources of information about the competitive dynamics in the marketplace.

Questioning by the Commissioners is the key part of the hearing. These questions try to clarify the arguments of the parties, and to test the assertions being made against the evidence on the record. It is common for Commissioners to take a point made by the lawyers in written submissions or oral statements, and then rephrase the point as a question to witnesses. By doing so, the Commissioners often find the witnesses disagreeing with their own arguments. For this reason, witnesses need to be well prepared before the hearing.

The hearing is much less formal than many expect, and is not like cross-examination in a courtroom. The questioning by Commissioners is relatively informal. Questioning of one side by the other side is extremely rare. The time spent answering the question is subtracted from the time allocated to the questioning side, and a poorly framed question can lead to a meandering, unhelpful answer that uses up critical time.

Post-hearing briefs

After the hearing, the parties also submit post-hearing briefs. These briefs are usually limited to those issues raised in the pre-hearing briefs of the other parties, and those issues raised at the hearing itself. The post-hearing briefs also provide an opportunity to respond to any specific requests for information that were made by the Commissioners or the Commission staff during the course of the hearing.

Final staff report

After the post-hearing briefs, the staff prepares the 'final staff report'. This revised report adds any information that may not have been available for the pre-hearing staff report, corrects any errors identified in the earlier information, and sometimes reacts to arguments raised by the various parties. This final staff report, along with various supplementary memoranda that the individual Commissioners may request the staff to prepare, becomes the key basis on which the Commission makes its decision. The quality of this report can vary tremendously depending on the quality of the staff assigned and the nature of the information gathered during the case.

There may or may not be a meaningful public version of this report. Although in principle the staff will prepare a public version, the staff will not deem aggregate information to be public unless there are enough responding companies so that the aggregate numbers do not reveal anything about the individual companies responding. In many instances, the key issues relate to the circumstances of particular firms within the domestic industry, or to foreign industries which may have only a single large exporter in a particular country. This reality often means that the most interesting data are not disclosed in the public version of the staff report.

Comments on data

After all the briefs and hearing, the Commission officially closes the record. Once this is done, usually five business days after the final staff report, no new factual information may be submitted. The parties then have one final chance to comment on any new factual information that has been collected by the staff or provided by any of the parties since their post-hearing briefs.

These final comments can be crucial. At this stage, the issues are well developed, and the parties generally know the key issues they need to win to persuade the Commissioners to vote in their favour. A well-written set of final comments, persuasively recapping why the factual record requires the Commission to decide in a certain way, can be very important.

Commission vote

Finally, the Commissioners vote on whether they believe there is injury or threat of injury to the domestic industry. The basis for the vote is the final staff report summarizing the data collected in the investigation, and the briefs submitted by the various parties in the course of the investigation. The vote is usually scheduled about one week before the actual decision is due. This gives the Commissioners a chance to decide on the rationale for their decision, and gives the staff an opportunity to draft the formal decision of the Commission. The vote is always public (unlike the vote at the preliminary stage, which may be closed to the public), and sometimes the Commissioners ask questions of the staff at the public meeting at which the vote is taken.

Considerations in defending the investigation

In preparing its defence of the final injury investigation, the foreign company must consider a number of issues. Some of these issues relate to issues already considered during the preliminary injury investigation. Other issues are new, and must be considered for the first time during the final injury investigation.

The most important general consideration at the final stage is the importance of having lawyers who immerse themselves in the facts of the industry, and learn enough about the competitive dynamics to present an effective defence. Final injury investigations can often be won if the lawyers take the time to learn the industry, and take the time to present the case properly. If the lawyers promise to do the case for a very low price, they are really saying that they are not willing to spend the time necessary to do the case properly.

Reconsidering the defence team

In most cases, the foreign company retains the same defence team throughout the anti-dumping investigation. The company need not do so, however. If the company has doubts about the ability of the lawyers or economists involved, it should consider replacing those advisers.

Involving new advisers is not very difficult for the final injury investigation. As a practical matter, it is difficult to replace advisers during the Commerce Department investigation. It would be extremely difficult for a new adviser to learn the background of the case in the short time available. The final injury investigation, however, is different. The preliminary injury investigation takes place so quickly that it generates only a limited amount of information that a new adviser would need to review. Moreover, there is a relatively long period of time for the final injury investigation, a period during which the new adviser can review the background material and catch up.

The most common change is for companies to involve new economists. Sometimes these economists join the other economists already on the defence team. Sometimes the new economists replace those used earlier. These changes take place principally because as the lawyers learn more about the case, they better understand what type of expert witnesses are necessary. In particular, the preliminary decision of the Commission often suggests critical areas that will be explored in more detail during the final investigation. The lawyers try to identify those experts who can best address these critical areas.

Redefining the product or the industry

As noted in chapter 12, the preliminary injury investigation devotes considerable time to deciding the scope of the investigation – the products under investigation (the 'like products') and the domestic industry to be evaluated. In many cases, the parties do not challenge the decisions made in the preliminary injury determination concerning these issues. The scope of the investigation remains the same.

In some cases, however, the parties may try to redefine the scope of the investigation. Sometimes the Commission invites such reconsideration in the preliminary injury determination, by asking the parties specifically to address certain issues in the final injury investigation. If a foreign company thinks there is some benefit to redefining the scope of the investigation, the company and its lawyers should pursue this issue.

It is important to alert the Commission to such issues as soon as possible. The best time to raise such issues is during the preliminary injury investigation. If the issues do not arise until after the preliminary investigation, it is crucial that the lawyers alert the Commission staff to the issue that the company wishes to raise in the final injury investigation. Once the Commission staff drafts the questionnaires and begins to receive responses, it is often too late to collect additional information. If the Commission does not collect the information needed to consider the foreign company's argument, the argument will almost certainly fail.

The company should distinguish arguments that seek to expand the scope of the investigation from those that narrow the investigation. It is usually easy for the Commission to exclude certain data that it has collected. If the company wants to expand the scope of the investigation – for example, to include aluminium car wheels in addition to steel car wheels – the company must alert the Commission staff so that it can collect the relevant information.

Commenting on the questionnaire

It is possible to comment on drafts of the questionnaire that the Commission intends to use in the final injury investigation. Since the time allowed for the final injury investigation is more generous (the Commission staff works separately while the Commerce Department is busy with its own work), the Commission can be more careful and deliberate in its final injury investigation. The staff provides a copy of the draft questionnaire to both the domestic industry and the foreign industry, usually through the lawyers for each group. The staff is generally open to constructive suggestions from each side.

By commenting on the draft questionnaire, the foreign company can often improve it significantly. The comments can help eliminate any confusion or ambiguity in the questions posed by the Commission staff. Such clarification can make responding to the questionnaire much easier. The company can also sometimes expand the scope of the information the Commission collects. As noted above, gathering additional information can often be critical to proving an argument that the foreign company wishes to make later in the investigation.

Checking petitioner's information

The Commission now releases confidential business information submitted by the petitioner and other parties under certain circumstances. Counsel must sign an application for an administrative protective order (APO), promising not to disclose the information to any other parties, not even to the lawyer's client. The penalties for disclosure are severe. Note that the Commission releases this information only to the foreign company's outside counsel, or a consultant or expert hired to assist that counsel. The staff and managers of the foreign company cannot receive the information. An in-house lawyer for the foreign company (or its United States subsidiary) may or may not be allowed access under APO, depending on the nature of the lawyer's position and responsibilities. Basically, lawyers involved in business decisions, and not focusing on narrower legal issues, are not permitted access under APO.

The information disclosed includes the responses to detailed questionnaires that the Commission sends to petitioners and other parties. These contain, together with the various briefs filed, the economic and financial data upon which the petitioner's injury argument is based. The lawyers can scrutinize this information, test the arguments made in the petitioner's briefs, and offer counter-arguments.

Although this access to confidential information is available at both the preliminary and final stages, its importance at the final stage is much greater. The time allowed for a preliminary investigation is so short that the foreign respondents are too rushed to be able to make the most effective use of the APO access. In the final stage, in contrast, there is much more time and a much more meaningful opportunity to test the information being submitted by the other side. That information can be tested for both internal consistency (whether the various domestic companies provide consistent data about the market and their financial accounting systems) and external consistency with other data about the industry in question. In some instances, there is a wealth of public data about the companies and industry in question, and this data can be used to challenge what the domestic industry is reporting to the Commission.

Working closely with economic consultants

Economic consultants play a particularly important role in Commission final injury determinations. As economic analysis assumes a more prominent role in the analysis performed by the Commission, the role of the economists will increase. Economists sometimes become involved in the preliminary injury investigation, but often there is insufficient time to undertake any serious economic analysis. This problem affects both the Commission staff economists and any outside experts hired by companies involved in the investigation. It is therefore much more common for the economists to become involved in the final injury investigation.

Economists provide two kinds of analysis in injury investigations. First, they provide descriptive analysis – they help collect information that describes the United States market and the role that imports play in the market. Second, they provide analytic analysis – they explain why the United States market behaves a certain way, and how the imports interact in the market. The Commission staff economists sometimes use formal economic models to analyse the United States market and the effect of imports. The economists hired by foreign companies often give comments to the Commission staff on the use of these economic models. With these analyses, the economists help develop arguments for the lawyers to present to the Commission.

The most effective approach is for the lawyers and economists to work together closely when developing legal and economic arguments. Doing so is not always easy, however. Lawyers and economists each use a specialized jargon unique to their profession. Experienced lawyers and economists often learn the jargon of the other (in fact, some lawyers have earned advanced degrees in economics), but not everyone has such 'bilingual' skills.

Overall coordination among companies

If the investigation involves many parties and complex issues, overall coordination becomes essential. Since cumulation became mandatory under United States law, domestic industries have usually filed anti-dumping complaints against many foreign industries at the same time. The injury investigation therefore may involve not just several foreign companies, but foreign companies from many different countries. In complex cases, it is not usual for 20–30 companies from numerous different countries to be involved.

There are several approaches to solving this coordination problem. When there are many smaller companies in the foreign industry, it is common for the industry as a whole to hire a single lawyer and share the cost. Each foreign industry is thus represented by a single counsel, and the number of advisers becomes more manageable.

In some foreign countries, it is common for each company (especially the larger multinationals) to want its own lawyer. A foreign industry involved in an anti-dumping investigation therefore may have several lawyers speaking for it. In some cases, the individual companies have somewhat different interests, so the industry does not have a single voice.

Sometimes the industry (usually through an industry association) will hire its own lawyer to serve in the role of coordinating counsel. The coordinating counsel sometimes helps to create a more unified position on the part of the industry.

Even if companies have somewhat different views about the best approach for the defence, they should try very hard to reach a unified position. A unified position, usually reflected in a joint brief filed by all the companies, is more persuasive to the Commission. As a practical matter, the Commissioners and staff will have more difficulty reading four 100-page briefs than a single 150-page brief. Moreover, if companies prepare independent arguments, they risk taking inconsistent positions that will undermine each other's arguments.

If the industry does not have a single counsel, or someone serving as the coordinating counsel on behalf of the industry, the various foreign companies should try to appoint one of the individual company's lawyers to serve as an unofficial coordinating counsel. Often the lawyer for the company with the largest import volume assumes this role. How the lawyer is chosen does not matter very much. It is crucial, however, that someone coordinate the efforts of the industry.

Chapter 14

Settlement of trade disputes

Foreign companies confronting a trade remedy case often ask if there is some way to 'settle' the case. This question is not surprising. After all, many lawsuits in the United States are settled. Moreover, in other countries 'undertakings' to settle anti-dumping cases are quite common. The situation in the United States, however, is more complicated. Settlements of anti-dumping and countervailing duty cases are the exception rather than the rule.

This chapter discusses the specific rules and policies involved in trying to settle unfair trade cases, including the somewhat different rules for anti-dumping and countervailing duty cases. It then discusses briefly settlement issues for other types of cases.

Settlement of anti-dumping and countervailing duty cases

During the course of an anti-dumping or countervailing duty investigation, many companies ask whether there is some way the case can be settled. Usually, the answer is no. There is a mechanism under United States law to enter into what is called a suspension agreement, by which the respondents agree with the Commerce Department to undertake certain actions in lieu of an order. However, the law makes it very difficult for these agreements to be reached. When the law was being drafted, United States industry representatives expressed concern that the use of these agreements could lead to the settlement of cases for political reasons wholly unrelated to the existence or absence of dumping or subsidies. They therefore insisted that the ability to settle anti-dumping or countervailing duty cases be subject to numerous and sharp restrictions. As a result, agreements to settle dumping and countervailing duty cases short of the imposition of additional duties have been few and far between. Often, the only reason such agreements are signed is because the President and his staff have decided that doing so is in the broader global interests of the United States, notwithstanding the objections of the United States industry.

Suspension agreements in anti-dumping cases

Up until 1980, while the United States Treasury Department had jurisdiction over dumping and subsidy investigations, a foreign manufacturer could avoid importer liability for the payment of dumping duties by engaging in a 'price undertaking'. Under such an undertaking, the Treasury Department would agree upon a satisfactory price for the product under investigation, presumably because Treasury felt that the price would be high enough to eliminate the dumping or remove the injury. So long as the exporter sold to the United States at or above that price, the Treasury Department would not collect any dumping duties. The Treasury Department would, through the Customs Service, periodically monitor the foreign exporter's prices to confirm that it was living up to its undertaking.

When the provisions of the anti-dumping law were extensively rewritten in the Trade Agreements Act of 1979, the provision for price undertakings did not survive in the new statute. Instead, the new law provided for 'suspension' agreements, under which the dumping investigation would be suspended, with no dumping duties imposed, provided certain conditions were met.

The new statute permits three types of suspension agreements in anti-dumping investigations: (1) agreements to cease exporting the investigated product to the United States; (2) agreements to eliminate dumping; and (3) agreements to revise prices so as to eliminate the injurious effects of dumping. The first type is virtually useless, since there is no incentive for the exporter to enter into it; an exporter that intends to stop exporting to the United States could as easily withdraw from the case and accept whatever dumping margins are found in the investigation without its participation, rather than struggle through the procedural difficulties of negotiating an agreement. In a practical sense, therefore, there are only two types of agreements: one to eliminate dumping and one to eliminate injurious effects.

Agreements to eliminate dumping

Agreements to eliminate dumping are relatively uncommon. These agreements must be signed by exporters accounting for 'substantially all' of the imports into the United States. Commerce Department regulations define the term 'substantially all' to mean exporters that account for at least 85% of imports of the subject merchandise. For industries that comprise several exporters, meeting the 85% threshold requirement can be difficult.

More importantly, it is extremely difficult for exporters to promise that they will 'eliminate completely' all dumping. The amount of dumping depends upon a number of complex factors, including product comparisons based on the Department's choice of characteristics, transportation and selling expenses, costs of production, and exchange rates. Many of these factors, such as exchange rates, can change abruptly and without notice. A manufacturer could well find after the fact that it had sold at dumped prices even when it had made good faith efforts to sell at non-dumped prices.

As a result of these and other problems, suspension agreements to eliminate dumping have been largely confined to non-market economies. Agreements with non-market economies are easier to reach because the basis for calculating normal value for these countries is the value of certain 'factors' of production which the Department chooses based on similarly situated market economies. The Department can therefore set a static normal value upon which the exporters can base a non-dumped United States price.

Agreements to eliminate injurious effects

Agreements to eliminate the injurious effects of dumping provide more flexibility than agreements to eliminate dumping. In practice, however, they are not necessarily more workable.

Such agreements must meet three conditions: (a) they must completely eliminate the injurious effects of the exports of that merchandise; (b) they must assure that each entry of merchandise is sold at a price that will not produce dumping margins greater than 15% of the average dumping margins found during the course of the investigation; and (c) they must prevent suppression or undercutting of domestic prices. Each of these requirements presents special problems.

First, the requirement that the revised prices eliminate the injurious effects of dumping implies a review of the injury question by the Commission. The statute provides for such a review, provided that it is requested within 20 days of the suspension of the investigation. Such a review is not automatic, in the absence of a request, since all sides could presumably agree that the suspension agreement eliminates injury. If it is referred to the Commission, however, the Commission has 75 days to consider whether the agreement in fact eliminates injury. If the Commission finds that the agreement does not eliminate injury, the suspension agreement is terminated and the investigation is resumed as soon as the Commission's determination is published.

The second requirement of the provision is that the revised prices under the agreement must reduce dumping margins to less than 15% of what they were determined to be during the investigation. Since the 15% rule must be satisfied individually by every future entry, the same difficulties discussed above with regard to agreements to eliminate dumping exist.

Finally, the rule against price suppression or undercutting often results in setting minimum prices that make it very difficult for exporters to remain in the market. The Department has found that the only way to meet this requirement is to set a minimum price below which the exporters' price cannot fall, while also permitting the price to increase if the market adjusts upward. This often means that the price at which the exporters must sell is above the market price, thus making it difficult to compete (particularly in commodity markets).

Although agreements to eliminate injury do provide more flexibility than agreements to eliminate dumping completely, they are still not common remedies. In large part, this is because the statute requires that before they can be accepted, the Commerce Department must find that there are 'extraordinary circumstances'. Extraordinary circumstances exist when: (1) the Commerce Department determines that suspension of the investigation would be more beneficial to the United States industry than continuing the investigation; and (2) the case is complex. In only a handful of cases has the Commerce Department made these findings. Furthermore, the Commerce Department will only try to meet these criteria if the President decides that it is in the broader global interests of the United States to enter into such an agreement. This is rarely deemed to be the case.

Suspension agreements in countervailing duty cases

The types of suspension agreements available in countervailing duty cases are roughly parallel to those in dumping cases. There are agreements to cease exports, to eliminate subsidies completely, and to eliminate the injurious effects of subsidies. While the agreement to cease exports is the same in countervailing duty as in dumping cases, the other two types of countervailing duty suspension agreements present significant differences from their counterparts in the dumping area.

Agreements to eliminate the subsidy

Agreements to eliminate subsidies completely contain a provision not available in dumping cases. The countervailing duty provisions permit a suspension agreement based on the elimination of the subsidy or on an agreement to offset the subsidy with an export tax. This provision is substantially more attractive as well as substantially more practicable than the corresponding provision for dumping cases. Unlike the situation in dumping cases, the exporter need not assure that every individual export is free of subsidies as it enters the United States. All the exporter needs to do is to renounce any benefits it might otherwise be entitled to under its government's subsidy programmes. This is much easier for the exporter to do.

In some cases, it may not be possible for the exporter to renounce or eliminate a subsidy. For example, if the Commerce Department has found that a company's exports are subsidized as a result of government loans or equity investments that occurred years before, it may well be physically impossible for the company to eliminate the impact of those prior subsidies. In this event, however, the suspension agreements provide for the offsetting of the benefit by an export tax.

The offsetting export tax provision, which is not available in dumping suspension agreements, permits the exporter to renounce that portion of the subsidy which the Commerce Department has determined affects United States sales, without at the same time foregoing the benefits of the subsidy on domestic sales or on exports to third countries. This makes it very attractive to exporters. It is also attractive to the foreign government involved, since in essence it permits the amount of the countervailing duty to be collected by the foreign government itself, rather than by the United States Government.

In the first few years following the introduction of the suspension agreements provisions, agreements to offset the full amount of the subsidy based on export taxes were frequently used. Eventually, however, United States interests claimed that these types of agreements were meaningless, since the foreign government could simply refund whatever export tax it was collecting by means of a new or increased subsidy to the exporter. In part as a response to these complaints, the Commerce Department has discouraged such agreements, and few have been signed in recent years.

Agreements to eliminate injury

The provisions for suspension agreements eliminating injury in countervailing duty cases closely resemble, in most respects, the corresponding provisions in dumping cases. The exporters must eliminate or offset at least 85% of the subsidy, and the agreement must result in the elimination of the suppression or undercutting of United States prices. As with anti-dumping agreements, there are provisions permitting referral of the matter to the Commission for a determination of whether the agreement in fact eliminates the injury.

Agreements of this sort in countervailing duty cases differ from their anti-dumping counterparts in one important respect. While quantitative restrictions are not permitted in anti-dumping cases, agreements to eliminate injury in countervailing duty cases can limit the quantity of subject merchandise exported to the United States.

This is often an attractive alternative for exporters as they can remain in the United States market – albeit restrained in terms of quantity, but without the restraints of countervailing duties.

Procedures for suspending investigations

To suspend an anti-dumping or countervailing duty investigation, the party desiring suspension must submit a proposed suspension agreement no later than: (1) 15 days after the Commerce Department issues a preliminary determination in an anti-dumping proceeding; or (2) 5 days after the Commerce Department issues a preliminary determination in a countervailing duty proceeding. The Commerce Department must then notify and consult with the petitioner concerning its intent to suspend the investigation, and must do so no less than 30 days before it suspends the investigation. The parties are then given an opportunity to comment on the proposed suspension agreement by a date set by the Commerce Department, but not later than: (1) 50 days after the preliminary determination is issued in an anti-dumping investigation; or (2) 35 days after the preliminary determination is issued in a countervailing duty investigation or a regional industry case.

If the Commerce Department decides to suspend the investigation, it must issue a public notice to that effect. If the agreement is to cease exporting or to eliminate the dumping or subsidy, then the Commerce Department will also end any suspension of liquidation that might have occurred prior to the agreement, and will refund any deposit or other security paid.

If the agreement is to revise prices to eliminate the injurious effects of dumping, or to eliminate the injurious effects of subsidies, the procedure is somewhat different. In those cases, the Commerce Department does not end the suspension of liquidation; indeed, if liquidation of duties has not previously been suspended, Commerce orders that liquidation be suspended. This suspension continues for 20 days, until the time has passed for interested parties to request a review of the injury issue by the Commission. If a party requests the Commission to review whether the agreement eliminates the injurious effects of dumping, suspension of liquidation continues for the term of the Commission's review (75 days). If the Commission finds that the agreement does, in fact, eliminate the injurious effects of dumping, the suspension of liquidation will be ended, and any deposits or other security refunded, on that date.

Continuation of the investigation following suspension

Except for the Commission review of agreements to eliminate injurious effect, the signing of a suspension agreement ends the investigation. There is no final dumping or countervailing duty determination and no final injury determination by the Commission. This situation could leave either foreign exporters or the United States industry dissatisfied. If exporters feel that they have a strong case that they are not injuring the United States industry, they will want to have the Commission rule on the injury question in order to have the investigation dismissed and the suspension agreement nullified. If the domestic industry believes that it has a strong injury case, it will want to have the case go forward to a final injury determination in order to have the possibility of an immediate dumping or countervailing duty order if the suspension agreement should ever be terminated.

For this reason, both the subsidy and the dumping suspension agreement provisions include the possibility of continuing the investigation after the suspension agreement is signed. They provide that interested parties may, within 20 days of the date when the Commerce Department publishes its notice of suspension, request that the investigation be continued. In that event, the case goes forward to a final dumping determination by the Commerce Department and a final injury determination by the Commission.

The continuation of the investigation does not have any direct impact on the suspension agreement itself. Imports of the subject merchandise enter the United States without duty deposit requirements or suspension of liquidation. Exporters must continue to abide by the agreement, whether it be to eliminate dumping or subsidies, or to eliminate the injurious effect of either.

The results of the investigation, however, may have a significant impact on the suspension agreement. If the Commission finds no material injury or threat of material injury, the suspension agreement is dissolved. If the Commission finds material injury or threat of material injury, the suspension agreement remains in effect and the parties must live by the terms of the agreement.

If the injury case appears strong to petitioners, they can still gain an advantage by seeking to continue the investigation. In the event that the suspension agreement is violated, the Commerce Department is required to reinstitute suspension of liquidation and continue the investigation if it had not previously been pursued to a final injury determination. In most cases, however, violations of suspension agreements will occur years after the agreement was signed. The situation with respect to injury may be very different at that point from what it was when the investigation was originally instituted. Petitioners who had a strong injury case at the time the case was filed may find that the case is much weaker when the suspension agreement terminates.

Petitioners who believe that they have a strong injury case at the time they file the petition are therefore well advised to request that the case go forward to a final injury determination. If the final injury determination is affirmative (material injury or threat of material injury), then when and if the exporters ever violate the agreement, that violation will result in the immediate institution of a countervailing duty or anti-dumping order. The final injury determination made during the original investigation will carry forward into the time that the agreement is violated.

In short, both sides usually have an incentive to continue the investigation to a final injury determination even after the suspension agreement is issued. Petitioners have an incentive to request continuation if they believe the injury case is strong, and exporters have an incentive to request continuation if they believe the injury case is weak. As a result, a high percentage of suspension agreement cases continue to a final determination.

Settlement of other trade remedy cases

For other trade remedies the rules are less formal. There is no equivalent of a 'suspension agreement' for a Section 201 safeguards case. Since these investigations do not involve allegations of unfair trade, and since they involve all import sources, it is much harder to imagine settling such a case. The remedy phase of a Section 201 investigation, however, involves elements that are in some respects similar to a settlement. It is quite possible for a country to craft arguments in the remedy phase to exclude substantial portions of its trade from the remedy being imposed. It is also common for individual countries to press the interests of their exporters when the President is debating the form and scope of the Section 201 remedy.

Section 337 investigations of intellectual property violations can be settled. If the two companies can reach some agreement with respect to the intellectual property at issue, the petitioner can withdraw the complaint and the proceeding disappears.

The same pattern often occurs in Section 301 market access cases. Merely initiating the case and beginning consultations often can trigger some change by the foreign government or foreign company that satisfies United States concerns. If the petitioner withdraws the complaint, the proceeding can be dismissed or suspended indefinitely.

For all of these settlement options, however, foreign companies need to bear in mind that United States antitrust laws still apply. Thus, competitors cannot discuss or reach agreements about their respective prices or quantities. It is permissible to discuss other topics, such as licensing intellectual property or eliminating practices the United States has challenged as market barriers. Foreign companies often think such commercial proposals are the best way to satisfy their United States competitors. But such proposals to United States competitors are extremely risky from a legal perspective. If the United States and foreign governments force a settlement that involves price or quantity issues – such as an official suspension agreement under the anti-dumping law – that government involvement creates substantial (but not complete) insulation from challenge under the antitrust laws. The less government involvement, the greater the risk of such company-to-company arrangements.

Chapter 15
Post-order issues

Even when the case is finished, it is not really over. After the order has been imposed, the foreign company still has several issues to consider. This chapter discusses the three most important post-order issues.

First, foreign companies must realize that the final Commerce Department decision is really only an estimate of potential duties. The final duties are determined later in an administrative review, which involves basically similar rules but applied to a different time period and with some unusual twists. Foreign companies need to understand these differences as they plan.

Second, foreign companies need to be aware of United States laws to stop circumvention of the unfair trade orders. Steps that the foreign company may believe are legitimate commercial efforts to avoid the scope of the order can sometimes trigger an anti-circumvention proceeding to bring the imports at issue back within the scope of the order.

Third, foreign companies should remember the requirement for a 'sunset' investigation five years after the order has gone into place. Both the Commerce Department and the International Trade Commission must make new findings to continue the imposition of the duties beyond this five-year period.

Administrative review to determine ultimate anti-dumping liability

General overview of Commerce Department anti-dumping administrative review process

Under United States law a final Commerce Department determination at the conclusion of an anti-dumping investigation does *not* establish an exporter's ultimate anti-dumping liability. Rather, the anti-dumping rate announced in the Commerce Department's final determination is simply an *estimated* rate used for purposes of setting the cash deposit amount applicable to imports after an anti-dumping duty order is issued. The actual amount of anti-dumping duties paid is based on the results of an administrative review, which is commenced one year after the anti-dumping duty order is issued. Consequently, no one can know with absolute certainty what the ultimate anti-dumping liability will be until the Commerce Department issues a final administrative review determination.

The United States process is very different from other countries' laws. For example, under Canadian law anti-dumping duties are applied on a prospective basis. Accordingly, under Canadian law, following a final determination by Revenue Canada, an exporter is able to know what its ultimate liability will be *before* the export shipment is made to Canada. In contrast, under United States law, an exporter does not know what its anti-dumping liability will be until long after it makes its shipments to the United States. United States law establishes final anti-dumping liability only *after* the shipments have already been made.

The United States system is best illustrated by way of example. Assume the following situation:

On 28 April 2000, the Commerce Department issues a final anti-dumping determination establishing a 15% anti-dumping rate. On 15 June 2000 an anti-dumping duty order is issued after a final affirmative injury determination by the Commission. The order requires a cash deposit of estimated anti-dumping duties equal to the amount stated in the Commerce Department final determination.

A review is requested in June 2001 (the anniversary month of the order). The Commerce Department begins an administrative review on 1 July 2001 for all shipments made from the preliminary determination of the previous year; i.e. from 19 February 2000 to 31 May 2001. The administrative review is based on a comparison of home market and United States prices between 19 February 2000 and 31 May 2001.

The Commerce Department completes its administrative review by June 2002. The Commerce Department's final determination for the administrative review establishes an anti-dumping rate of 5%.

The Commerce Department would then instruct the United States Customs Service to refund the difference between the cash deposits received on the imports subject to the administrative review (i.e. imports on which cash deposits of 15% have been made) and the rate found in the final determination in the administrative review (i.e. 5%). In addition, interest on the overpayment (i.e. the difference between the amount of cash deposits paid based on 15% margins and the actual amount of duties owing as a result of the 5% margins found in the review) will be paid. The current interest rate on overpayment is about 7%, and varies with market rates.

Assuming that a single importer had imported merchandise worth $1 million between 1 February 2000 and 31 May 2001, it would have paid $150,000 in cash deposits of estimated anti-dumping duties. Commerce's final determination in the administrative review finding a 5% margin would reduce the importer's actual liability to $50,000. The importer would be refunded the difference, $100,000 and would also receive interest on the $100,000.

The final determination in the administrative review would also change the cash deposit rate for estimated dumping duties effective as of the date of that determination – 1 June 2002. Thus, all entries after this date would pay a 5% cash deposit rate, not a 15% cash deposit rate.

On each subsequent anniversary date of the order, an administrative review may be commenced; when completed it will provide the basis for ultimate duty liability. For example, if a review is commenced in June 2002, and the result is a final determination of a 10% margin, the importer would have to pay the difference between the cash deposits made (5%) and the 10% margin found in the review, plus interest on the underpayment.

As is evident from the above discussion, the importer's actual anti-dumping liability will not be determined until after the Commerce Department completes its administrative review process. Because the Commerce Department always applies the law in effect at the time it makes its determination, the administrative review process could very well be based on a different law from the determination which established the cash deposit rate for estimated anti-dumping duties. The review will always be based on facts for a different period of time. In other words, it is possible the cash deposit rate could have little relationship with the actual amount of anti-dumping duties ultimately assessed.

Note that the Commerce Department's current practice is to calculate *importer-specific* anti-dumping assessment rates. The Commerce Department does this by using the database submitted by the exporter during the administrative review process. In this database, the exporter is required to identify the name of the importer and the entered quantity and entered value for each United States transaction. The Commerce Department calculates total PUDD (potential uncollected anti-dumping duties) for each importer and divides the total importer-specific PUDD by the total entered value of the shipments imported by that importer. The resultant dumping ratio is then applied against the entered value of each entry of that importer to derive the anti-dumping assessment amount for the shipment. Accordingly, if an exporter ships to several United States importers, it is possible, depending on type of product and price, that the actual assessment rates for individual importers are very different from the new overall margin found for the exporter (e.g. one importer-specific rate could be 20%, and another 1%, while the overall margin for the exporter is 5%).

Finally, it is important to note that for the time period from the start of the administrative review period until the Commerce Department's final determination, importers can take advantage of the application of a cap on ultimate liability. In conformity with the WTO Anti-Dumping Agreement, United States law imposes a cap on the actual anti-dumping assessment of those shipments entered from the start of the review period until the date of the Commerce Department's final determination. The cap is equal to the anti-dumping rate set forth in the Commerce Department's preliminary determination. For example, if the Commerce Department found a 15% margin in its preliminary determination, but one of the importer-specific assessment rates determined in the administrative review was 20%, then that importer would be able to limit to 15% the assessment of those entries made from the start of the review period until the date of the Commerce Department's final determination.

For shipments between the Commerce Department's final determination and the date of the Commission 's final determination, a cap equal to the rate found in the final determination applies. For shipments made after the Commissions' final affirmative injury determination, there is no cap on ultimate anti-dumping liability.

Special dumping margin calculation rules applicable to administrative reviews

Although for the most part the Commerce Department's approach during an administrative review is very similar to that followed during an investigation, there are two particularly important differences. (There are other differences, but they relate more to the degree to which Commerce enforces other policies.)

Comparison of average home market prices to individual United States prices

During an administrative review, the Commerce Department resorts to its prior dubious practice of calculating the applicable anti-dumping margin by comparing monthly average home market prices to individual United States prices. After employing its model-match methodology (described below), the Commerce Department compares an *individual* United States transaction sales price to a *monthly average* of home market prices of the matching control number

(CONNUM). This means that it is quite possible for the Commerce Department to find dumping margins when no such margins were found in the original investigation. Consider the following simple example, with three sales that total $600:

Sales date	Home market price	Weighted average home market price	United States price	Commerce Department dumping in review
1 March	$100	$200	$100	$100
15 March	$200	$200	$200	No dumping
30 March	$300	$200	$300	No dumping

Dumping margin in original investigation: 0.0%

Dumping margin for administrative review 16.7%: [(100)/600)]

Although this practice is dubious in light of WTO standards, the practice continues. The Appellate Body has declared 'zeroing' to be WTO-inconsistent, but has considered this issue only in the context of an original investigation. The applicability of this same logic in the context of an administrative review has not yet been tested. Given the wording of Article 2 of the Anti-Dumping Agreement, however, it may be difficult to challenge such practices in administrative reviews. There have been other WTO panel decisions accepting the idea that different rules should apply to original investigations and administrative reviews.

Modification in model-matching methodology

During an administrative review, the Commerce Department will follow the same practice of using the applicable CONNUM to find identical or most similar home market matches. In an administrative review, however, there is also a time element that does not exist during an original investigation. During an administrative review, the Commerce Department limits its search for an identical or similar match to a six-month period which includes the month of the individual sale plus three months before and two months after. In short, the six-month period becomes part of the model-match test.

For example, for a United States transaction in April 1999, the Department would limit it search for the most similar CONNUM to home market sales from 1 January 1999 through 30 June 1999. If no identical or similar match (which passes the 'difmer' test) can be found in this six-month period, then the Commerce Department will use constructed value to calculate the dumping margin for that transaction.

United States provisions to combat circumvention

United States anti-circumvention provisions are designed to counteract alleged circumvention of the anti-dumping duties imposed. These actions by and large consist of expanding existing anti-dumping measures to different products or to products from different countries. It is important to remember that the WTO Anti-Dumping Agreement does not address the issue of circumvention; indeed it is very much silent on the issue. This means that it is somewhat unclear whether any anti-circumvention anti-dumping law is valid. Whether valid or not, the United States applies this law.

The United States anti-circumvention law has gone through significant changes over a short period. Anti-circumvention provisions were first added to United States law in 1988. Interestingly, notwithstanding this specific new authority for the Commerce Department to target alleged circumvention, the domestic producers were rather disappointed in the effectiveness of the new law, as they lost several early cases brought under it. Accordingly, as they often do, domestic producers convinced Congress to strengthen the new law. Somewhat ironically, even though the Uruguay Round Anti-Dumping Agreement does not address circumvention issues, it was through the Uruguay Round Agreements Act that Congress completely rewrote the United States anti-circumvention law.

Like its 1988 predecessor, the current anti-circumvention law provides specific statutory authority for the Commerce Department expand anti-dumping duty orders to address *four* situations, four types of alleged circumvention. Each one is discussed below.

Minor alterations

The first situation involves minor alterations. The minor alteration provision can be traced to Congress's reaction to just one anti-dumping case. In 1980 the Commerce Department issued an anti-dumping duty order on portable electric typewriters from Japan. After a few years of being subject to this order, however, some manufacturers discovered that if they attached a simple four-function calculator to the typewriter (at a cost of less than $5), the machine would be reclassified as a business machine and, initially at least, would not be subject to the anti-dumping duty order. Although the Commerce Department ultimately determined (in response to the Court's decision) that the modified typewriters were, in fact, subject to the scope of the anti-dumping duty order on portable electric typewriters, domestic manufacturers became concerned that foreign manufacturers could, by repeatedly altering merchandise in an almost infinite number of ways, avoid the effect of the original anti-dumping duty order indefinitely.

In response to these concerns Congress created a provision that would permit anti-dumping and countervailing duty orders to apply to merchandise that is 'altered in form or appearance in minor respects' from the merchandise subject to the original order. The statutory provision concerning minor alterations does not define the term 'minor respects', and the Commerce Department has only had a couple of occasions to interpret the term. It does make clear, however, that even if the minor alteration results in a change in the tariff classification of the product, it may still be subject to the order if the alterations are minor.

Later-developed merchandise

The second situation concerns later-developed products. The later-developed product provision also can trace its roots directly to the typewriter case. Shortly after the anti-dumping order against Japanese portable electric typewriters was issued, the electronic revolution overtook the electric typewriter industry, with the result that simple typewriters were largely replaced in home and office use by word processors and personal computers. Of particular concern to United States typewriter producers was a small and relatively simply machine which was lighter and smaller than original typewriters, but contained a small amount of memory, plus a single line text display.

The United States producer of portable electric typewriters, Smith Corona, claimed that this machine was fundamentally a portable electric typewriter subject to the anti-dumping duty order. The manufacturer countered that it was a completely different product – a personal word processor – which by virtue of its memory and display functions could perform tasks not within the capacity of an ordinary portable electric typewriter.

The Commerce Department initially agreed with the Japanese manufacturers. In a 1987 determination, the Commerce Department ruled that portable typewriters with memory were not within the scope of the anti-dumping duty order because they had not been identified in the petition, and because they fell into a tariff classification not covered by the anti-dumping duty order. The United States producer, however, ultimately won. The Court of International Trade overturned the Commerce Department's initial decision and ruled that the personal word processor was within the scope of the original anti-dumping duty order on portable electric typewriters. Domestic producers were sufficiently concerned about the cost and effort of proving the case, however, that they got Congress to include a modification in the statute specifically providing for the inclusion of 'later-developed' merchandise within the scope of the original anti-dumping or countervailing duty order. Indeed, in its report on the 1988 legislation, the Senate specifically chastised the Commerce Department for its position in the typewriter case.

Inclusion of later-developed merchandise within a prior order is, however, a delicate matter. Since, by definition, the merchandise did not exist at the time of the original anti-dumping or countervailing duty order, it was not (and could not have been) subject to the original injury determination by the International Trade Commission. It is at least possible – as indeed was argued in the case of personal word processors – that the market that contains the newly developed merchandise is a fundamentally different market from that originally considered by the Commission. It thus can never be demonstrated to a certainty that the Commission would have reached the same conclusion on the question of injury had the later-developed merchandise been under investigation.

Congress sought to respond to these concerns by including a series of factors that must be considered in order to assure that the later-developed merchandise brought under the scope of an earlier order is fundamentally the same as that included in the original order. These factors are:

❑ Whether the later-developed merchandise 'has the same general physical characteristics' as the original merchandise;

❑ Whether the 'expectations of the ultimate purchasers of the later-developed merchandise are the same as for the earlier product';

❑ Whether the 'ultimate use' of the later and the earlier products are the same;

❑ Whether the 'channels of trade' of the later-developed product are the same as those for the earlier product; and

❑ Whether the later-developed merchandise 'is advertised and displayed in a manner similar to the earlier product'.

These statutory factors are virtually the same as those developed by the Commerce Department administratively in determining whether any new merchandise is within the scope of the original anti-dumping or countervailing duty order. Their codification in the statute means that Commerce may not now depart from these criteria in future decisions.

The third and fourth types of situations which the United States circumvention law seeks to address concern parallel but distinct situations. One addresses manufacturing operations in the United States, and the other addresses manufacturing operations in countries not subject to the anti-dumping duty order.

Assembly in the United States

This section of the United States anti-circumvention law addresses the situation in which a foreign manufacturer attempts to circumvent an anti-dumping or countervailing duty order on a finished product by importing parts into the United States and assembling them there. If the order itself applies only to the finished product, parts imported into the United States would not normally be subject to the order. Hence, a foreign manufacturer could import sub-assemblies or relatively finished parts into the United States free of dumping or countervailing duties and assemble them into the finished product at minimal additional cost.

However, Congress did not want this provision to be used to interfere with real manufacturing operations in the United States. So it required that, for the anti-circumvention provision to apply, three conditions must be met: (1) the merchandise sold in the United States must be made from parts or components produced in the country subject to the anti-dumping or countervailing duty order; (2) the value of the parts or components imported from the country subject to the order must be 'a significant portion of the total value of the [completed] merchandise'; and (3) the process of assembly or completion in the United States must be 'minor or insignificant'.

If all of these conditions are satisfied, the Commerce Department has the authority to apply the original anti-dumping duty order to the importation of the component parts.

Note that the key phrases of the second and third conditions, namely, 'significant portion of total value' and 'minor' assembly, are not defined by the United States law. Such determinations are left for the Commerce Department to decide on a case-by-case basis.

However, with respect to the issue of the magnitude of the assembly or completion, the United States law sets forth five factors that the Commerce Department *must* consider in reaching its determination. These factors are:

(1)   The level of investment in the United States;

(2)   The level of research and development in the United States;

(3)   The nature of the production process in the United States;

(4)   The extent of production facilities in the United States; and

(5)   Whether the value of the processing performed in the United States represents a small proportion of the value of the merchandise sold in the United States.

Assembly in third countries

The fourth situation addressed by the United States anti-circumvention law concerns assembly operations in third countries. Assembly operations in third countries present different problems from those presented by assembly operations in the United States. In this case, the merchandise being imported into the United States is not parts or components but rather the finished product itself. However, since an anti-dumping or countervailing duty order applies only to countries named in the order, if the merchandise is assembled in a country not subject to the order it may avoid anti-dumping or countervailing duties.

Despite the differences between assembly operations in the United States and those in third countries, the statute treats them in the same manner. The value of parts or components from the country subject to the order must be a 'significant' portion of the value of the merchandise exported to the United States, and the process of assembly in the third country must be 'minor or insignificant'.

The factors in determining whether the operations in the third country are 'minor or insignificant', and in determining whether to apply the order to the merchandise from the third country, are the same as those that apply to assembly operations in the United States.

Sunset reviews to terminate orders

The sunset review process results from changes to the WTO Anti-Dumping Agreement that were made in 1994 as a result of the Uruguay Round of multilateral negotiations. Before the changes to the Anti-Dumping Agreement, United States law allowed anti-dumping orders to remain in existence indefinitely. For example, the anti-dumping duty order on steel jack from Canada was imposed in September 1966 and was in effect until July 1998 when it was formally abolished as a result of this new sunset review process. Another example is the anti-dumping duty order on colour televisions from Japan that was imposed in March 1971 and remained in effect until 1999 when it was revoked as a result of the new sunset review process.

The WTO Anti-Dumping Agreement now contains a specific provision calling for the revocation of anti-dumping orders after they have been in place for five years. An anti-dumping duty order may be continued after this period only if a review is initiated and it is determined that revocation would be likely to lead to the continuation or recurrence of both dumping and injury. This provision is referred to as the sunset provision and reviews under it are called sunset reviews.

The Anti-Dumping Agreement has required a dramatic change to United States law, which previously had no automatic mechanism for terminating anti-dumping duty orders. United States law now requires both the Commerce Department and the Commission to initiate and conduct a sunset review to determine whether 'termination of the anti-dumping order would be likely to lead to continuation or recurrence of dumping and of material injury'.

Commerce Department and Commission sunset reviews are separate proceedings. An anti-dumping duty order can be revoked by a negative finding of either agency, regardless of the outcome of the other agency's proceeding. The Commerce Department's sunset review examines whether termination of the order would be likely to lead to recurrence of dumping, and if so, what the extent of the dumping margin would be. The Commission examines whether termination of the anti-dumping order would be likely to lead to continuation or recurrence of material injury. The sunset review process takes a little more than one year to complete.

Commerce Department responsibilities in sunset reviews

The sunset law imposes two tasks on the Commerce Department in a sunset review. First, the Commerce Department must decide whether revocation of the anti-dumping duty order is likely to lead to recurrence of dumping by the foreign exporters. Second, if the answer is yes, the Department then determines what the future dumping margin would be.

In April 1998 the Commerce Department issued a policy bulletin that set forth the Commerce Department's thinking on how it would make its sunset determination. The heart of this policy bulletin is contained in a series of presumptions. The bulletin states that the Commerce Department normally will determine that dumping would be likely to recur if any of the following three scenarios exists:

❑ Dumping continued at any level above *de minimis* (defined as 0.5% or less) after the issuance of the anti-dumping duty order;

❑ Imports of subject merchandise ceased after issuance of the order; or

❑ Dumping was eliminated after the issuance of the order or suspension agreement, and import volumes declined.

Under the Commerce Department's approach, if any of these factors are present; there is a presumption that the foreign exporters are not able to ship merchandise to the United States without dumping. In short, rather than undertaking a serious analysis, the Commerce Department simply imposes presumptions about the likely resumption of dumping.

Commission responsibilities in sunset reviews

The Commission examines whether revocation of the anti-dumping order would be likely to lead to continuation or recurrence of material injury. Unlike the Commerce Department sunset review, the Commission takes its sunset analysis seriously. In cases in which both sides participate, the Commission undertakes a fresh examination of whether the anti-dumping order needs to be continued. The sunset law requires the Commission to:

❑ Determine which product manufactured in the United States is 'like' the imported product under review;

❑ Define the composition of the relevant domestic industry producing the product 'like' the imported product under review; and

❑ Determine whether that domestic industry is materially injured by reason of the imports under investigation.

In making this determination, the Commission examines 'the likely volume, price effect, and impact of imports of the subject merchandise on the industry if the order is revoked'.

Chapter 16

Judicial and WTO review

If a foreign company is not happy with the results of trade remedy case, it can pursue two possible forms of appeal. First, the company can appeal the decision to United States courts. There is a well-established and frequently used system of judicial appeals for anti-dumping and countervailing duty cases. Section 337 decisions can also be appealed. Section 201 and Section 301 decisions are subject to very limited (if any) judicial appeal and are only rarely taken to United States courts. Second, the company can pursue an appeal to the WTO. Technically, such appeals are brought by the foreign government, not the foreign company. Most foreign governments, however, are sympathetic to WTO appeals that raise valid issues against trade remedies that block exports by the country. This chapter briefly reviews each of these two types of appeal.

Review in United States courts

If both the Department of Commerce and the International Trade Commission make affirmative determinations, the Commerce Department automatically issues an anti-dumping order. The foreign company must then decide whether to file a court appeal to challenge the anti-dumping order. In most situations, the company has the legal right to file a court appeal. The more difficult issue, however, is whether it is a good strategy to file the appeal.

This section explains the background to filing a judicial challenge to Commerce Department and Commission determinations. First, the circumstances under which the foreign company has a right to seek judicial review are reviewed and the various stages of the court appeal are summarized. Finally, the relationship of a court appeal to the foreign company's overall strategy for defending itself is explored. Foreign companies should understand the way in which the court appeal can contribute to the overall strategy for the case. Too often foreign companies waste money filing court appeals that have little if any hope of helping the company. This chapter seeks to explain when a foreign company should turn to the court, and when the company should instead pursue other strategies.

Right to judicial review

When it amended the anti-dumping law in 1979, the United States Congress expanded the right to judicial review of anti-dumping duty orders and the underlying determinations. Since then, more and more anti-dumping investigations have ended in litigation.

As a practical matter, judicial review is available at the end of the proceeding. The United States statute gives a clear and unambiguous right of appeal once the Commerce Department has issued an anti-dumping or countervailing duty order. Although there have been a few instances where parties have filed a court appeal earlier in the process, those instances are quite rare.

In particular, there is no right to appeal a preliminary determination by either agency. This fact surprises many foreign companies. Since the preliminary determination has a very real impact in the market, and triggers the beginning of legal liability, many companies wonder why they cannot appeal an unfavourable decision – particularly one in which the Commerce Department essentially admits to having made a mistake. The rule of law, however, is clear that such appeal is not allowed. The logic is that since the errors can be corrected in the final determination by the agency, there is no need to bother the courts.

Although the right to appeal anti-dumping and countervailing duty proceedings is clear, the right to appeal other trade remedies varies. Some remedies – such as Section 337 decisions – can also be appealed. But other remedies – such as Section 201 safeguard actions and Section 301 market access actions – do not have a clear right to appeal. In these instances the degree of Presidential involvement is larger, and Congress has decided to limit the degree of judicial review of the President's policy decisions. Depending on the particular circumstances in a case, there may be some legal theory for bringing the issue to court. (For example, there has been at least one judicial challenge to a safeguard remedy.) Bringing such a case to court, however, will be a real challenge, and a foreign company should not assume it will have any right of judicial review.

Nature of proceedings

Proceedings before the Court of International Trade (CIT) differ greatly from proceedings before the Commerce Department and the Commission. The most fundamental difference lies in the timetables for each. The Commerce Department and Commission have rigid statutory frameworks within which they must make their decisions. Beyond a certain point, extensions are not permitted. In contrast, the CIT has the freedom to set its own schedule. Although different judges have different personal preferences for timing, they all allow extensions if the circumstances warrant. There is no ultimate deadline. Because of this fundamental difference, CIT litigation can drag on for years after the final Commerce Department and Commission decisions. With the exception of the summons and the complaint, all of the stages discussed below can be delayed indefinitely if the judge permits.

In addition, CIT proceedings are slightly more formal. The parties pay more attention to technicalities, and generally prepare more polished documents. The parties need the court's formal permission to take certain actions, such as delaying the submission of a brief.

File summons

The appeal starts when either the foreign company or the United States petitioner files a summons. The summons is a very short statement of an intent to start an appeal, which must be filed within 30 day of the publication of the anti-dumping order in the *Federal Register*. Sometimes both sides file appeals. The Commerce Department or Commission never starts the appeal, because it is the agency decision that is being challenged.

It is common to file what is known as a 'protective summons'. Under United States law, if one party files an appeal and the other side does not, the appeal is limited to those issues raised by the appealing party.

This rule sometimes places the non-appealing party at a disadvantage. There may be issues that the non-appealing party would like to raise, but that are not important enough to justify the expense of an appeal by themselves. If the party has to participate in an appeal anyway, however, it might be interested in raising these issues.

To avoid finding themselves in this dilemma – forced into an appeal, but not being able to raise the issues of interest – foreign companies sometimes file a summons even though they do not intend to follow up the appeal. During the period between the summons and the complaint, the lawyers can confirm the intentions of the other parties. The cost of filing the summons is minimal – just a few hundred dollars – and filing the summons protects the company's ability to raise its own issues if the other side decides to appeal.

File complaint

Within 30 days after the summons, the appealing party must file a complaint. The complaint is a longer document that describes the basic facts and lists the various issues the party wishes to raise. It does not include a detailed explanation of the argument. If both sides have appealed different issues, both sides must file their own complaints.

Intervention by other parties

If one side files an appeal, the other side may intervene in the lawsuit. Thus, even if the foreign company does not want to bring its own complaint, it can intervene in the lawsuit filed by the domestic industry to protect its own interests.

Such intervention is quite common if a foreign company has benefited from some agency decision. In theory, the United States Government will defend itself. In practice, however, the quality of the defence can vary enormously. Depending on the skill and workload of the government attorneys, they may do a good job or a bad job. Foreign companies often decide that they want to have their own lawyers intervene, to help ensure that the favourable decision is well defended in court.

Administrative record

After the complaint has been filed, the Commerce Department or the Commission files the administrative record with the court. The administrative record is the collection of all the papers submitted to the Commerce Department or the Commission during the course of the investigation. It includes all the formal submissions as well as all the documents collected by the Commerce Department at the verification, or collected by the Commission during its injury investigation. This collection of papers is the basis on which the CIT makes its decisions.

In theory, the agency should file the administrative record within 40 days after the complaint is filed. The agencies generally try to meet this deadline, but often must ask for an extension. The delay results from several factors. First, preparing the record is not particularly easy, or enjoyable, work. The staff avoid this work whenever possible. Second, the staff is often too busy meeting the strict deadlines on other ongoing investigations to worry about the flexible deadlines for the CIT litigation. Third, the judges on the CIT have been very willing to grant repeated extensions to file the administrative record. As a practical matter, the agency usually files the record 60–90 days after the summons is filed.

Discovery

CIT appeals of trade remedy decisions generally do not involve discovery. This fact surprises many foreign companies with experience with normal litigation in the United States, in which discovery is almost the entire process. CIT appeals are administrative litigation, and in most cases the judge must limit consideration to the information that was before the agency – the administrative record.

In theory, a party can seek to supplement the administrative record – for example, by taking the deposition of the Commerce Department staff who made the decisions. The CIT, however, has been extremely protective of the Commerce Department and the Commission. Various legal doctrines say that courts should not allow litigants to probe into the internal decision-making of the agency. The Commerce Department and the Commission, with the CIT's approval, have used these doctrines to avoid discovery. Efforts to convince the court to make exceptions have been largely unsuccessful. But in a particular case, if the circumstances were extreme enough, it might be worth trying to take discovery.

Summary judgement and other briefs

Once the administrative record has been filed, the appealing party can begin to prepare its motion for summary judgement. Known technically as a 'rule 56.1 motion', this document presents all the factual and legal arguments that the party believes supports its claim that the Commerce Department or the Commission made mistakes. The document is often very long – sometimes over 100 pages – and very detailed.

The timing of this brief can vary. The parties agree to a scheduling order in which all of the relevant deadlines for briefs are set forth. The complaining party generally receives 60 days to file its brief. Extensions are permitted, but only for good reason.

Once this motion for summary judgement is filed, the other side then has 30–60 days to file its response brief. The precise timing is usually set forth in the scheduling order. This response brief lists all of the arguments – factual and legal – in opposition to the arguments made by the other side.

The appealing party then files its reply brief. Again, the precise timing is set forth in the scheduling order, but usually the appealing party has 15–30 days for this brief. The time may be longer if the parties have negotiated deadlines to avoid conflicts with holidays or other work commitments. This brief is limited to rebutting the arguments made in the response brief, and elaborating on themes from the original brief. The appealing party cannot now raise new arguments.

Although this explanation seems easy, the realities of actual litigation are often more complex. Various parties ask for extensions. Other issues may arise. One party may decide to add a new claim later in the litigation, which the court can allow as long as the other side does not suffer any prejudice. Actual cases may have various different wrinkles, which are beyond the scope of this section.

Oral arguments

After the briefs have been filed, most cases involve an oral argument before the judge. This oral presentation allows both sides to focus their arguments. More importantly, the oral argument offers the judge the opportunity to question the parties, and explore each side for weaknesses. Often the oral argument can be the crucial stage at which one side persuades the judge to accept its position in the litigation.

CIT decision

After the oral argument, the judge makes a decision. Some judges decide quickly; others take quite a long time. There is no deadline. It is not unusual to wait 6–12 months for the judge's decision.

Appeal to CAFC

Decisions by the CIT can be appealed to the Court of Appeals for the Federal Circuit (CAFC). In many cases, the parties stop after the CIT stage. But if the issue is very important to either party, that party can continue the process to the next stage.

Historically, the CAFC has been more deferential to the agency decision-making, whereas the CIT often disagrees with the agency decision. If the agency feel strongly about its decision in a particular case, it appeals to the CAFC, where it finds a more sympathetic audience.

More recently, however, even the CAFC has begun to express some skepticism about agency decisions that seem to go too far. For example, the CAFC recently has ruled:

❑ The Commission must carefully consider the impact of imports not subject to investigation, and cannot assume that all of the harm being suffered by the domestic industry is due to the imports that are being investigated.

❑ The Commerce Department cannot abuse 'facts available', and can only resort to this form of punishment when the proceedings show that the agency genuinely asked for the information it says that it needs.

These examples illustrate that the CAFC can reverse agency decisions when it feels the legal basis for doing so is strong enough.

Role of court appeal in overall strategy

Basic concepts

Before reviewing the various strategic considerations involving a court appeal, two basic concepts need to be reviewed. First, the foreign company should understand the limited standard of review that applies to court appeals – the court generally defers to the agency decision.

Second, the company should understand the problem of timing – if the appeal does not proceed quickly enough, the court may dismiss the appeal for 'mootness'.

Under United States law, the court generally defers to agency decisions. The presumption is that agencies have expertise in the matters entrusted to them, and the court should reverse the agency decision only in limited circumstances. Thus, the standard of review limits the court to two situations. First, the court can reverse decisions where the agency action is contrary to law (ignores the clear instructions of the statute). Second, the court can reverse decisions where the agency action is not supported by 'substantial evidence on the record' – in other words, if the decision is inconsistent with the factual information that has been collected. The court is not supposed to replace the agency's judgement with its own. If the agency decision is a reasonable interpretation of the evidence, the judge must accept that interpretation, even if the judge would have made a different decision.

Beyond this standard of review, the unusual structure of the duty assessment process creates a timing problem. Recall that the original investigation only sets a deposit rate of estimated duties, and the Section 751 administrative review determines the actual duties owed. This difference has created a special legal problem for foreign companies who seek judicial review of Commerce Department final determinations.

The problem results because of the long delays that usually occur in CIT litigation. Often the appeal drags on so long that the Commerce Department finishes its first Section 751 review of the anti-dumping order before the court makes a decision concerning the original Commerce Department determination. Finishing the Section 751 review means that the actual anti-dumping duties owed on the prior shipments have been determined in accordance with the results of the Section 751 review, and the deposit rate on future shipments is based on the margin found in the Section 751 review. Under these circumstances, what is the role of the original dumping determination?

Several court decisions have said that there is no role for the original determination. Since whatever decision the court makes concerning the original determination has no effect– either on the assessment of duties, or on the setting of the deposit rate – these decisions have said the original appeal is 'moot' – in other words, it has no legal effect. Therefore, there is no need for the lawsuit to continue. (The one exception would be if the issues raised in the appeal could lower the original dumping margin below *de minimis* – in which case the anti-dumping order itself would be dismissed.)

None of these problems apply to appeals of either Commission final determinations or Section 751 determinations. If the court overturns an affirmative Commission final determination, the anti-dumping order must be revoked. Under both United States and international law, an anti-dumping order cannot remain in effect unless there has been a finding of injury to the domestic industry. The court decision therefore determines whether there is any legal basis for the order to continue. Similarly, if the court overturns some aspect of the final decision in the Section 751 investigation, that decision affects the amount of anti-dumping duties that the foreign company must pay. Again, the court decision is outcome determinative. In both cases, the court will proceed with the appeal.

These court decisions mean that if a company cannot proceed quickly enough, there is a serious risk that the court will dismiss the appeal. The company will receive no benefit for its efforts.

Suggested strategies

Anticipate a possible court appeal while defending the case before the agencies

Because of the special nature of judicial review, it is crucial that the foreign company begin anticipating the possibility of a court appeal from the beginning of the investigation. The court's review is limited to what has been submitted to the agency during the investigation. If certain facts or factual arguments have not already been submitted to the agency, they cannot be raised in the court appeal. Companies must therefore plan ahead.

During the investigation, the company and its lawyers should consider whether the necessary information is being made part of the administrative record. There are two major opportunities to submit information. First, most of the basic information is submitted as part of the response. Second, the company is able to elaborate on this basic information during the verification. For purposes of the appeal, it does not matter when the agency receives the information, as long as the information becomes part of the administrative record.

Waiting until the verification to submit crucial information, however, can be a risky strategy. It has the advantage of delaying the release of the information to the lawyers for the other side, but there is no guarantee that the Commerce Department will accept the information as a verification exhibit. The Commerce Department staff has almost complete discretion to decide what documents to take as exhibits. Documents shown at the verification but not taken as exhibits are not part of the administrative record and cannot be used in court.

Decide whether to pursue an appeal

Many factors will enter into the decision to appeal the Commerce Department or Commission decision. The foreign company should evaluate the following considerations.

How important is the issue to the company? The more important the issue, the greater the potential benefit of a court appeal. The company should consider both the importance of the issue to this case, and to possible Section 751 reviews. Moreover, the Commerce Department is likely to treat the same issue the same way in investigations against the same company of other products.

The importance of the issue must be evaluated in light of the great uncertainty, however. In Section 751 reviews, the issues are often treated differently by the new Commerce Department staff than they were in the initial investigation. Therefore, even without a court appeal, it may be possible to persuade the Commerce Department to decide an issue differently.

Moreover, the company may be able to restructure its sales in such a way as to make the issue irrelevant, or at least to increase the likelihood that the new staff will decide the issue in the company's favour.

Because of these opportunities for changing the adverse decision, the company should not overestimate the value of the court appeal for future cases. The only certain benefit is that the court may order the agency to reverse its decision in this particular investigation.

How likely is the company to succeed? This judgement can be difficult, but is an important part of any litigation strategy. Is the issue legal or factual? Courts are more likely to overturn agencies on legal than factual issues. How complete is the record? Depending on the issue, the completeness of the record could help or hurt the likelihood of success.

Can the agency defend itself? Depending on the issue, the foreign company may be willing to play a more or less active role in helping the agency. Although particular cases depend on those circumstances, two rules of thumb are useful. First, the Commission tends to be better at defending itself than the Commerce Department. The Commission staff attorneys who work on the cases are allowed to defend them when they go to court. The Commerce Department staff attorneys, however, must turn their cases over to the Department of Justice when they go to court. Since the Department of Justice attorneys have less experience with the details and nuances of trade law – and since they did not 'live' the case during the agency proceedings, they are usually less effective.

Second, the government attorneys usually do a better job with legal rather than factual issues. For factual issues, there is no substitute for having been actively involved in building the factual record at the agency level. The Government often does not have lawyers with that advantage.

What is the estimated cost? Court appeals are not cheap. Since the process is more formal, and the stakes are often high, the cost can be substantial. The actual cost, of course, varies depending on the case.

If the company decides to appeal, decide whether to push the appeal or delay it

If the company decides to pursue an appeal, the company and its lawyers should push the case as quickly as they can. Much of the process is beyond the control of the parties. But a commitment to move a case quickly can help speed the process.

Note, however, there may be cases where the foreign company wants to delay. If the Commerce Department has made an adverse decision, and the company now owes a large amount of additional duties, the company may want to delay the process. There are ways to delay the litigation, if that is the company objective.

Review in the WTO

Scope and nature of WTO dispute settlement

Many companies think of the WTO as a 'court' sitting in Geneva that hears trade cases. At one level, this perception correctly reflects the creation of binding dispute settlement during the Uruguay Round. This new binding dispute settlement represents perhaps the single greatest accomplishment of the WTO. Under the old GATT dispute settlement system, the losing party had the legal ability to 'block' the panel decision and thus preclude any legal consequences; the new WTO dispute settlement system eliminates this ability to block panel decisions. Under the new system, there are unavoidable legal consequences from losing a panel decision. Moreover, this new system will over time interpret the new WTO Agreement, clarifying the nature of the obligations.

Notwithstanding the new binding dispute settlement, however, characterizing the WTO as a 'court' overstates the nature and the function of dispute settlement. WTO review is *not* the same as national judicial review.

Most importantly, WTO panels and the Dispute Settlement Body (DSB) that supervises the overall dispute settlement system have no power to order compliance with panel decisions. This limited power to enforce panel decisions represents the most frequently misunderstood part of the WTO dispute settlement system. Under the new system, there are legal consequences from losing a panel decision, but that does not mean that WTO panels can invalidate domestic laws. Panels can simply note that a domestic law does not comply with a country's international legal obligations. It is then up to the country to decide what to do: either modify the law to comply with the international obligations, or work out some arrangement to pay compensation to the other country. If the losing country refuses, the WTO response does not involve invalidating the national law; rather, the WTO simply authorizes the winning country to impose compensatory sanctions (usually higher tariffs) against the losing country.

Procedural framework

As a general matter, cases take at least a year, and complex cases often take longer. After the panel makes a decision, delays in implementation can take even more time. Although this process may seem time consuming, compared to many domestic legal systems and other systems of international dispute settlement the WTO in fact moves rather quickly.

Consultations

The process begins with a request from one country to another country for consultations. Parties cannot go directly to a panel; the process must begin with a good faith effort to resolve the dispute. The party receiving the request must respond within 10 days after receipt. The complaining party must describe the measures being challenged and the legal basis for the claim. Requests for consultation are typically one or two page letters with few details. After 60 days, and at least one round of consultations, the complaining party can go to the next stage.

As a practical matter, many consultations serve no real purpose but to delay the inevitable formation of the panel. Although the Dispute Settlement Understanding (DSU) calls on parties to seek a settlement in 'good faith', many trade disputes simply cannot be settled. Reflecting this reality, countries often simply treat the consultations as a formality to be completed – the officials read prepared statements, refuse to answer questions in any meaningful way, and conclude the consultations as quickly as possible.

Panel request

After the consultations have finished, the request for a panel starts the more formal process of the dispute settlement. The request for a panel circulates among all Members, and the formation of the panel must then be approved by the DSB. The target of the complaint can block the first request, which is common, but cannot block the second request. The right to block the first request serves little purpose but delay; this right reflects the old, consensus-based origins of WTO dispute settlement.

The written request for a panel is a crucial legal document. In setting forth the specific measures at issue, and the legal theories for alleging a WTO violation, this written request sets the 'terms of reference' for the panel. The terms of reference define the panel's jurisdiction – what measures and legal theories the panel may consider. Panels have become quite strict in construing their terms of reference. If the complaining party later raises some measure or legal theory outside the scope of the terms of reference, the panel will refuse to consider that item.

Panel procedures

A panel generally has three members, typically government trade officials currently or formerly in Geneva or professionals with experience in trade matters. Panellists who are officials of member country governments serve in their individual capacities and not as government representatives. The secretariat provides an 'indicative list' of suggested panellists, but this list is just a starting point. If the two countries cannot agree on panellists, the Director-General chooses three panellists. Depending on the nature of the dispute and the nature of bilateral relations between the two countries, selecting the panellists can be either easy or extremely difficult. Many frequent users of the WTO dispute settlement system are reluctant to accept panellists who have previously ruled against the country in a prior dispute. Consequently, the WTO secretariat and WTO Members often find themselves looking for 'fresh faces' to whom no country has any reason to object.

The DSU has created more fixed expectations about procedures and timing than existed under the prior system. Appendix 3 of the DSU on working procedures includes a suggested timetable for disputes, stage by stage:

The panel proceedings themselves involve exchanges of written arguments, and meetings with the panel. Both sides exchange written first submissions, and then meet with the panel. At this meeting, the parties present oral statements, and respond to questions from the panel. This initial meeting often takes two or three days, particularly if there are third parties to the dispute.

After this initial round, both sides then submit their second submissions, rebutting the other side's arguments. At this stage, the two sides must file second submissions on the same date. Although the party being complained against will typically have already responded to the complaining party's first submission, the written answers to panel questions usually raise issues that need responses. The parties then meet again with the panel. Unlike the first meeting, however, third parties are not involved in the second meeting with the panellists. The panellists can pose another round of questions, and the parties provide another round of written answers.

Table 7 Timetable for panel procedures	
Receipt of first written submission by the complaining party	*3–6 weeks*
Receipt of first written submission by the party complained against	*2–3 weeks*
Date, time and place of first substantive meeting with the parties: third party session	*1–2 weeks*
Receipt of written rebuttals of the parties	*2–3 weeks*
Date, time and place of second substantive meeting with the parties	*1–2 weeks*
Issuance of descriptive part of the report to the parties	*2–4 weeks*
Receipt of comments by the parties on the descriptive part of the report	*2 weeks*
Issuance of the interim report, including the findings and conclusions, to the parties	*2–4 weeks*
Deadline for party to request review of part(s) of report	*1 week*
Period of review by panel, including possible additional meeting with parties	*2 weeks*
Issuance of final report to parties	*2 weeks*
Circulation of the final report to the Members	*3 weeks*

Panel conclusions

Once the panel has finished its work, it releases its preliminary conclusions in the form of an interim report. At this point, the panel invites another round of comments. Panels never change their basic conclusion, but they sometimes change or adjust the rationale adopted for the decision in response to comments from the parties. Although interim reports should remain confidential to encourage any final efforts to settle the dispute, in practice they often are leaked to the press, particularly in high-profile cases. The press has proved quite resourceful in finding out what has happened in such cases, and in reporting the outcome long before it is known officially. The early press reports often trigger 'no comment' reactions from government officials speaking on the record, but the stories usually quote unnamed sources who seem willing to talk off the record.

The 'final report' comes when it is ready. Since the work involved in each dispute varies, there is no fixed deadline to meet. Panels usually set themselves a tentative deadline, but they can extend that deadline if they need to do so. The report goes first to the parties, usually in the English version. At this stage, the report remains confidential. The entire document must then be translated from the English version into French and Spanish versions by the WTO secretariat. Since the final report and its rationale must be adopted by the DSB, the final report circulates officially and publicly to all WTO Members in all three official languages of the WTO.

Appeal options

Either party can appeal the panel decision to the Appellate Body. Within 60 days after the final panel report has circulated to the members, a party to the dispute (but not third parties) can notify the DSB of its intention to appeal the panel decision. This new feature reflects the concern that, with the new binding dispute settlement, the system needed some mechanism to ensure the quality and consistency of the legal interpretations being made of the WTO treaty text. Different panels might well embrace divergent treaty interpretations, which could seriously disrupt understandings about the proper scope of the treaty obligations.

Reflecting this institutional concern, the Appellate Body consists of a standing judiciary of seven members. Unlike panels with ad hoc members, the Appellate Body has more continuity. The members are chosen by consensus by the DSB, with a view to geographic diversity. Each member serves for four years, and is eligible for one reappointment. In any given case, three members sit to review the panel decision at issue.

The most important characteristic of the Appellate Body process is its speed once the process begins. The 60–90 day appeal process goes very quickly. After serving notice of the appeal, the appellant (the party raising the appeal) has 10 days to make its submission. This submission must focus on the specific legal issues being appealed. The Appellate Body is limited to 'issues of law covered in the panel report and legal interpretations developed by the panel', and does not reconsider factual issues unless those issues are intertwined with relevant legal issues. The appellee (the party defending against the appeal) then has 15 days to file its response.

Implementation

The losing party is expected to bring its laws into conformity with the ruling, or to otherwise offer some acceptable compensation. This may involve a change to a law or policy, or repealing the law. In general, the losing party must implement the decision within 15 months, or earlier. If the losing party does not implement the panel decision, the DSB can authorize the country bringing the complaint to retaliate against the other country.

Implementation has been one of the major issues with the new system. Particularly in high-profile cases, the losing country often faces intense political problems in trying to implement panel recommendations. In many cases, the WTO decision that a country has violated its international obligations provides the impetus needed for that country to overcome domestic political opposition to change. For example, differential taxes on various types of alcoholic beverages have long resisted international efforts at change. Yet with the arrival of binding dispute settlement, a series of successful WTO challenges forced several countries to make the politically painful decision to change their rates of tax on certain alcoholic beverages.

In other cases, the domestic political pressure proves too great. For example, the EU resisted changes to its domestic regulations on hormone-fed beef and on the tariff treatment of bananas, and the United States issued rather strong statements refusing to concede that its 'foreign sales corporation' tax system must be changed. It remains to be seen whether WTO Members will work out these implementation issues, or if the system needs to be changed again.

Private party access to the system

Only governments can be members of the WTO. Therefore, only governments can be formal parties to the WTO dispute settlement proceedings. If private parties have concerns about the policy of another government, the private parties must motivate their government to take action and begin the dispute settlement process.

Some countries have a formal mechanism for their nationals to petition the government to pursue violations of WTO obligations. One of the current purposes of the internationally infamous Section 301 under United States law is to facilitate this private sector access. The EU has a comparable law.

Even countries without a formal mechanism work closely with affected private sector interests. Given a strong enough private sector interest, most governments will act. A review of WTO disputes to date reveals few examples where there was not some significant private sector interest at stake. For example, the United States complaint against the EU tariff treatment of bananas was driven by the private interests of Chiquita Banana, a United States corporation involved in the banana trade.

Whether the mechanism is formal or informal, the government may face conflicting interests. Sometimes the conflict is between industry sectors affected differently by a policy in another country. Sometimes the conflict is within the industry sector, based on the divergent interests of individual companies. Even more problematically, sometimes the government may have a different perspective on an issue than the private sector. The government may be reluctant to pursue cases in one sector that might hurt the country in other sectors.

The role of the private sector will vary. It is quite common for the private sector to work closely with its government to develop the case. Since the private sector has both specialized knowledge and greater financial resources, it is not surprising that governments usually seek to exploit those assets. If the dispute requires private sector technical expertise or historical experience, the government may not be able to present the case effectively on its own. The private sector will often hire outside experts to help the government. The government will sometimes hire its own outside experts. The Appellate Body has now made clear that a government can nominate a private lawyer, an industry representative, or anyone else to participate in the process; governments are free to decide who makes up their delegation to the proceeding.

WTO review of trade remedies

Trade remedies have been generating more and more WTO disputes. It is no coincidence that, of the 10 most recently issued panel reports as at July 2001, seven involved trade remedies of some sort. Moreover, of the 16 panel requests filed in 2000, 8 involved trade remedies. Much of the litigation has involved countries other than the United States. But the lessons from all these cases will affect the United States system of trade remedies over time.

WTO decisions on anti-dumping

There have been numerous panel and Appellate Body decisions on anti-dumping remedies. Given the frequency of use of anti-dumping remedies – both by developed countries against developing countries, and by developing countries against each other – these WTO precedents will take on more importance. These sections discuss a few of the most important recent decisions.

Standard of review

The 'standard of review' is crucial in any legal system. The more deferential the standard of review, the less likely it is that someone reviewing the decision will be able to reverse that decision. The issue may seem technical, but it is extremely important.

At the very end of the Uruguay Round, the United States Government pushed for language in Article 17.6 of the Anti-Dumping Agreement calling for only limited and deferential panel review of decisions by the administering authorities. This language was unique for anti-dumping; all other WTO disputes took place pursuant to a different standard of review. There was concern after the Uruguay Round that this special standard of review for anti-dumping measures would make meaningful review of such measures impossible.

These fears have proven to be exaggerated. Panels have not shied away from careful review of anti-dumping measures. The panel decisions have found numerous practices by administering authorities to be wrong. Indeed, in every challenge so far, at least some part of the authority's decision has been overturned.

On legal issues, it is now clear that 'permissible' interpretations do not mean 'any possible' interpretation. The effort by the United States Government and others to read 'permissible' broadly has failed.

On factual issues, some panels are probing rather deeply into the underlying facts and not just deferring. The best example is *Stainless steel sheet and plate*. In that case, brought by the Republic of Korea, the panel engaged in very careful review of the factual basis for the United States Department of Commerce's decision on dumping margins.

Calculation of dumping margins – zeroing

In determining dumping margins, many authorities – including the United States – have engaged in a practice called 'zeroing', in which any negative dumping margins are treated as 'zero' in determining the overall margin. The result of this practice is to exaggerate dumping margins. Instead of negative margins offsetting positive margins, the average is based only on those transactions with positive margins.

Zeroing has its largest impact when there are many sales with negative dumping margins – usually cases where the overall dumping margins are below 10%. In such cases, zeroing can make the difference between margins being above and below the legal *de minimis* level.

This practice was attacked during the Uruguay Round, and new language was added to Article 2 in an effort to outlaw it. The United States and EU, however, interpreted the new language of Article 2 as requiring them only to consider average prices within a particular model type, and not as requiring the elimination of the old practice of zeroing out negative dumping margins when determining the overall weighted average dumping margin.

This interpretation has now been rejected. In the *Bed linens* case, both the panel and the Appellate Body found this practice of zeroing to be inconsistent with Article 2. This decision is a huge victory for respondents.

Remember, though, that the *Bed linens* decision is very new, and it is still not clear how the case will be implemented in various countries. The United States, for example, has not implemented this decision. Also, at present, this precedent applies only to original investigations. The WTO has not yet considered this issue with respect to other types of decisions, such as administrative review proceedings or sunset reviews.

Use of 'facts available'

When exporters do not provide the information necessary to determine the dumping margins, authorities often use 'facts available' to create high dumping margins. In some countries, such as the United States, the abusive use of 'facts available' is quite high. The use of 'facts available' is often politically motivated, as a way to find high dumping margins against imports that might otherwise not be dumped or dumped at very low margins.

In *Hot-rolled steel*, the WTO panel condemned two examples of United States-style 'facts available' and found them to be inconsistent with Article 6.8 and Annex II of the Anti-Dumping Agreement. First, the panel attacked the Commerce Department decision to reject information about weight conversion factors. The Commerce Department had refused to consider the information because it was submitted after the response deadline, although prior to verification. The panel rejected this strict rule and said authorities must consider all the circumstances and accept information when they can.

Second, the WTO panel attacked a decision to punish a company that could not obtain information from an affiliated company that was a petitioner in the same case. The Commerce Department had ignored this obvious conflict of interest, but the panel found the use of adverse 'facts available' in that circumstance to be unfair.

This issue is crucial to all respondents in anti-dumping cases. Limiting the ability of authorities to ignore the real facts and to punish respondents for minor problems will help reduce the frequency of high dumping margins.

The United States Government appealed this adverse panel decision to the Appellate Body. The Appellate Body ruled in July 2001 that the panel had correctly condemned the United States practices in that case, a rather stinging rebuke to the United States.

Non-attribution

The Appellate Body recent addressed the issue of non-attribution in the context of anti-dumping cases. Article 3.5 of the Anti-Dumping Agreement explicitly requires authorities to ensure that they do not attribute to imports any injury caused by other factors. This issue was critical in the anti-dumping investigation of hot-rolled steel from Japan.

In *Hot-rolled steel*, the panel agreed with the United States argument that Article 3.5 did not require authorities to isolate alternative causes, and to distinguish carefully the effect of alternative causes. The Appellate Body, however, reversed this finding. The Appellate Body found that the language of Article 3.5 does require authorities to separate and distinguish alternative causes.

This decision builds on similar decisions in the safeguards context (see below) and is very important. If the International Trade Commission begins to examine alternative causes more carefully, it will help foreign companies in making arguments that their exports are not the cause of any injury being suffered by the domestic industry.

Factors to decide injury

Administering authorities have a tendency to consider only those factors that help justify their desired decision. Article 3.4 of the Anti-Dumping Agreement lists about 15 factors that authorities should consider in deciding whether a domestic industry is being injured by imports.

Some authorities have viewed this list as permissive, meaning they could consider whatever factors on the list they consider relevant in each case. Several WTO panels and the Appellate Body have now confirmed that the list is mandatory, not permissive. Each of the factors must be considered in each case.

This new rule will make it harder for administering authorities to ignore inconvenient facts that argue against finding a domestic industry to be injured. This, in turn, should produce more findings of no material injury and will limit the number of anti-dumping measures.

Requirement to consider the domestic industry as a whole

In all injury cases, the authorities must decide what 'domestic industry' should be evaluated. The definition of the domestic industry can dramatically affect the outcome of the analysis.

WTO panels have begun to attack arbitrary definitions of the domestic industry. For example, in *High fructose corn syrup*, the panel found that authorities may not consider a single industry segment without considering the relationship of that segment to the industry as a whole. Authorities also cannot arbitrarily expand the industry. In *Bed linens*, the WTO panel rejected an EU effort to include companies in the injury analysis that were not part of the domestic industry as defined by the EU.

The controversial United States law on 'captive production' is still being litigated. Under this United States law, the International Trade Commission can focus on merchant market sales and largely ignore captively consumed material used to make downstream products.

This provision is particularly important to the steel industry. For example, when investigating hot-rolled steel, the question is whether the authorities should consider only the hot-rolled steel that is sold on the merchant market or also consider the hot-rolled steel transferred internally to make cold-rolled steel and other downstream products (such transfers are referred to as 'captive production').

In *Hot-rolled steel*, the WTO panel upheld this United States law as consistent with the WTO. The panel found that, since the United States law did not mandate *exclusive* focus on the merchant market but rather a *primary focus*, the United States law did not preclude consideration of the industry as a whole.

On appeal, the Appellate Body agreed that the United States law on its face was consistent with WTO obligations. But the Appellate Body reversed the panel finding that the Commission decision in this particular case had been consistent with WTO obligations. By the end of 2002, the United States still had not indicated how or whether it would undertake any reconsideration of its injury finding. It will be up to Japan to decide when and whether to challenge in the WTO this United States recalcitrance.

WTO decisions on safeguards

Safeguard measures have been less common than anti-dumping measures, largely because the legal standards are tougher. But the impact of safeguard remedies can be broader, because they limit imports from all countries, not just those countries targeted by an anti-dumping petition.

Several important Appellate Body decisions have helped define the permissible scope of safeguard actions. Most are helpful, but some raise potentially troubling issues.

Expanded explanations

Unlike anti-dumping measures, safeguard measures are subject to the normal standard of review found in the Dispute Settlement Understanding, which calls for an 'objective examination' of the facts. WTO panels have not hesitated to review safeguard measures carefully. When authorities have not provided sufficiently logical or detailed explanations, panels find the measures to be WTO-inconsistent.

In *Dairy products*, for example, the panel found that the authorities had not evaluated all the relevant factors and had not provided an adequate explanation of those factors considered. The more detailed the explanations, the harder it will be for authorities to justify a wrong decision.

Most recent period

Safeguard investigations typically involve longer periods of time than anti-dumping investigations – five years rather than three years. This longer time period gives the authorities more opportunities to manipulate the period being considered to find an increase.

In *Footwear*, the Appellate Body emphasized the importance of considering the most recent period of time and finding a sudden and significant increase in imports. One cannot justify safeguard actions based on any increase in imports.

Unforeseen developments

There has been a debate over the extent to which the sudden increase in imports must be due to 'unforeseen developments'. The Appellate Body has now made clear, in both *Dairy products* and *Footwear*, that the authorities must demonstrate as a factual matter that the sudden increase in imports was due to unforeseen circumstances.

This principle represents an important limitation on the use of safeguards. If the increase in imports is the natural evolution of market forces, safeguards simply are not justified. It remains to been seen, however, how this requirement will evolve over time.

Non-attribution and causation

The most important safeguard decisions have involved the crucial issue of causation. In the majority of cases, causation is the most contentious issue in the proceeding.

The Appellate Body in *Wheat gluten* made it clear that injury due to other factors must not be attributed to imports. This decision clarifies an important principle of causation. But in the same decision the Appellate Body reversed the panel finding that imports alone must be the sole cause of injury. Both of these findings were reaffirmed in *Lamb meat*.

These findings are troubling. The *Wheat gluten* and *Lamb meat* cases do not provide any useful guidance to authorities on applying the principle of non-attribution. The Appellate Body seems to be saying that other factors can make some contribution to injury, but that the injury from those other factors must not be blamed on imports. There is a tension between these two ideas. If read too broadly, this precedent could represent a significant relaxation of the causation standard in safeguard actions. It remains to be seen how *Wheat gluten* is interpreted and refined in future cases.

WTO decisions on countervailing duties

Although there have been several WTO decisions about export subsidies, there have been limited WTO decisions about countervailing duty measures. The WTO jurisprudence on subsidies more generally is beyond the scope of this chapter.

The one applicable decision involved a United States policy with respect to privatized companies. The Commerce Department argued that government equity infusions into a company still had a lingering subsidy effect, even after that company had been privatized. In *Lead and bismuth bar*, however, the Appellate Body disagreed with this argument. The Appellate Body found that a privatization transaction eliminates any prior government-provided subsidies, and held that the United States could not impose countervailing duties in such a situation.

Even though the WTO precedent on countervailing duties is more limited, foreign countries should consider WTO decisions about trade remedies as a group. Decisions in the anti-dumping and safeguards context, for example, can shed very helpful light on how a WTO panel might consider injury issues even in a countervailing duty context.

Implementation issues

The substantive WTO decisions about anti-dumping and safeguard measures have been encouraging. But will these decisions change the behaviour of the administering authorities? Implementation has been a controversial issue more generally. Several high-profile disputes between the United States and the EU (such as bananas, beef hormones, and the Foreign Sales Corporation tax law) have shown that it is politically difficult for the losing side in a WTO dispute to implement the decision. This general problem is also quite acute in the area of trade remedies. The United States has been particularly reluctant to implement meaningful changes to its trade remedy laws.

For example, in *Lead and bismuth bar*, both the WTO panel and the Appellate Body found that a United States policy on subsidies – whether privatization extinguishes subsidies that a company previously received – was inconsistent with the Agreement on Subsidies and Countervailing Measures. Rather than change its policy, the United States persuaded the petitioners to withdraw their petition, thus ending the order but also rendering moot the need to change the policy. Since then, the United States has insisted on case-by-case challenges to this policy.

As another example, consider the *DRAM* case. The panel had found in favour of the Republic of Korea, ruling that the Commerce Department standard for revoking anti-dumping measures was inconsistent with Article 11. The United States made a change in the wording of the regulation but then made precisely the same decision that revocation was not justified.

Some might consider these examples and become very pessimistic about change. For several reasons, however, there are reasons to be somewhat more optimistic over the longer term.

First, it may take more time, but the WTO process does eventually force changes to national trade remedies. Case-by-case litigation is burdensome, but it still eventually leads to change in the remedies. There are now pending cases that may push the WTO system to address the issue of 'generally applicable policies' more effectively. The EU and other countries are now fighting this battle in the context of ongoing WTO litigation about privatization.

In the *DRAM* example, the Republic of Korea took the United States back to the WTO, challenging the WTO consistency of the Commerce Department decision after the regulation change. Although the panel never issued a formal decision (because Hyundai Electronics was able to settle the dispute by having Micron agree to terminate the anti-dumping order in the context of the ongoing sunset dispute), there were various indications that the panel would have ruled for the Republic of Korea in that case.

Second, the United States position is becoming more internationally isolated. For example, after its loss on zeroing in the *Bed linens* case, the EU announced that it would begin a systematic effort to change the policy in all its anti-dumping cases. The EU also argued that it hoped other countries would begin to do the same – a message clearly directed at the United States. If other countries support this EU approach, it will become harder for the United States to sustain its isolated position indefinitely.

Third, even when the authorities do not officially change their policies, they often quietly change their analysis. They do so to minimize the risk of future trade remedies being attacked in WTO disputes. For example, when authorities consider all specifically listed factors in their injury decisions, the authorities are less likely to find injury. Decisions with respect to 'facts available' are another example. If authorities know their decisions are going to be carefully scrutinized by panels, they will be less likely to make bad decisions.

WTO decisions thus steer national administering authorities into making better decisions. The system is far from perfect – some authorities will still ignore WTO principles and make bad decisions in politically tough cases. But the decisions in close cases now have a better chance of being made fairly.

Finally, under WTO rules, when a country loses a dispute and refuses to implement a WTO decision, the winning country can obtain the right to retaliate against the losing country. It takes time to win the right to retaliate, but that retaliation can be used to generate political pressure for change.

Some trade remedy cases involve levels of trade that are too small to matter very much. But other cases – such as lumber from Canada and DRAMs from Korea – have such large volumes of trade that retaliation could have economic and political significance. For retaliation to work, however, countries need to be willing to use it strategically.

Internet guide to United States trade remedy law under Title VII and Section 201

United States trade remedy laws are perhaps the most well-documented trade statutes on the Internet in terms of practice, procedure and historical application. Electronic forms of United States statutory and regulatory language, actual decisions, statistical information, and practice manuals used by staff-level United States trade authorities are literally a few mouse clicks away from anyone with access to an Internet-capable computer. The section below describes the most valuable resources on the Internet for researching United States trade remedy law issues, concentrating on available information from the principal administering agencies, offices, and courts.

The Department of Commerce

The Department of Commerce is responsible for initiating anti-dumping and countervailing duty (AD/CVD) cases. In the bifurcated process established under United States law, its principal responsibilities include quantifying dumping and subsidy margins in original investigations and reviews, as well as establishing the scope of investigations and orders. These responsibilities are handled by the Import Administration, contained within the International Trade Administration, which is one of the 11 principal divisions of the broader Department.

The Import Administration maintains its own web page, which may be accessed through the main Department web page (*www.doc.gov*), or directly at *www.ia.ita.doc.gov*. The Import Administration provides access to the following information concerning the Department's administration of the AD/CVD laws:

❏ **United States Code, Title VII (i.e. AD/CVD statutory language).** A complete statutory recitation, with amendments resulting from the Uruguay Round Agreements Act of 1994.

❏ **Current AD/CVD Departmental regulations.** A complete recitation of applicable regulations covering Department investigations.

❏ **The 'Anti-dumping Manual'.** The 'Anti-dumping Manual' serves as a training tool and reference for staff-level administrators at the Import Administration, but serves equally well as a training tool and reference for private parties involved in AD/CVD investigations. In 20 chapters, the manual covers: (1) analyses of petitions and initiations of investigations; (2) the administrative record; (3) Access to information; (4) questionnaires; (5) analyses of responses; (6) fair value comparisons; (7) export price and constructed export price; (8) normal value; (9) data submission, computer processing, and calculation review; (10) critical circumstances; (11) preparation of preliminary and final determinations, other *Federal Register* notices, and other documents; (12) postponements of determinations; (13) verification; (14) hearings and briefs; (15) terminations and suspensions of investigations; (16) International Trade Commission injury determinations; (17) preparation of anti-dumping orders; (18) administrative reviews and other post anti-dumping duty order activities; (19) court records and litigation; and (20) international agreements.

❑ **A glossary of terms used in AD/CVD cases.**

❑ **Standard and non-market economy questionnaires issued in AD/CVD cases.** Boilerplate questionnaires issued in AD/CVD cases.

❑ **Databases for petitions filed, orders in effect, and their disposition, including statistical information.** This includes a number of Excel spreadsheets listing pertinent data.

❑ *Federal Register* **notices.** As issued in specific cases, sorted by month, year and country.

❑ **Unpublished decision memoranda.** The Import Administration no longer publishes in the *Federal Register* the entire discussion on margin calculations in specific AD/CVD cases. The full record, including the unpublished decision memoranda, can be accessed on the Internet.

❑ **Court-ordered remand determinations.** Cases on appeal to the Court of International Trade or Court of Appeals for the Federal Circuit may be remanded to the Import Administration for further consideration.

❑ **Currency exchange rates.** These are exchange rates published by the Federal Reserve and used to calculate dumping margins.

❑ **Databases of recorded subsidy programmes in various countries.** A catalogue of material on foreign subsidy programmes identified by the Import Administration.

❑ **Scope information, by order.** Precise definitions of products covered (or not covered) by AD/CVD orders.

❑ **Data on prior and current suspension agreements.** Useful reference in terms of the mechanics of suspension agreements.

❑ **Foreign AD/CVD cases against United States firms and exports.**

International Trade Commission

The Commission is responsible for ruling on the issue of injury in AD/CVD cases as well as Section 201 cases. Like the Department of Commerce, it maintains a wealth of electronic data on practice and procedure, specific opinions of the Commission, and related material. The Commission's web page is located at *www.usitc.gov*, and makes available the following information and resources:

❑ **Published AD/CVD and Section 201 opinions of the Commission.** The Commission keeps more recent determinations directly available, while the titles of other cases can be searched for in the Commission Library's electronic catalogue, also available through the Commission web page.

❑ **Summaries of statutory provisions related to Commission AD/CVD and Section 201 investigations**. An excellent primer for Commission statutory authority and responsibilities is contained in a single publication – 'Statutory Provisions Related to Import Relief'.

❏ **An 'AD/CVD Handbook'.** The 131-page document is similar in purpose to, though less dense than, the Import Administration's Anti-dumping Manual. The emphasis is on Commission practice and procedure.

❏ **Import and Export Statistics.** The Commission's 'Data Web' provides up-to-date import and export statistics searchable at the 10-digit HTS level, which may be organized by country, port of entry (imports), and other criteria.

❏ **EDIS.** EDIS contains electronic versions of public submissions filed by parties in AD/CVD and Section 201 investigations.

❏ **Other miscellaneous topical reports prepared by the Commission on trade flows, developments, and trade agreements.**

Court of International Trade and the Court of Appeals for the Federal Circuit

The Court of International Trade (CIT) has primary jurisdiction over international trade matters within the federal judicial system. Decisions of the Department of Commerce and the International Trade Commission are appealed to the CIT, which may lead to court-ordered remands of agency actions. Information regarding the CIT can be found at *www.cit.uscourts.gov*, with opinions of the CIT found at *www.cit.uscourts.gov/slip_op/slip-op.html*.

Rulings of the CIT may be appealed to the Court of Appeals for the Federal Circuit (CAFC). Information regarding the CAFC may be found at *www.fedcir.gov*. Opinions of the CAFC may be found at *www.fedcir.gov/#opinions*.